Admired Man Why?

THANK YOU VERY MUCH BRYCE
FOR THE ENGAG.-G CONVERSATION
AND KNOWLEDGE. CLEARLY
YOU ARE AN ADMIRED MAN!!

DR CHRIS LA___ 52

Admired Man Why?

The Making of an Admired Man

CHRIS L. HICKEY, SR. PH.D.

ISBN: 1943626006
ISBN 13: 9781943626007
Library of Congress Control Number: 2015943095
Admired Man Leadership Institute, Inglewood, CA

Dedication

This book is dedicated to the loving memory of my first teacher, my first friend, and the smartest person I have been blessed to know, Ardelphia Hickey, my mother. You will always be at my side and in my heart.

I love you, Momma.

Your #1 son, Chris.

Save my seat in Heaven, next to you.

Border to border; shore to shore.

The man that is Fatherly we always adore.

Whether Grandfather, Brother, Husband, or Friend,

Being Honest and Loving is respected in Men.

A Hardworking Father whose Family comes first

With Loving support you are always well versed.

So, raise your hands in Pride and take your rightful stand,

For to those who Matter,

You are An Admired Man.

Table of Contents

Preface

THIS BOOK WAS initially inspired by my personal experience growing up without a father. Much, much later in my adult life, I was inspired by the many men I had the privilege to talk with during the completion of my doctoral dissertation. During the final stage of data gathering for the dissertation, I had the "luminous" idea to conduct a survey of men, where I asked them to name a man who knew them personally, that they admired, and to explain why. I also asked them if they grew up with their father in their life. Lastly, I allowed space for additional comments, which was very much utilized. This survey ignited some of the most interesting and inspiring conversations I can recall ever having. While I decided not to include this particular data in my dissertation, after I was awarded my doctoral degree, I was eventually re-inspired to resume this topic of inquiry. However, this time I wanted to include women in the survey. This book chronicles the results of my revised national survey of over 4,500 responses to my questionnaire on this topic, as well as the contribution of over 64 face-to-face and focus group interviews and at least 3,000 people I randomly stopped during my daily life and travels to ask the quick questions about the man they admire and why. The purpose of this book is to inspire and encourage men to understand and embody the personal Quality, Behavior, and Characteristics (QBC) that inspire others to admire them, as a man. This is not to say that women would not also be inspired by the revelations excavated from these pages. Mothers, wives, sisters, aunts, grandmothers and the like will benefit equally by understanding the Quality, Behavior, and Characteristics

(QBC) they can encourage the men in their life to personify. To assist me in making this book relevant and precise, I spared no effort in researching existing scholarly and common sense literature on various topics around male studies and leadership. As I share what my research subjects have shared with me about a man they admire and why, I shall also explore a collection of what I refer to as L(ife)eadership Skills that facilitate the adoption and personalization of the Quality, Behavior, and Characteristics (QBC) that people admire in a man.

I have to admit, I am somewhat surprised at the response to what appeared to be a very innocuous inquiry—simply, a dialogue about an "Admired Man, and Why?" Clearly, throughout all of our lives we are inundated with various connections and associations with men, both directly and indirectly. Beginning in our immediate family, our father, brothers, uncles, husband, and so on are often the men to which we have the strongest connection, with obvious exceptions. Our extended family includes our cousins, stepbrothers, grandfathers, stepfathers, and others. Beyond our immediate and extended family the men we tend to think of include friends, neighbors, co-workers, boyfriends, bosses, teachers, mentors, coaches, and teammates. While this latter group of men may initially be thought of as somewhat remote and impersonal, clearly, a significant number of such associations occasionally have profound meaning to many of us, which is reflected, in many cases, by them being included among the list of our most admired man. Then, of course, there are the thousands of men that cross our weekly path who have ostensibly a less than remote association with us: bus drivers, airline passengers, supermarket cashiers, subway passengers, etc., that interesting enough are often considered in our subconscious consideration of possessing Admirable Quality / Behavior / Characteristics (QBC). One need only to reflect back on an ever-so-slight feeling of pride or admiration you may have felt watching a young man who you did not know, say, on the bus, who is nicely dressed, or is acting in a conspicuously respectful way to an elderly passenger. So, why do you have this seemingly instinctive emotion? Does the behavior of the young man remind you of another man you admire? Do you have a set of Quality/Behavior/Characteristics (QBC) that you instinctively admire? In either case, why do you admire such Quality/Behavior/Characteristics (QBC)? How likely are others to admire the same QBC's of the young lad on the bus? Why?

While the generally accepted perspective on which men we admire, including why we admire them—considering the aforementioned scenario—seems almost universally shared, consider an alternative reality for many men and women. It is so easy to assume that everyone has a network of immediate family, extended family, remote associates, and day-to-day interactions that facilitate experiences that engender emotions of either lasting admiration, or at the least an impetuous moment of admiration for the Quality/Behavior/Characteristics (QBC) of a man. In reality, this is not the case. The reality is that there are throngs of individuals, both men and women, that, when asked about what man they admire, are as quick as those who profess, "...my father"; "...my uncle"; "...my friend"; "...my brother"; to spout, "...nobody." Furthermore, they are equally articulate about their reasoning: "Men have never done a damn thing for me that did me any good," said a 32-year-old woman, responding to my national inquiry.

These realities abound: The societal norm of experiencing either a sustained admiration of a man (or group of men) or temporary/sudden experiences of admiration are not shared with all men or women. Why and how is this possible? Are there alternative perspectives about admirable Quality / Behavior / Characteristics (QBC) experienced by individuals who suggest they admire no man? If so, what are the Quality/Behavior/Characteristics (QBC) they consider admirable, that they suggest they are not experiencing from any man they consider in their sphere of relationships? Moreover, how is it possible that those who insist that there is no man in their sphere of relationships, whom they admire, share the same perspective of admirable Quality / Behavior / Characteristics (QBC) considered as the norm for most others?

Clearly, these almost contradictory co-existing paradigms are profoundly counter intuitive to our common sense of reasonableness. How can most people report the existence of numerous men they admire with profoundly consistent reasoning, share daily experiences with others who report no such realities at all? Subsequently, such paradoxical realities, related to men, have not eluded the curiosity of scholarly inquiry and research over the past few decades. Since the 1970's a number of colleges and universities have embarked on the creation of men studies programs and courses. Often referred to as men and/or masculinities programs, this type of interdisciplinary curricula generally focus on such topics as men, masculinity, power, gender, and politics. Additionally, some university men's studies programs were adopted in correlation with women's studies programs, as a supplement to a more comprehensive gender studies program. The men and masculinities academic field was proposed in the influential book *Masculinities*, by Australian sociologist and University of Sydney Professor Emeritus R.W. Connell, and encouraged the concept of plural masculinities, or diversity of masculinities.[1] These programs subsequently evolved into a number of variations to the initial concept, culminating in a rich selection of diverse courses and research literature. There is no shortage of scholarly books, papers, articles, and conferences on topics relevant to men's studies, father studies, and men-mentoring-men topics, to name a few.

The American Men's Studies Association (AMSA) advances the study of men and the development of teaching, research, and clinical practice in the field of men's studies. AMSA has held an annual conference each year since 1993, which is the largest annual men's studies conference in the United States. The Men's Studies Association (MSA) is another association of scholars with an interest in the interdisciplinary field of men's studies. *Men's Health Magazine* provides their readers with actionable information that they can put to work—information that helps men be healthier, smarter, more fashionable, more confident and more successful in their relationships and family life. These are examples of the ever growing list of organizations and magazines that focus on men and masculinity. The popularity of such topics, particularly on the importance of fathers in the lives of children, has also proliferated interest in the sphere of public media. In mid 2013, Oprah Winfrey dedicated an entire program, on her OWN network, on *The True Role of the Father-and the Devastating Effect of an Absent one,* which can be found on YouTube by that same name. In September of 2014, Unites States President, Barack Obama challenged cities, towns and counties across the country to become actively involved in the White House's "My Brother's Keeper" Initiative, designed to address "...persistent opportunity gaps faced by boys and young men of color and ensure that all young people can reach their full potential."

(https://www.whitehouse.gov/my-brothers-keeper#section-about-my-brothers-keeper).

Correspondent with the growing popularity of academic courses and opportunities that examine various critiques relevant to males and masculinity, a growing interest in diverse non-academic arenas evolved. A number of groups, organizations, books, biographies, magazines, websites, support groups, journals, and the like began to proliferate. Moreover, issues of males and masculinity began to be explored on much deeper levels of analysis: Black men; Hispanic men; gay men; shared child rearing arrangement (co-parenting); single men raising their children; custody sharing; violence against men, stay-at-home fathers and other 21st century paradigms began to infiltrate the consciousness of acceptable inquiry related to the role of men.

Literature abound in reference to evolving and inclusive perspectives on the role of men and masculinity. Sexuality, ethnicity, and culture have now entered into the discussion on all levels, both in academia and general non-academic arenas of inquiry. Such discussions are especially explored in the context of fathering. Dr. Charlotte J. Patterson, professor in the University of Virginia Department of Psychology and the Center for Children, Families, and the Law shares, "Social science research on gay fathers is a relatively recent phenomenon. Because the research has arisen in the context of widespread prejudice and discrimination against members of sexual minorities, much research has been concerned to evaluate negative stereotypes about gay father families."[2] In my survey, a 36-year-old man and a 56-year-old man both stated that the man they admired most in their life was their husband.

In a review of research on the evolving practices of Latino fathers, co-authors Dr. Natasha J. Cabrera, University of Maryland Associate Professor of Developmental Science Program Human Development and Quantitative Methodology, and, Dr. Cynthia Garcia Coll, Brown University Professor of Education, Psychology and Pediatrics write, "In one study that looked at shared and divided parental task in school-related and learning experiences in the home of Mexican American families, researchers found that Latino fathers who shared child-care tasks with their wives were also more likely to read to their children and engage in other learning activities with them than were fathers who divided parental tasks with their wives."[3] Illuminating on the significance of Black father parenting skills, researcher authors Leon D. Caldwell, from the University of Nebraska, Lincoln and Le'Roy Reese, from the Center of Disease Control and Prevention enlighten, "Seeking the knowledge base and developing critical parenting skills such as prioritizing the importance of quality time spent with children, nurturing the brilliance of children in what can and at times will be a hostile world, disciplining children with a focus of correction and teaching, communicating and modeling self-love, self-respect, and responsibility are among the many important attributes required of responsible Black fathering."[4] Clearly, these and other L(ife)eadership Skills such as time management, getting along with others, patience, perseverance, and communication are essential elements of the ingredients that facilitate the attributes most often associated with the Quality/Behavior/Characteristics (QBC) that embody the essence of a man that is admired.

My initial interest in men as a topic of scholarly research focused on *The Phenomenal Characteristic of the Son-Father Relationship Experience.*[5] The central question addressed in my doctoral dissertation was constructed to determine the specific ways that leadership development is influenced by the phenomenal characteristics of the son-father relationship experience; including how sons articulate their feelings about the relationship in the moment of the experience and over time. A series of sub-themes that also formed the foundation of my methodology (were) built upon the following theory-based questions:[6]

a) What are the perceptions adolescent boys and men have about the son-father relationship experience?
b) How do adolescent boys and men describe their feelings and emotions about their own son-father relationship experiences?
c) In what ways do adolescent boys and men describe leadership characteristics and qualities in the context of their own son-father relationship?

Ultimately, I summarized the answer to the central question as follows: "Men and boys are enthusiastically expressive in their articulation of their feelings about their son-father relationship experience, at and over time. However, while they are somewhat expressive and articulate about leadership characteristics that may or may not exist in them and/ or their fathers, they tend not to be very expressive of any influence on leadership development deriving from their son-father relationship experience."[7] The research gathered for this book bore the same interesting disconnect. There was scarcely anyone that specifically attributed leadership qualities, behaviors or characteristics as the impetus for their admiration of a man. It is my hunch that this is primarily attributed to a disassociation of the broader more comprehensive understanding and perspective relevant to various attributes and characteristics of leadership. I qualify this hunch on the bases that the most profound Quality/ Behavior/Characteristics (QBC) most often cited and attributed to an admired man, clearly embed the tenets of leadership, in spite of the scarce occurrence of the term "leadership" being used. More often than not, when we think of leadership it is in the context of an individual who has been ordained a specific role, commensurate with power, rather than a process where people are motivated and enfranchised to act, change, and/or transform. In his seminal book on leadership, American historian and political scientist (and friend, I might add) James McGregor Burns illuminates the broader perspective from which to understand leadership. He shares:

The concept of value is so crucial to our concept of leadership here that we must establish definitions. Values have a special potency because they embrace separate but closely interrelated phenomena. Values indicate desirable or preferred end-states or collective goals or explicit purposes, and values are standards in terms of which specific criteria may be established and choices made among alternatives. Thus social equality can be both a goal and a standard by which to measure policies, practices, other goals. We will use the term end-values to designate these two intertwined meanings of values as goals and standards. Values are also defined as modes of conduct, such as prudence, honor, courage, civility, honesty, fairness.[8]

In this context, leaders are not merely observed from afar as power brokers who lead a flock of powerless followers, but rather are seen as value-added participatory agents of collaborative engagement, modeling and influence; who inspire others to self-reflect and aspire to appreciate, emulate, and seek the presence/influence and example of leadership. In light of the fact that, "…we may have some difficulty in laying bare precisely and definitively the components of leadership and the working relationships among those components,"[9] writes author John W. Work, the senior principal in Work Associates, Inc., an New York City-based management consulting firm, "…we do seem to think that we know leaders when we see them: they are those individuals who, in their inimitable ways, inspire confidence, undermine despair, fight fear, initiate positive and productive actions, light the candles, define the goals, and paint brighter tomorrows."[10] While leadership and organizational consultant Richard Beckhard cites the first principle of leadership being that it is a relationship between a leader and followers, he adds that the second, and significantly relevant principle is that effective leaders are both, "...aware of and consciously manage the dynamics of this relationship."[11]

Leadership co-authors Dr. Barbara F. Schaetti, Dr. Sheila J. Ramsey, and Dr. Gordon C. Watanabe add, "Leadership is, at root, about understanding and managing our own internal experience. Extraordinary leaders know that experience is subjective: we feel and think and behave in the way we do, we see what we see and hear what we hear, because of the way we've been taught by our families, our school, our culture."[12] And, I add, by the men who directly and indirectly touch our lives, on various levels. "While practicing Personal Leadership is therefore very relational, its focus begins with the 'self' rather than with the 'other.'"[13] It is this experience of "relational" leadership that is embedded, yet not necessarily articulated, in the Quality/Behavior/Characteristics (QBC) of an admired man. A 24-year-old man from Atlanta, Georgia shares, "I really admire my 19-year-old brother. He always knows what to do and say to make others feel important. I am really working on trying to be more like him. I want others to feel about me as they feel about him." A 16-year-old girl from Detroit, Michigan promises, "I am going to marry a man that treats me like my father treats my mother." I will elaborate more on how relational leadership is embedded in the Quality/Behavior/Characteristics (QBC) of the admired man throughout the book.

It is understandingly plausible that this strand of inquiry would lead to even richer questions around the nature of men in the context of how they influence and affect the thoughts and emotions of another, regardless of the varied nature of their relationship and connection. Parenting experts, Professor emeritus Dr. John M. Gottman and his colleague Joan DeClaire help us understand the significance of emotions in the context of this inquiry. "In the last decade or so, science has discovered a tremendous amount about the role emotions play in our lives. Researchers have found that even more than IQ, your emotional awareness and ability to handle feelings will determine your success and happiness in all walks of life, including family relationships."[14] The family phenomena plays out significantly in my research findings. You will find much more on this topic as you read and discover the emotional connections many of us embody related to family and the man we admire. Inquiry into the Quality / Behavior / Characteristics (QBC) of an admired man naturally follows the aforementioned general public and academic inquiry and perception regarding men as fathers—a rapidly evolving interest shared by both men and women. The conjunction between these related inquires is, of course, dependent upon whether the respondents grew up with their father in their life; with the possible correlation between their phenomenal child/father relationship, and, who and why a respondent admires a particular man.

In a study presented by the National Health Statistics Report, men evaluated the job they are doing with their children. "In general, fathers aged 15-44 who lived with their children ages zero-to-eighteen were about twice as likely as fathers who did not live with their children to say they are doing 'a very good job' as a father (44% compared to 21%). While 0.6% of coresidential fathers think they are doing 'a not very good or bad job,' 24% of noncoresidential fathers think they are doing 'a not very good or bad job'"[15] Ultimately, this book will share the attributes of an admired man in order to excavate the type of L(ife)eadership Skills conducive for cultivating admirability.

As mentioned, over the last few decades there has been an understandingly escalating interest in the role of fathers in the lives of their children. In the last decade this conversation has grown to monumental levels, which is again, clearly understandable. Research clearly elucidates the disruptive nature of fatherlessness in the lives of children; as well as the enormous advantages in the areas of social adaptability, emotional stability, academic achievement, and psychological development for those who experience a present and nurturing father in their life. Subsequent to these findings there has been an enormous effort on all levels to make available resources for a man to understand and learn how to be a "good" father; and I, for one, applaud these efforts with all of my strength, support, and involvement.

What this book does, however, is extend the conversation relevant to the role that an admired man plays in the lives of not only their own children, but to others who either directly or remotely cross their path. In this book I share how the Quality/Behavior/Characteristics (QBC) of an admired man affect the consciousness of just about everyone he comes in contact with; and, how an admired man's relationship with others creates an avalanche of optimistic positivity, spirited graciousness, appreciative goodwill, and philanthropic sharing in those who are attracted by his relational leadership and influence.

The objective of this book is to undertake a phenomenological inquiry and discussion of how the cultivation, adoption, practice and perfection of evolving L(ife)eadership Skills facilitate the embodiment of "admired" Quality / Behavior / Characteristics (QBC) in boys and men. Renowned research expert Michael Quinn Patton explains, "Phenomenological analysis seeks to grasps and elucidate the meaning, structure, and essence of the lived experience of phenomenon for a person or group of people."[16] As boys go through various stages of life toward manhood, they are confronted with evolving (age/stage of life relevant) challenges that require the perfection of selected L(ife)eadership Skills, correspondently appropriate for the challenge(s) at hand. This book explores the "meaning" and "structure" of these challenges and skills. Research methodology gurus Valerie M. Benz and Jeremy J. Shapiro clarify, "...phenomenology attempts to take seriously the fact that we are conscious beings and that everything we know is something that we know only in and through consciousness...[it] makes us stop taking for granted the things that we normally take for granted, and that is part of mindfulness."[17] I will make the point that L(ife)eadership Skills evolve and are correspondently perfected through (age/stage of life appropriate) mindful practice; similarly to the way athletic skills (such as dribbling a basketball) are perfected, through sustained/committed practice, for evolving and more challenging levels of competition/opportunity. As I mentioned to a group of 30 young middle school boys about preparing to play high school, college, or even professional basketball, "...the ball will be the same, it is just the challenge(s) that will get bigger and stronger. So, you will need to be able to dribble the same size ball much better than you do now, which means you will need to adopt the 'practice' of mindful practice."

But, first things first. After a short bit of self-disclosure and introduction of the book content, I will share the survey responses, conversations, antidotes, experiences, feelings, and emotions of everyday people who were more than willing to share their perspective about the man they admire, why they admire the man, their relationship with their father, and how that relationship may have influenced their perspective on what are, and are not admirable Quality/Behavior/Characteristics (QBC) of a man. Let's say, I will examine the cognitive, emotional, and spiritual perspectives people have about their relationship with men. That is, what they think and how they feel about such relationships. Oh yes, let it be known now, an examination of emotions as well as the mind/body relationship will play a significant part in my exploration and understanding of the nature of relationships. Noted University of Southern California Professor and neuroscientist, Dr. Antonio Damasio, eloquently elucidates the significance and relevance of the emotion/mind/body connection. He contributes, "It does not seem sensible to leave emotions and feelings [body] out of any overall concept of mind. Yet respectable scientific accounts of cognition do precisely that, by failing to include emotions and feelings in their treatment of cognitive systems."[18] Elaborating on the significance of a deliberate examination of the emotions and feelings underlying the shared accounts of the individuals contributing to this effort, emotion researcher Michael A. Jawer and Georgetown University professor of physiology and biophysics Dr. Marc S. Micozzi discuss the primacy of feeling. They explain:

Regardless of what researchers (or anyone else) means by the terms "feelings," "emotions," or "feeling states," we should all be able to agree that this aspect of being is not merely an essential component of consciousness. Our deepest feelings inevitably dictate who we are as individuals, what's important in our life, what we choose to do, and what we become. "For human beings," remarks one observer, "the reality that ultimately matters is the reality of their feelings."[19]

With respect to spirituality, writer and scholar Matthew Fox uncovers the hidden spirituality of men. He shares, "One of the best kept secrets of our culture is that many men are deeply spiritual and care deeply about their spiritual life. It is a secret, however, because it is hidden—sometimes...even from the men themselves. Sometimes the hiding is deliberate."[20] In many of the accounts that men share in this book, you will be able to get a sense of not only the hidden spirituality, but the hidden vulnerability of men as well. Fox continues, "...research of young boys is giving us this extraordinary insight that boys get shamed for their vulnerability at a very young age, right around kindergarten, and that's the time at which they really learn to hold off from expressing their feelings and experience."[21] Resulting from my clear and deliberate authenticity, I managed to break through many of the emotional barriers that men often shield themselves behind. The men I talked with were open to share, laugh, and cry about their emotions, feelings, and experiences. To no one's surprise I'm sure, the women I talked with had no problem at all showing and expressing their emotions freely and openly.

I conclude the book with a summary review of some very significant literature on various topics relevant to admiration, masculinity, fathers, friends, mates, and leadership. Clearly, my exploration of survey responses, interviews, and discussions will surely elicit a myriad of experienced thoughts, feelings, and emotions about a significantly topical inquiry: Admired Man: Why? – The Making of an Admired Man.

Who am I?

The Discovery of my Purpose

THE MONTH WAS September. The year was still 1965: One month after the original, and now infamous, Watts Riot. I had finally entered the much anticipated junior high school. All of my lessons were in place, and I really felt like I knew what I was doing. I had a pretty clear understanding of my authority to create my own identity. I was bilingual on issues related to Black people: I could quote with convincing eloquence both Martin Luther King, Jr., and Malcolm X. My personality was one of incontestable confidence and self-respect. When I spoke, people listened—this included old friends, new friends, and new teachers. I was considered to be a very smart kid by the authority vested in the school's academic leadership. Everyone liked me. Then, it happened. In all of the reading, conversations, and observations I had made over the last six years; over the course of all that I had examined about my life, my purpose, my joys, my family, and my belonging, there was a huge oversight that had not been addressed for years. I'm still very convinced that this oversight was probably the most classic case of denial one could imagine. On a nice September night in Los Angeles, I was about to come face-to-face with what I think troubled me for the last six years of my life without ever coming to the surface, until now.[1]

The elementary school that I had previously attended was located very close to the housing projects in which I lived, and was populated primarily by kids from these same projects. There was very little difference in the life styles, family structures, and income levels of most of the kids in the school. Many of the kids were brothers and sisters living in different households, as a result of men making babies with multiple women, and not living with any of them. In my own family there were now two more kids from two different men, neither of which were anywhere to be found. The point is, an overwhelming number of the kids in my elementary school were from fatherless homes, just as I and my brothers and sisters were. The junior high school I now attended was in an area that drew from a more diverse pool of kids, many of which were from different family structures and income levels, but this was not a subject of any conversations I had with my new classmates and friends. As a leader so to speak, most of the conversations, activities and other things me and my new friends were engaged in were generated by me.[2]

During the second or third week of school it was announced by one of the gym teachers, who I might add were the first men I had been exposed to for years that I had any respect for, announced the school's annual Father/Son Night. They handed out flyers that described a wonderful night of fun for us to take home to invite our fathers. Since the flyer did not say Mother/Son Night there was of course no reason for me to take it home, not that it would have mattered, in that my mother had not spent very much time doing things like attending school events. In the days leading up to Father/Son Night this was all that was talked about by most of the boys at the school. My friends and I talked endlessly about how much fun it was going to be, running around and playing at the school as much as we wanted, without the interruption of classes. I could not wait. Then, it came, Father/Son Night.[3]

I will never ever forget, or get over, the agonizing pain I suffered that night. I went up to the school anticipating the fun I would have, dressed in the same clothes I wore all day, expecting the same from my friends. My friends were there all right, but they were dressed (as my fifth grade teacher would have described) like they were intelligent, with their fathers. Along with their fathers they were having fun conversations with the gym teachers about things dads and sons talk about. Their behaviors were not at all what I had seen and anticipated. They had respect for their fathers and their fathers showed respect for them. The gym teachers had respect for both the boys and their fathers. I was devastated. I could scarcely feel the shame I had through the debilitating pain in my chest. It seemed that everywhere I turned and everywhere I looked, people turned their back. I was nobody at all. I felt worthless. It didn't take long at all for the tears to move up from deep in my heart, and roll from my eyes, back down to my chest. I began to think that my tear filled eyes were a blessing, because I could no longer see what was happening around me, assisted by the palms of my hands, covering my face. It appeared that I was not the only one blinded by my tears, because I could feel that none of my friends could see me at all. Why should they? They were with their fathers, and their fathers were with them, just where they belonged. I managed to find the path back to where I belonged. But, with each step I took the pain grew stronger. I realized that with each passing moment it was closer to the time I would have to be back at school the next day, and the thought of hearing my friends and gym teachers talk about what a fantastic night it was made my heart scream with wretchedness.[4]

As was typical of me I starting searching my mind for an answer to what was happening to me. Why did this feel so bad? Why didn't I know what was going to happen? What was I going to do about it? I reflected back on the lessons from my mother: Nothing. I thought about Martin Luther King, Jr.; Malcolm X; The Sons of Watts: Nothing. I thought about my fifth grade teacher—OKAY: This was clearly not my fault. The pain and tears started to make room for anger and tears. I became very mad, but I didn't know who I was mad at, or couldn't face in my own mind who I was mad at. I just knew that this should not have happened to me. I knew that I deserved better. I decided that I was going to have better. Before I made it home I made a vow before God and country that I was going to have this experience again, only I would not be the kid. I would be the father. I vowed on that night that I would not allow myself to die before I had kids that would attend Father/Son Night and/or Father/Daughter Night, and any other day or night, and they would always, as long as they were kids, have their father right there, every time. I decided that night that everything that I did from now on would be with this promise in mind. I decided on that night what a true leader was. I decided on that night that I could not consider myself a leader of anything unless I was first someone that my kids could depend on and respect. My job was to be their leader first, and everything else would evolve around that. I was angry and determined. I discovered my purpose that night.[5]

Introduction

"When a nation gives birth to a Man who is able to produce a great thought, another is born who is able to understand and Admire it."

— JOSEPH JOUBERT
(18th-century French essayist)

To be Admired

Ad·mire
/əd'mī(ə)r/

THE MERRIAM-WEBSTER ON-LINE dictionary defines admire as: "…to feel respect or approval for (someone or something): to look at (something or someone) with enjoyment." Vocabulary.com elaborates, "If you hold someone in high esteem or look up to someone, you *Admire* that person. If you ask four-year-olds who they most *Admire*, they are likely to list their mom, dad, and grandparents—or superheroes and comic book characters." According to Thesaurus.com, "…other words that often suggest Admiration are: adored; applauded; appreciated; hailed; honored; idolized; praised; treasured; revered; and, respected."

Throughout the course of early modern history some of the most renowned and thought provoking philosophers have found the subject of admiration as a source of their own creative expression. Ludwig Van Beethoven once stated, "This is the mark of a really admirable man:

steadfastness in the face of trouble." The renowned ancient Greek poet Homer shared, "There is nothing more nobler or admirable than when two people who see eye-to-eye keep house as man and woman, confounding their enemies and delighting their friends."

Two pretty simple questions, right? "Name a man that you admire." "Why?" These two "seemingly" harmless questions are flanked by the question, "Did you grow up with your father in your life?" which in and of itself illuminates volumes of discussion with respect to why men are, or, are not admired. Consider; of the respondents who indicated that they "Grew up with their father in their life," 44% also listed their "father" as the man they "admire"; with 16% listing "family" as the primary reason. In my research on the son-father relationship experience I shared, "...in the case of boys who grow up in families without a live-in father, they often articulate experiences of feeling like it is their responsibility to be the secondary protector of the family (after their mother), even when they have older sisters. These feelings begin to develop at the time they witness the role of the father in other families; however, they find that they are challenged with constructing the [Quality / Behavior / Characteristics (QBC)] of protector without a primary example, relying instead on what they think they witness in other families. Often, these men and boys are expressive of how such early experiences affect other relationships in their lives, and how they perceive their role accordingly."[1] In this book, I disclose, not only do these men and boys study the perceived Quality/Behavior/Characteristics (QBC) of such surrogates, but often, they also develop an admiration for the men they attempt to emulate, however laudable; or, misguided. This tendency lends to an interesting perspective about the mentoring relationship experience.

I posed these questions far and wide and received an array of extremely interesting and provocative answers. Starting with the men admired (by role) I received the follow (top 5) results:

1. Father
2. Friend

3. Husband
4. Brother
5. Grandfather

Honorable mentioned include: Pastor, Uncle, Boyfriend and Mentor. I will also address those who indicated that there is no man in their life they admire. There are some very interesting implications about how those responses fleshed out. There are also revealing accounts on why some respondents admire some of the honorable mentioned. A 42-year-old man who only partially grew up with his father and listed four mentors as the men he admires explains, "These four mentors—though different in age, race, and ethnicity—collectively supported me in deepening three core educational leadership values: (1) keep the students at the center of decisions; (2) ask courageous questions to improve the effectiveness and efficiency of schools and districts such that they increase the educational outcomes for children; and (3) embrace a diverse team to ensure that schools and districts are open to ethical and creative possibilities." I cannot help but notice how impersonal this testimony seems, in contrast to the many accounts from others who reported an admiration of their father, friend, husband, brother, and grandfather. While this is generally not the case with respect to the attachment mentees have with mentors, male studies author Dr. Samuel Osherson, Doctoral Faculty at the Fielding Graduate University School of Psychology, elaborates on the sometimes vulnerability of the mentor-mentee relationship:

When the mentee comes to a mentor as a needy little boy in search of an all-knowing, all-loving father, both men are put in a difficult position: The mentor may feel angry, constrained, and confused (without being sure why, since the parental overtones to the relationship are often hard to see), while the mentee will easily feel disappointed, guilty, and angry. When both mentor and mentee feel comfortable enough with their feelings, values and identity—with each other—to express themselves honestly and to explore relatively openly their mutual vulnerabilities and strengths, there is less difficulty. Clearly, that happens in some mentoring relationships, but we must understand that the issue of male vulnerability becomes highly charged for both mentor and mentee from their own relationship with their fathers.[2]

A 53-year-old woman who did grow up with her father in her life shared that her boyfriend was the man she admires discloses, "He is a widower. Married to his wife for 41-years and stayed with her to the very end. Worked hard, raised his children, recovering alcoholic (32-years sober)...allowed me into his life and is the MAN in the relationship. Even though he only has a high school education, he is not threatened by my three advanced degrees...He is well read and a loyal friend. He is an all around good person."

The top five reasons (Quality / Behavior / Characteristics (QBC)) given for why a man is admired are:

1. Family
2. Hardworking
3. Loving
4. Honest
5. Fatherly

Likewise, the honorable mentioned Quality/Behavior/Characteristics (QBC) include: Caring, Kind, Strong, Role Model, Supportive, and Intelligent. Leadership expert and writer Kevin Cashman, Founder and CEO of LeaderSource, an international leadership and executive coaching consultancy writes, "Why is one of the most powerful words in our language. 'Why?' is the question that calls us to meaning; it forces us to look beneath the surface into the deeper essence of things. 'Why?' is the question that directs us onto the path of purpose."[3] A 14-year-old girl who partially had her father in her life, listed her older brother as the man she admires, stating, "My biological dad left when I was two; I have a step dad who plays the father role. I admire my brother because he has made the best out of nothing."

Now, of course before we all retire from reading further—feeling like we got the point—a closer more compendious look at the survey responses, fact-to-face interviews, focus group dialogue sessions, and informal conversations with hundreds of individuals across the country reveals much more elaborate complexities about admired men, with particular focus on the reasons given for why certain men are admired, and the affinity between the admired men and the reasons they are admired. A close analysis of these various sources reveals a provocative web of relationships associated with how and why individuals admire a particular man; both in and outside of their daily lives. I will share how and why certain emotional connections are made and/or destroyed with men, via the intricacies of experience, fantasies, and expectations. My research reveals that by-and-large we want to have men in our lives that we admire. When the men we expect to admire are either absent or lack admirable Quality/Behavior/Characteristics (QBC) we will seek other men to admire. While the men (in relationship to the role they play in our life) may differ, the Quality/Behavior/Characteristics (QBC) we deem admirable are substantially uniform. Moreover, these quality characteristics spawn from a substantially uniform set of mindfully practiced behaviors that can be acquired.

At first, the information coming in from the surveys seems pretty simple to understand. However, the more I looked it over and compared different elements of the data from different perspectives, the more I began to excavate less obvious intricacies about the real stories; the hidden elements that reveal the more significant issue: Why are men admired? Let's go over the survey findings in a simple to understand and digestible summary that is, of course, graphically supported.

What do we have here?: The initial data that I collected for this book was derived from a short survey that was distributed nationwide. I distributed the survey, and received responses through the collective use of: electronic means, social media, snail mail, telephonic, and face-to-face conversations. The final number of responses used for the book are: n=4,784. Of the total responses, 67% indicate that they grew up with their father: 21% said they partially lived with their father in their life, with 12% saying they did not grow up with their father in their life. The average age of the respondents is 41 years of age, with 68% of the responses coming from women.

The ethnic distribution is:

Black 41% | White 38% | Hispanic 10% | Asian 6%|Bi-Racial 4%|Native American/Other 1%

The geographic distribution is:

West 54% | South 23% | North East 11% | Mid West 10 % | International 2%

The survey consisted of the following:

1. Name for me a man, by their role (not their name) in your life (for example: my father, my brother, my husband, a friend, my cousin, my pastor, or none) that you know; and that knows you, that you admire (free text).
2. Briefly describe why you admire the man you listed (free text).
3. Did you grow up with your father in your life (Select from the following)?
    a. Yes
    b. No
    c. Partially
4. What is your ethnicity (free text)?
5. In what city and state do you live (free text)?
6. What is your age (free text)?
7. What is your gender (free text)?
8. Other comments you would like to share (free text)?

So, what did they say?: The first question is: Name for me a man, by their role in your life that you know; and that knows you, that you admire. In the following summaries I *italicized* key words to remind you of the man admired and the Quality/Behavior/Characteristics (QBC) noted:

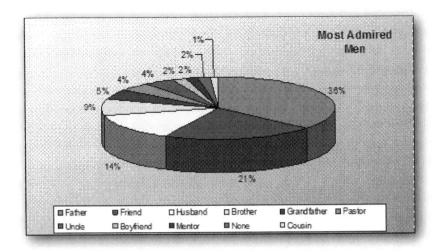

As this chart illustrates, the tabulation for the men admired are:

Father 36%	Friend 21%	Husband 14%	Brother 9%
Grandfather 5%	Pastor 4%	Uncle 4%	Boyfriend 2%
Mentor 2%	None 2%	Cousin 1%	

A 27-year-old man who had his father partially in his life indicated that his *brother* is the man he admires. He shares, "I do most of the cooking and cleaning at home because I'm studying and not employed. And, it is how I've been helping my *brother* since before he started working." A 52-year-old woman who also had her father in her life and indicated that a *friend* was the man she admires, adds, "He is *honest, hardworking* and well intended. He has learned to consider the impact of his life choices on his *family* and others. He is a committed *father* to three sons."

Before I go on to the second question, I am compelled to add a bit more on the topic of fathers. In my travels, it is not infrequent that I hear someone proclaim something on the order of, "It does not take a man to raise a boy to be a man." Obviously, in no way would I dispute this statement as it is stated, nor do I have objections with the intent of the argument on its face. However, I will suggests, it does take an admired man to expose a boy or man to the experience of relating to and emulating an admired man. Only an admired man can provide the consistent and sustained modeling of an admired man; and, it is only through shared/relational modeling that a boy or man can directly experience the physical, emotional, and spiritual essence of how it feels to be in the presence of an admired man. This matters greatly. Moreover, it is through the consistent accumulation of such direct experiences with an admired man that allows a boy or man to comprehend the embodiment of being an admired man. Additionally, I would be remiss if I did not share the following statistics on fatherless children. Consider this from *The Fatherless Generation* website:

- 63% of youth suicides are from fatherless homes – 5 times the average (U.S. Dept. Of Health/Census)
- 90% of all homeless and runaway children are from fatherless homes – 32 times the average (The Fatherless Generation)
- 85% of all children who show behavior disorders come from fatherless homes – 20 times the average (Center for Disease Control)
- 70% of juveniles in state-operated institutions come from fatherless homes (U.S. Dept. of Justice, Special Report, Sept 1988)
- 80% of rapists with anger problems come from fatherless homes –14 times the average (Justice & Behavior, Vol 14, p. 403-26)
- 71% of all high school dropouts come from fatherless homes – 9 times the average (National Principals Association Report)
- Children with fathers who are involved are 40% less likely to repeat a grade in school. (The Fatherless Generation)
- Children with fathers who are involved are 70% less likely to drop out of school. (The Fatherless Generation)
- Children with fathers who are involved are more likely to get A's in school. (The Fatherless Generation)
- Children with fathers who are involved are more likely to enjoy school and engage in extracurricular activities. (The Fatherless Generation)
- 75% of all adolescent patients in chemical abuse centers come from fatherless homes – 10 times the average. (The Fatherless Generation)

Enough said!!

On the second question, "Briefly describe why you admire the man you listed," I summarize the following results:

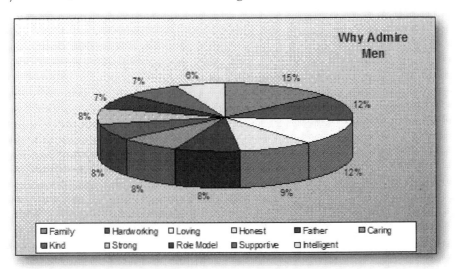

As this chart illustrates, the tabulation for the reasons a man is admired are:

Family 15%	Hardworking 12%	Loving 12%	Honest 9%
Fatherly 8%	Caring 8%	Kind 8%	Strong 8%
Role Model 7%	Supportive 7%	Intelligent 6%	

A 53-year-old woman who lived with her father indicates that she admires her *father*. She shares why she admires her father. "I just miss my *dad. Honest* and straight, *loving* and *caring, hardworking,* always supporting our projects and advises us. Participates in all activities at school, involved us in social activities; provide us anything, never count what he did for us. Was always there for us and for others. Made us laugh and smile. Gave us strength and took school very seriously."

On the third question, "Did you grow up with your father in your Life?" I summarize the following results:

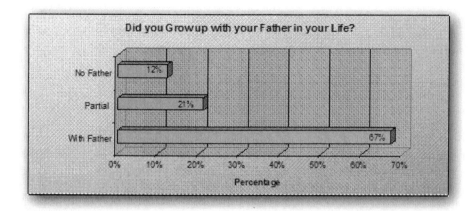

What is the relationship between the men that are admired with the reasons (Quality/Behavior/Characteristics (QBC)) they are admired?: As I delved deeper into the reasons men were admired, I found it prudent and informative to excavate how the role hierarchy of admired men correlates (aligns) with the Quality / Behavior / Characteristics (QBC) exhibited by admired men. The following charts summarize the role hierarchy of each of the top five Quality/Behavior/Characteristics (QBC) exhibited by admired men, starting with family:

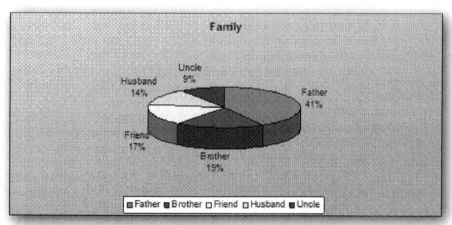

A 31-year-old Black man who indicated he partially had his father in his life; his *Uncle* as the man he admires shares, "My *father* was partially in my life. But there is no way I can view him as a man. He is totally content with being a slave. My uncle supports his *family*, he is active in the fight to save our people and at the age of 15 he gave me reading material that would eventually have me seeking freedom." Another Black man, 54-years of age, who indicated that he did grow up with his father, who he admires, says, "I look at myself and feel I pale in comparison to my *father*. He's been dead for more than 17 years and he still comes up in conversation with *family* and friends. My *father* was never a grandstander and never sought attention, yet people remember him because of his character and devotion to *family*. Even on his deathbed, the *family's* welfare took precedence over his fight against stomach cancer. He thought himself half a man because he was very weak and confined to a bed, unable to support his *family* the way he felt he should. That [could not have been] further from the truth."

The following chart indicates the role hierarchy for the Hardworking Quality / Behavior / Characteristics (QBC):

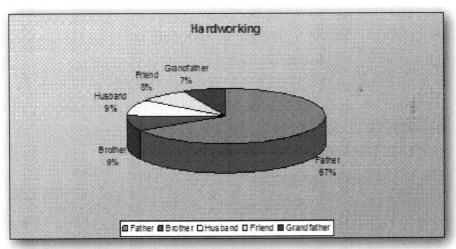

A 28-year-old man who grew up with his father, and indicated his *father* as admired, brags, "My *father* is the greatest man on the face of the Earth. That is not an opinion. His strength, kindness, knowledge, and sense of humor are second to none. He has the physical prowess of Chuck Norris and the ingenuity of MacGyver. His ability to reason rivals that of Spock, but his ability to connect with others surpasses the most popular person you know. He is a *hardworking*, everyday American with a heart of gold-plated steel."

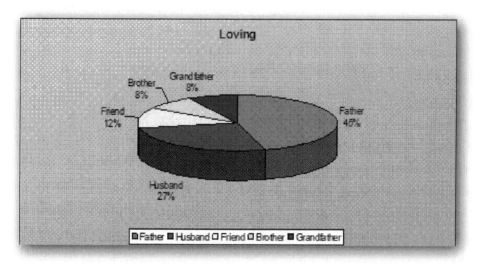

The following chart indicates the role hierarchy for the Loving Quality/Behavior/Characteristics (QBC):

In very much the same tone people speak of admiring men for being a *family* man; *hardworking, loving* is also considerably appreciated. A 49-year-old woman who did not grow up with her father, indicated that she admires a *friend*. However, in her comments she does not mention the *friend*. She states, "We need to show others God's love by being an example every day. Forgiveness, building up what the world torn down (souls, peoples spirits), *loving* unconditionally not just when convenient. Jesus came for more than forgiving us; He was the perfect example for us to follow. He experienced everything one can think of that makes life at times seem unbearable but he did not fall into the trap Satan sets to snare us. Rather he said if it be thy will..., then he fulfilled the rest of the prophecy and in his final words he asked God to forgive us, because we know not what we do. I want all I know to be like him."

A 28-year-old woman, who did grow up with her father in her life, listed her *grandfather* as the man she admires. She shares, "He overcame many obstacles, made a crap load of money and is the nicest, most compassionate and *loving* man I know."

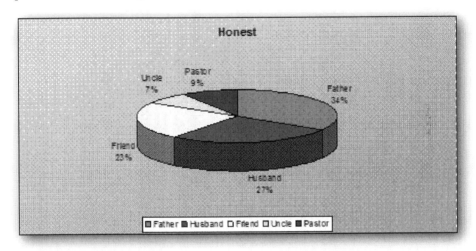

The following chart indicates the role hierarchy for the Honest Quality/Behavior/Characteristics (QBC):

A 39-year-old woman, who did not grow up with her father in her life, speaks fondly of her pastor. "I admire my pastor because he *loves* his sheep. He prays for us and he *loves* his wife. He respects her and they show what a Christian couple is supposed to look like. When I was sick my pastors called me personally to pray with me. They are an example of what *love* and *honesty* looks like every day and not just behind the pulpit."

A 47-year-old man who partially lived with his father, but listed his *father* as the man he admires suggests, "I think forthright, *honest*, principled are undervalued male traits."

The following chart indicates the role hierarchy for the Fatherly Quality/Behavior/Characteristics (QBC):

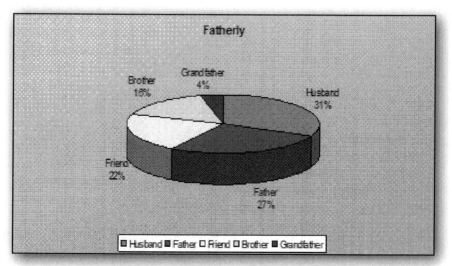

You may notice that the number one spot for this Quality/Behavior/ Characteristics (QBC) is *husband*, replacing *father*, which held the top spot on the other top four QBC's. A 31-year-old woman, who grew up with her father, and stated her *husband* was the man she admires, boasts, "My *husband* and *father* are the best men that I know."

Another woman, age 32, who also indicated that she grew up with her father, and admires her *husband*, adds, "I admire any man who recognizes the importance of his role as a *father*."

Speaking of her brother as the man she admires, a 48-year-old woman, who indicates that she did grow up with her father in her life explains, "He is a good *husband* and *father* and has been a good *uncle* to my son, whose *father* has been absent most of my son's life."

If one were to combine these five Quality/Behavior/Characteristics (QBC) of admired men into a single reference, it might sound something like, "People admire a *father-like, hardworking, family man,* who is *honest* and *loving.* This being the case, the consolidated chart combining the Quality / Behavior / Characteristics (QBC) together follows:

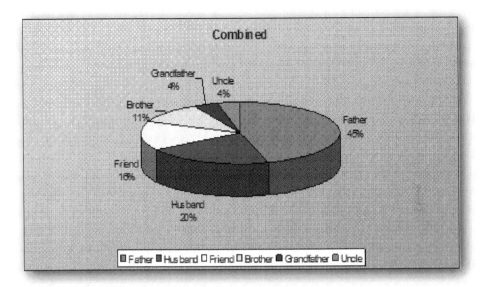

This chart represents the composite hierarchy of roles that represents a, "*Father-like, hardworking, family man,* who is *honest* and *loving.*" A 32-year-old woman who grew up with her father listed her *father, boyfriend,* and *brother* as admired. She explains, "What makes a man admirable is selflessness, putting their children first before any other person including the mother, and leaving behind childishness for their children's sake."

A 35-year-old man who also grew up with his father, listed his *grandfather* as the man he admires states, "He demonstrated many of the traits I try to emulate."

Interestingly, a 54-year-old woman, who wrote that she grew up with her father, but declared there was no man she admired, reflected, "My father was in my life until my parents were divorced and after that he was partially in my life. We always maintained a relationship, but he wasn't there day-to-day because he and my mother were divorced." A more than uncommon sentiment, expressed by more than a few respondents.

Before we leave this part of the book, I would like to point out a few observations about the charts I have just presented.

1. *Father* is at the top of the list for all but one (*fatherly*) Quality/Behavior/Characteristics (QBC) category people admire in a man.

2. The difference between father (67%) and the second role, brother (9%), is greatest in the hardworking Quality / Behavior / Characteristics (QBC) category. The least difference is between husband (31%) and father (27%) in the fatherly Quality / Behavior / Characteristics (QBC) category.

3. The role *brother* appears in the 2nd position on two of the Quality / Behavior / Characteristics (QBC) categories (*family* and *hardworking*); the 4th position on two other Quality/Behavior/Characteristics (QBC) categories (*loving* and *fatherly*); and, not at all with the Quality / Behavior / Characteristics (QBC) category *honest*. However, *brother* appears in the 4th position on the combined chart.

4. The role *husband* progressively moves up the hierarchy from *family* (4th position), *hardworking* (3rd position), *loving* and *honest* (2nd position) to *fatherly* (1st position). Husband appears in the 2nd position on the combined chart.

5. The role *friend* appears in 3rd position on four of the five Quality / Behavior / Characteristics (QBC) categories (*family, loving, honesty* and *fatherly*). It appears in the 4th position on the *hardworking* Quality / Behavior / Characteristics (QBC) categories. *Friend* appears in the 3rd position on the combined chart.

6. *Grandfather* appears in the 5th position on the *hardworking, loving* and *fatherly* Quality/Behavior/Characteristics (QBC) categories. *Uncle* appears in 5th position on *family*, while *pastor* appears in 5th position on *honesty*. *Grandfather* and *uncle* appear in the 5th and 6th positions respectively on the combined chart.

Additionally, there are a few other points of interest from the data I received, that are not obvious on the charts I have shared. These data facts will be reiterated at the start of the appropriate chapters to come.

1. Not too surprisingly, in all the Quality/Behavior/Characteristics (QBC) categories, 99% of the responses that list *husband* as the man they admire are women. Only two men had the response of *husband* as the man they admire.

2. Every one of the respondents (100%) who select their *father* as possessing the *family* Quality/Behavior/Characteristics (QBC) also indicate that they at least partially had their father in their life. Comparatively, of those who select their *brother* with the *family* Quality / Behavior / Characteristics (QBC), five-out-of-every-six (83%) indicate that they had their father in their life. Additionally, those who list a *friend* in this category, five-out-of-every-seven (71%) indicate that they had their father in their life. As we move down the role hierarchy, from *father* to *friend* in the *family* Quality / Behavior / Characteristics (QBC) category, it is less likely the respondent had their father in their life growing up. However, for those women who indicate their *husband*, in the *family* category, the percentage jumps back up to 100%, for at least partially having their father in their life. This suggests an interesting correlation between how women feel about their husband, at least in the *family* Quality/Behavior/Characteristics (QBC) category, when they have had their father in their life. I am compelled to propose a closer examination of the subconscious mate selection process / experience between women who admired their father, or at least had him partially in their life while growing up, in contrast to those who did not admire their father, or have him in their life. Clearly, there is something to learn about the similarities between the Quality / Behavior / Characteristics (QBC) of an admired man (or not)

in the beginning and early years of a girl's life, and the Quality/ Behavior/Characteristics (QBC) of an admired man (or not) they choose (or not) to start a *family* (or have children) with. Moreover, what might this say about the selection of mates for women who <u>did not</u> have an admired man, or father in their early years of life?

3. Of the respondents, who select their *father* as possessing the *hardworking* Quality/Behavior/Characteristics (QBC), 96% indicate that they at least partially had their father in their life. Comparatively, of those who list a *friend* in this category, five-out-of-every-six (83%) indicate that they had their father in their life. Similarly, of those who select their *brother* or *husband* with the *hardworking* Quality / Behavior / Characteristics (QBC), four-out-of-every-six (67%) indicate that they had their father in their life. All of those who list their *grandfather* in this category (100%) did at least partially have their father in their life.

4. Every one of the respondents (100%) who selected their *father, friend,* or *grandfather* as possessing the *loving* Quality / Behavior / Characteristics (QBC), indicate that they at least partially had their father in their life. Of the respondents, who select their *husband* or *brother* as possessing the *loving* Quality/Behavior/ Characteristics (QBC), five-out-of-every-six (83%) indicates that they had their father in their life.

5. Every one of the respondents (100%) who selected their *father* as possessing the *honest* Quality / Behavior / Characteristics (QBC) indicated that they at least partially had their father in their life. Five-out-of-every six (83%) of the women who selected their *husband* in this category indicated that they had their father in their life. Only two-out-of-every-five (40%) of those who list *pastor* as having *honest* Quality / Behavior / Characteristics (QBC) indicate that they had their father in their life. All (100%) of these respondents are men. All (100%) of the women who listed *pastor* as having *honest* Quality/Behavior/Characteristics (QBC) also indicated that they <u>did not</u> have their father in their life growing up.

6. Not surprisingly, every one of the respondents (100%) who selected *husband, father,* or *friend* as possessing the *fatherly* Quality / Behavior / Characteristics (QBC) indicated that they at least partially had their father in their life. Four-out-of-every-six (67%) of those who select *father* are men, while 91% of those who select *friend* are women.

7. Of the respondents who indicate that there was no man they admired, 68% are men, with a somewhat surprisingly low one-out-of-every-five (20%) of them indicating that they <u>did not</u> have their father in their life, meaning 80% of these men *did* have their father at least partially in their life.

8. The concept of leadership as a Quality/Behavior/Characteristics (QBC) for an admired man is for all intent and purposes non-existent in the survey data. This oddity was addressed briefly in the preface, and will be addressed more in subsequent chapters of the book, particularly as I explore L(ife)eadership skills.

So, now that some of you readers have fulfilled your desire and need to somewhat run through the numbers, it is now appropriate to tell the personal stories that help us digest and understand the essence of the numbers. I share now with you a point made in the Prior Research chapter later in the book. Leadership co-authors, Dr. Boas Shamir, Department of Sociology and Anthropology, The Hebrew University, Jerusalem; and, Dr. Galit Eilam, School of Business Administration, Ono Academy College, Israel are emphatic in their argument that authentic leadership development is directly influenced by storytelling, for both the leaders and followers, on an aesthetic as well as practical level. They elaborate extensively on the research implications of storytelling and authentic leadership development, including the cross-cultural generalizability of this concept.[4] The following stories and anecdotes provide a foundation for formulating and grounding evidenced based perspectives and strategies for identifying the L(ife)eadership skills commensurate with being an *Admired Man.*

1

On Being Fatherly

"I married a man just like my father"

— A 31-year-old woman who admires her father

"There is innocence in admiration; it is found in those to whom it has never yet occurred that they, too, might be admired some day."

— Friedrich Nietzsche

THE FIFTH MOST frequently identified Quality/Behavior/Characteristics (QBC) of an admired man is *fatherly*. The men most selected as embodying *fatherly* Quality / Behavior / Characteristics are husband (31%), followed by father (27%), friends, (22%), brother (16%), and grandfathers (4%).

Data Facts: Not surprisingly, every one of the respondents (100%) who selected *husband*, *father*, or *friend* as possessing the *fatherly* Quality / Behavior / Characteristics (QBC) indicated that they at least partially had their father in their life. Four-out-of-every-six (67%) of those who selected *father* are men, while 91% of those who selected *friend* are women.

Friend for Being Fatherly

Alison

One of my most delightful interviews was with a 26-year-old young lady from Newport Beach, California. To say that Alison is all about fun and being happy is a bit of an understatement, to say the least. A community college student, studying nursing, Alison grew up as the single child in a two-parent, middle-class household. She can hardly think of a time when all of her needs were not being met. She shares nothing but fond memories of the loving family she experienced as a child. She declares, "I should be so happy to have a family; children and a husband like my father. All I can remember is how I always felt safe and happy. My mother seemed so happy also. Now, that I am older, I can imagine that; I'm sure they probably had disagreements—everybody, you know, all married people have an argument. But, I don't ever remember my father being mad—or my mother."

"Tell me about your relationship with your father." I asked. "Oh, I was such a happy child...all I can remember is being happy. My father was always there...always making me laugh, making sure I was having fun. He helped me when I needed it...maybe because I was an only child; it seemed that he and my mother were careful not to let me feel alone. And, they both knew how to make me happy." I asked her to explain. "It seemed like whenever there was something, you know, something that caused me to feel bad, or unsure of myself, my dad would like remind me of how it feels to have fun. He would help me...for example, if I was having trouble with a subject in school, he could help, but first he would make me feel good. He would build up my confidence...or distract me from feeling bad or feeling unsure. Then, after I felt better about myself we would talk about the trouble I was having…he always made sure I felt good about me first."

I reminded Alison of her answer to the question about the man she admires, who was not her father. "Oh, of course I admire my father. Yes, my father is my hero. But, I wanted to mention my friend Benjamin. I have known Ben for just about my entire life. His mother has always been a friend of my parents; he lived nearby; we attended all our schools together. And, we are still very, very good friends. We know all the same people. I wanted to say I admire Ben cause, very much like my father, he has always been in my life. I have always felt protected by Ben. Although we are the same age, he has always looked out for me…very much like my father."

"Can you give me some examples?" I asked. "Sure, let's see. Oh yea, I remember when I was in, I think, the seventh or eighth grade and was trying to play softball. I was not very good at all, but it seemed like none of the other girls would make fun of me, because they knew Ben was my friend. At first he would ask if I wanted him to practice with me…he was very good at sports and things…so, we practiced a little. I finally decided that I didn't want to play, and Ben was so supportive. He was like…you don't have to play softball. It is things like that which remind me of my father…that is how Ben is…always supportive…always there." Later in our discussion Alison talked about the relationship between her friend Ben and her father.

"Ben has been around our family for just about all of my life. His mother is a very good friend of my mother, and my father has been like a father to Ben, when he was younger. I'm not sure what happened with Ben's father…he would visit them from time-to-time, but that finally stopped. Ben has an older brother and sister, who he gets along with, but he really used to like talking with my dad. He would come over and help my dad work on his car, or talk about sports, clean up the yard, and things like that. Sometimes it was almost like having a big brother for me…it was really like my father was Ben's father as well. That might be why Ben was always so protective of me. But, as we got older, he reminded me of my father, more so than an older brother. It was like my dad was always there…if he wasn't there, Ben sure was." She laughed out loud, with affection. I laughed with her.

Our conversation about Ben was so engaging; how he is like a surrogate father to her, while interestingly enough, she has her own father that she profoundly admires. It seems almost as if her honoring Ben by saying she admires him, is a subliminal extension and expression of her admiration for her father. The more, particularly a child, has been directly exposed, influenced and affected by the modeling of admired man QBC's, by an admired man, the more instinctive it is for them to recognize its presence (or absence) in other men. This is profoundly significant for both boys and girls. Boys become not only more astute at recognizing these QBC's in other men, but they also sharpen their own sense of self-reflection; they recognize their own admired man QBC's. Likewise, for girls, their exposure to an admired man sharpens their senses about the QBC's they seek in a male friend or companion. It is almost like, if you see it, you get to know it (even if you are not consciously aware that you know it) …if you don't see it, you may not know, affectively, that it exist (consciously or sub-consciously); or, recognize its presents and/or value. You will recognize this tread of phenomena in many of the proceeding stories – the recognition of admirable quality/ behavior/characteristics (QBC's) in a particular man, preceded by and associated with the relationship and experience a person has had with a previous admired man.

Not surprisingly, I took an interest in talking with Ben. I am happy to say that an interview with Ben was arranged, so we will be revisiting this story later, in Chapter V—our discussion about families.

Beverly

Beverly, a 42-year-old divorced mother of two children, and resident of Phoenix, Arizona, also reflected on an old friend as a man she admires. "Several years ago I had a friend that I really admired. I haven't seen him in about 15 years, but I always think of him fondly. I knew him when I was in college. As a student at Arizona State, I met him…he was actually from some small town in Pennsylvania. I don't know exactly what it was, but he was always so much like a father figure…always paying attention to what I needed, and always willing to share. He talked a lot about his family and I really got the impression he had a great relationship with his own father…he was always talking about his father, and the things his father taught him about caring for others. His stories always reminded me of my father and older brother. I reflect back on how much my brother turned out to be just like my father. Both of them put nothing before the family. My father is the greatest grandfather my children could ever have. My old friend…I wish I could reconnect with him; reminds me so much of my father." I asked if she ever tried to contact him since college. "Naw, not too long after I graduated, I got married and started having children. Unfortunately, the marriage has not lasted, but my children's dad is actually very, very good to them. He spends a lot of valuable time with them and it makes a difference. We have a great relationship despite the marriage not lasting. We have a very healthy respect for each other, and I adore how he relates with our children. I guess I admire him too." She laughs.

Others Who Admire a Friend for Being Fatherly

Jen, a 52-year-old woman from Toronto, Canada, shares her thoughts about my only considering men that are admired. She wrote, "Why you don't do the same on women for women. Honestly, it was hard to find a man that I admire. But, there are many women around me that dedicate their life for their family, education, society." Your point is well taken, Jen.

A 48-year-old Los Angeles, California woman reflects on her father as she contemplated on her choice of an admired man. She states, "My Father, though a good guy and present, was a philanderer. I think I admire men that are faithful and consistent father figures."

Mildred, a 52-year-old woman from Nashville, Tennessee, who also selected a friend as her admired man, explains that he is a, "Christian;

excellent father role model for his son and daughter; remained in un-happy relationship for 12 years to be with his children."

Finally, a 49-year-old man from Philadelphia, Pennsylvania, consid-ers that his friend is a, "Great father and friend...very giving, even tem-pered, smart, and grounded. [He is the] best man that I know; teacher; consistency with his family and friends...[He] Will never leave a person wanting."

Father for Being Fatherly

Brent

Captain Brent Burton, Fire Captain, County of Los Angeles Fire Department, is a good personal friend of mine, and man that I admire. A 49-year-old, Brent shared with me that he admires his father. He shares, "My father is the number one man that I admired. He passed away at the age of 86 in 2013. He was the first example of a man that I saw. He was firm, manly, strong, brave, and no-nonsense. That's how I grew up. Under his disciplined eye. He taught me about respect, being prompt, and being serious about what I had to do."

Brent continues, "Mentoring is what many of us had growing up. We didn't call it that. It was more or less just being raised by the community members and extended family members. Today we have lost that effect. Mentoring has replaced what was once taken for granted. The village raising a child theory. It is so important for the men of the community and in organizations to invest in being a mentor. A young man with a father figure or a positive male role model, is most likely to do better in many aspects of life."

I mentioned that Brent is a man that I admire. This is largely on the bases of his commitment and conviction to making a difference in the lives of young men. In my discussions with Brent he speaks passionately about the need for mentors and mentoring programs for young men. However, he does so much more than talk about it. He has served as the chair of the Los Angeles Cares Mentoring Movement, and is currently the chair of the Mentoring Committee for 100 Black Men of Los Angeles.

Raul

"Even my friends love to hear me talk about my dad," says Raul, a 28-year-old college student from San Diego, California. "Nothing in the world could distract my dad from working hard and giving his family all that he can get his hands on for us. I am the second child of six children that he and my mother raised, and from top-to-bottom they take care of all their children, and spent time with other children in our neighborhood. Everyone is always welcome into our house...cause they all know that our parents are loving and caring for everyone. When my parents came to this country they considered it the land of opportunity, and they are committed to working hard to take advantage of those opportunities.

I was only four-years-old when we came here, and I don't remember much before then, but I do remember always being very happy...having lots of fun all the time...and my parents always being both appreciative and optimistic about their children's future. School was a very important part of our lives...my dad was not a very well educated man, but he always talks about the importance of education, and he never held his head down. He holds his children as examples of taking advantage of all opportunities regardless of his own lack of formal education. My dad is a very smart man...he just did not attend much formal schooling. He encouraged and made sure that his six kids, all of us, understood how important it is that we be educated and that we go to college." Raul is a third year Mechanical Engineer student at the University of California, San Diego. His 26-year-old sister attends the University of Arizona, where she is earning a degree in Public Health, with the goal of going to medical school. His oldest brother, Paul, attends law school in New York. His father still coaches a little league softball team in San Diego; the team one of Raul's younger sisters plays with.

I wanted Raul to summarize, in a few words, why he admires his father. "He is more than a father…he has this sort of fatherly leadership quality. When people are around him they seem to understand that he will look out for their best interest. He always wants people to know that they can count on him," Raul shared. He continued, "When I was little I wanted to play baseball like my brother…he was very good and I was really not that good. I remember feeling a little jealous cause my dad spent time going to my brother's game…cheering him on…being very proud. I told my dad that I wanted to play so he went to the club to sign me up. They found a team that I could be on but none of the kids on this team were very good and they could not find a coach for the team, so my dad said that he would be the coach." Raul laughed, "It wasn't until much later in life that I realized that my dad didn't really know much about coaching baseball, but he made us all feel good about playing….all of the boys. I think we lost most of our games, but we loved playing…and even the parents, mostly moms, of our team seemed to have a good time at our games. Everyone was so happy that he spent so much time with us…talking to us about doing good in school…making us feel important and smart…sharing funny stories with us about when he was a boy…just being a dad to all of us…there were some boys on the team that did not have fathers at home, and my dad made them feel just as good as the boys who did have dads."

I followed up, "So, how do you think this will affect the kind of man you are?" "Oh, I don't know. Right now I am just thinking about finishing school. One thing I have learned growing up is to finish what I start. I have struggled a bit with getting through the engineering program here…had to go to a community college first, but I am committed to being successful. I know that I have a responsibility to my family to be the greatest I can be…I watched my dad work hard to give us all we deserved and that is what I have learned from him. I am not really thinking about starting a family right now, but I do know it will be a challenge living up to the standards my dad set in motion for all of his kids." "Do you see yourself as an admired man?" I asked. Raul just laughed, moved his head from side-to-side; shrugged his shoulders and said, "I don't know." I smiled with him and gave him a fist bump. "Fathering [is] good for men as well as for children."[1]

Sarah

Eighteen-year-old Sarah, from Eugene, Oregon, cannot be more admirable of her father. She is the youngest of three children, with a 22-year-old sister and a 27-year-old brother. Her father is the school guidance counselor at her high school, and she loves having him there. "My daddy is awesome," she cheers. I am so proud all of the time to know that my daddy is helping other students, my friends, keep them on the right track. My daddy is able to show a tremendous amount of caring for others and still show so much affection to his own children." I asked Sarah to give me an example. She looked toward the ceiling for a few seconds and then shared, "Last year one of my friends at school was really devastated to learn that her father and mother were breaking up. They had been a very close family for years, and now, all of a sudden, they told my friend and her brother that they were going to separate. My friend confided in me that she was worried about what this would mean to the family financially, and how it would affect her ability to go to college. She was so worried and sort of embarrassed to go to the counseling office with this concern. I knew my daddy would be awesome."

"So, what happened?" I asked. She continued, "My daddy made her feel so good. He knew she needed more than just college advice. She needed to know that somebody cared for her and understands her fear of the family being disrupted. That is just how he is...he understands what teenagers need and he knows how to talk with us. He has always been able to really understand how we feel and what we are really thinking...not just what we say or how we may be acting. He knows how to help you feel good about yourself or the situation."

During the entire conversation she seemed to be smiling. I discovered that I was smiling along with her. "What do you know about your father's childhood?" I asked. "WOW!! He loves to talk about how he grew up. He is always talking about what it was like growing up with his three brothers and two sisters somewhere in Kentucky." "Where did he fit in?" I interrupted. "He was the youngest...the baby," she laughed. Continuing with the same bright smile, she shares, "He grew up somewhere in the country, but he always talks about how hard his father worked; how honest his father was, and how much his father loved helping other people. They lived on a farm with other farms around them, and his father was always helping and teaching others with whatever things they needed to do on their farms. He loves telling us stories about how his father would spend days helping his neighbors fix their truck; rebuild their fence; paint their homes, whatever they were working on. My daddy is so much like that. He loves helping other people...even our neighbors." She then let out a cheerful chuckle. "He was always having my big brother work with him on different projects, even if it was not at our house." "Really," I replied. "Oh yes," she chuckled. "My brother is just like him." "How so," I asked. "He is going to be such a fabulous family man. He is so honest, and works so hard. He is a teacher at an elementary school and he loves teaching and helping children understand things. He was like that with me and my sister when we were little...loved teaching us things. He is passionate and sincere about everything he does."

The thing that I found so profound about the conversation with Sarah is the multiple threads and relationships she shares, all resulting from her encouraging her friend to talk with her father about her family concerns. Clearly the generative nature of fathering[2] is evident in the accounts Sarah shares about the men in her family. She sheds illuminating light on the shared sense of caring about others that characterize her father, grandfather and her brother. Additionally she not only depends on these qualities, she is confident in encouraging others to take advantage of her father. I got a clear sense that her encouraging her friend to talk with her dad had more to do with her feelings that her dad would not only help her friend, but would genuinely care about her friend as well. She added, "I know that when I look for a man to marry, I am going to make sure I select a man that will be good to our children...that will be honest and caring, and know how to exhibit a caring heart for both me and his children....like my daddy has always done."

Jamal

My interview with Jamal was another fabulous experience: Fun loving; full of energy; enthusiastic; and, full of self-confidence. "For a long time in my life, my father was the best friend I had. I think my father is one of the smartest men I have ever met...I am so proud of him, and to be his son. He is so majestic and fatherly...everyone can see it in him...he is so much a model of what a father should be." Jamal is a 17-year-old high school from Lynwood, California, who grew up with his father and sister. His father has had custody of him and his younger sister since he was about six-years-old. I could tell early in our conversation that he really did not want to talk about the circumstances leading to this arrangement, so I wisely left it alone.

"Jamal, you seem so excited about talking about your father, why?" I asked, caught up into his enthusiasm. "Yes, how could I not be? I know how fortunate me and my sister are to have our father, not just in our lives, but actually taking care of us...for most of our lives. I would not hardly be the person I am today if it were not for the kind of man my father is. Admired man? You asked me about an admired man? Please." "So," I interjected. "Tell me a story." "WOW, I have hundreds. My father somehow found just the right balance of being manly and sensitive to our needs and our emotions. It is almost like he had to be a man for me and a mother for my sister," he chuckled. "I mean, my sister would go to school with her hair looking just as good as any other girl," he continued to chuckle. "And, then when it came to me, he was always there to show me how to be a man...I played a lot of sports and he always had time to teach me and workout with me. He always knew all of my coaches and my teachers. I can remember when he had to talk with my Spanish teacher when I was having trouble. She was a very small woman with a very light squeaky voice. You would think that my father, a six-foot-three Black man, would be sort of intimidating to her. My father knew how to make people feel really comfortable, particularly women…it was like they were talking with a woman. He really knows how to be our mother when it had to do with our welfare or our education." To say I was inspired by Jamal's fervency is an understatement.

I had to ask him, "What do you know about your father's relationship with his father?" "Not at all…he had no father, and he would always share with me that it was his life's goal to make sure that he was not only in his children's life, but wanted to be actively involved. I'm not going to go into what happened with our mother, but it was no way my father was going to break his promise to himself about being actively involved in our lives. It worked out that he was given custody of us, and he has been gracious with our mother. I mean, she can see us and spend as much time as she needs with us. But, he is extremely adamant about the type of influences we are exposed to…and that means everywhere…at school, our friend's homes, our relatives…everybody…he has the last word about us…to everybody, and he ain't playin'."

"So, what are your plans for the future?" I asked. "Well, my father has always been very serious about our school work, and I know that nothing short of me graduating from college will be acceptable. My father has always been very clear about his expectations. I mean, he makes a very decent living…we are very comfortable, but I think with him it is the principle of being college educated. He has told me a hundred times that he could not go to college like he wanted cause he had to get a job and earn money. He did very good economically, but the idea of his children having college degrees is something that is really important to him…he makes sure that we understand that. My sister, who is only 14-years-old, is already planning the college she wants to attend…UCLA. He started talking with her about college when she was seven-years-old, and she is an excellent student. I think I will probably study something in the social science area…I have very good grades and test scores, and I am fairly confident that I will be accepted into some good schools."

"Do you think about someday having a family?" I asked. While laughing, he uttered, "Not for awhile…gotta finish the education thing and make sure I can make a good living. There is no way my dad is going to accept me not being able to provide my children with way more than he provided for us…I mean, he did good…but he has very, very high expectations of both me and my sister.….naw, I am going to have to not think about that right now," he laughed.

I am sure it does not surprise the reader at all that this interview was conducted in Jamal's home, with his father in the other room, after me having to talk with his father a few times before he agreed to let me interview Jamal. I told him my story, and it really brought us close. Clearly, I wanted to also interview his father, but he declined. What did surprise me was that his father did not insist on approving my account of the interview. There was a real sense of trust between us, after our conversations. He just insisted on getting a free book after it is published. Of course!

Others Who Admire Their Father for Being Fatherly

An 18-year-old woman from Fresno, California, shared, "My father learned how to be a good father from his father. I am going to make sure I marry a man who has great memories and lessons from his father. Great fathers make great fathers."

A 29-year-old woman from Washington, DC, added, "My father is an awesome human being, whom I admire and love with all my existence."

Finally, a 30-old man from Cedar Falls, Iowa, explained why he admires his father. "Because he's my father and he loved me and raised me."

Husband for Being Fatherly

Yolanda

"Name a man that you admire: Why?" I asked a 33-year-old woman from La Mirada, California. "My husband, of course," answered Yolanda without a second of hesitance. "I mean this man is everything to me and has been since the day I met him. He is so fatherly to me and my son. When I met him, I could not believe how kind and understanding he was. I already had a five-year-old son, and he immediately started mentoring him. We were just friends for a long time; I met him at work. But, I could not help but love the way he was with my son; and, me. We have been married now for three glorious years, and trust me I am not letting this man go. I do everything to make him feel special, and like the man that he is. Even when we were friends, he would talk with me about things I could do to better the situation for me and my son. He encouraged me to continue taking college classes and put myself in a better financial position. He would take my son with him, got him interested in playing tennis, and just made my son feel love.

"My son's father died when he was just over a year old, so he really never had his father. I did my best to try to help him feel good about himself; my own brothers stepped in when they could, but it was very inconsistent, as they had their own challenges. Jim has been the best thing in the world to happen to my son and I feel so blessed. My son feels loved." I could not help but be moved by the glowing and continuous smile on Yolanda's face as she reveled in her reflections. It was generously clear that she is always this jubilant. She continued, "My husband also fit right into my family in a way you would not imagine. My mother, father, and brothers and sisters fell in love with him from the start. Don't get me wrong, they really loved my first husband as well. He was a kind and thoughtful man, who respected me to the utmost. Yea, he was a very good man. I have been so fortunate to meet some wonderful men in my life…men that remind me of how wonderful my father was to my mother and his children. This is how the men I have married have been. I am blessed."

Clearly, I became curious, as usual, about the paternal relationship the men in her life had with their fathers. I inquired, "What do you know about your father's father?" A big smile, "Oh let me tell you. My grandfather is one of the most fabulous men you can know. My father lived a glorious young life, as his father was so loving with his family." "Is he still alive?" I asked. "Oh yes he is, strong as ever. He also loves my husband, and he loved my first husband. He taught my father how to be a man. My father talked to my brothers all the time about how to be men; how to work hard, take care of their family, spend time with their children, and always love…he would make it a point to emphasize that this is what grandpa instilled in him."

"What about your husband? What kind of relationship did he have with his father?" I followed up. "Actually, I hadn't really thought about it before, but both of my husbands had great relationships with their fathers. Ummmm. Yea, I never really thought about that. I am treated and loved by both of my husband's fathers, and my son loves all of his grandfathers. You should see how my son loves to be with my husband and his father. It is so special…it brings tears to my eyes how they treat my son… they love him. My son is not missing anything in life. He is loved by so many men in his life, and I let them all talk to him and show him how to be a big boy and a man, just like my father taught my brothers."

Provocative and inspiring is this account of the generative nature of fathering.[3] It seems almost obvious that Yolanda attracted and was attracted to men that were not only similar in nature and values as her father, but, who themselves had similar, very positive and supportive relationships with their father. She reflected, "There is a long string of strong men in my life…I realize that now that I am thinking about it…I never really thought about it before, but I know that I would not have anything to do with a man that was not like my father…he takes care of family…gives advice…cares about everybody…would share his last dime with a stranger…loves life…and, knows how to make everyone around him feel special." I felt immensely special and honored to have Yolanda share this inspiring account with me about the admired man (men) in her life. Her son is most certainly on the way to being an admired man—like his fathers and his grandfathers.

Patricia

Thirty-one-year-old Patricia also demanded that her husband is the man she admires. Moreover, she suggested that her admiration is attributed to his fatherly nature among other admirable qualities and characteristics. Patricia and her husband of six years are recent transplants from Phoenix, Arizona, to Las Vegas, Nevada. At the time of our interview they did not have children; however, I understand that she is now two months pregnant (during the final writing of this book). My inquiry into Patricia and her husband's background reveals that while she only partially had her father in her life, her husband did not have his father in his life at all.

"My husband is a very loving man…he shows a lot of fatherly qualities, considering that we have no children and he did not grow up with his father." "Where do you think he got these fatherly qualities?" I asked. "Well, we have done a lot of talking during our relationship, and we know we are going to have a number of somewhat challenges. That might be why we have held off on having children. He has talked a lot about how much he missed having a father in his life, and how much he was teased growing up because he looks white." "What do you mean?" I asked. He is a mixed race of black and white. His mother is black and his father was white, so he caught a lot of hell growing up, a single child who looks white, in a black neighborhood. My husband talks a lot about dreaming about what kind of father he would be…basically looking at those fathers that were in his neighborhood and imagining how good the children felt who had fathers. Somewhere along the line he picked up some very admirable father qualities that he demonstrates much of the time…he volunteers as a little league coach and takes every opportunity he can to mentor young men…this is largely why I admired him the way I do…he is so giving and has overcome some personal challenges for most of his life…he really talks a lot about how he believes that having his father would have made all the difference in the world…he struggled in school…did not go to college…sometimes has struggles on his job… has had to change jobs a lot, you know, things like that."

"So, what about you?" I asked. "What type of relationship did you have with your father?" "That's funny, mine was not much better than his. My father was very abusive, causing him to have to leave the family home when I was about seven-years-old. I didn't see much of him at all after that...from time-to-time he would come by...usually have an argument with our mother...then we wouldn't see him for months. I was very resentful of my father...I wanted him to be a father and act like he cares for us...I didn't understand all the yelling and screaming and fighting he and my mother would do...I was scared all the time he would be at our house...so glad and sad when he left. It was like, while he was there, at least we had a father...I always loved saying things to him...saying daddy this, or daddy that...but the fighting would start and then I would not see him for months. I resented and loved him all at the same time... or, I should say, I loved the idea of having a father...and I wanted a father all of the time...but, it didn't really happen. It finally got to the point that my older brothers would want to jump in between our mother and father...they were getting very angry about the fighting and threatened to hurt our father if he hit our mother again...this is when he finally disappeared for good. I was about 15-years-old by then...I got used to it."

"How have your brother's lives been, considering their relationship with your father?" Abruptly, the mood shifted. Her facial expression transformed from content to anguish. I could see in her eyes the gathering of tearful reflection. Her lips folded inward as she slowly looked away from me. I knew I had touched a cord. This was not where she expected the conversation to go, nor did I. Reaching out my hand to her I said compassionately, "That's okay. Let's not talk about that." She held my hand tight and began to cry. There was little I could do other than allow her the space. Considering my experience with such conversation sometimes getting very emotional for both women and men, I always have tissues nearby. She took a couple of tissues and used them to hide her face with one hand, still clutching my hand with the other. She was not holding back...she let out her emotions without reservation... she allowed herself to cry, and it was evident that this was not the first time. I recognized the torment, but had no idea of the source...and, it really didn't matter. The pulsating rise and fall of her crying chest and abounding avalanche of tears reveals the whole story, the details of which were irrelevant. It is a story told over and over again. It was clear to me that our conversation was over, at least for now.

Glenda

Glenda shares, "I realize that my husband represents to me the father I lost in my life...I'm not sure whether that is right but it is the truth. At the age of 12, I had to actually go to therapy...which I believed did me some good...but I discovered how messed up it made me to not have a father anymore. My father left me when I was 10-years-old, and it really made me sad, and start really being very destructive; defiant at home; disruptive at school...I mean I was very messed up...it hurt me not to have my father. Finally, the school recommended that I see a therapist who helped everyone understand what I was going through."

Glenda, 29-years-old, lives with her husband of six months in Troy, Michigan. She elaborated, "I had real attachment issues with my father that, according to the therapist, caused symptoms related to emotional trauma. It is fortunate that I have been able to control the rage and anger I would suffer, and have developed a very normal life and ability to have a loving and trusting relationship with my husband." I asked Glenda, "How long did you know your husband before you were married?" "We knew each other about a year before we got married. It is really funny. We met each other at a mutual friend's birthday party. I thought he was amazingly charming and very smart. He talked about everything that came up, and was very opinionated...I like a smart man. That's what I thought of my dad... he was smart. Anyway, I was absolutely captivated by this man, and we started talking. He told me that he had been married a couple of times before, without children. He married his first wife when he was only 18-years-old...this lasted for only eight months. He explained that he was much too young and they should never have believed that they were a good couple.

"He married his second wife about six years later, a woman he met through his sister. He explained that this was more of a sexual attraction they had for each other, but, after they were married he discovered that she was really immature and unstable. They were only married for about a year and a half. He has been single ever since." I just listened. "I can't believe these women were not smart enough to hold onto this man...I mean he is so accomplished and articulate." "Are you planning a family?" I could not help but inquire. "No, we really haven't talked much about that. He says there is still a lot of things he wants to accomplish, and wants to really be sure that we are ready to give his children all the things they deserve in life." "How old is he?" I could not help but wonder. "He will be 41 this year."

I really wanted to understand this relationship, particularly in the context of her declaration that her husband represents the satisfaction of her "father hunger." I asked her, "What is it that you admire about your husband?" She replied, "He is so attentive and caring about my feelings. I talk to him about my desires and my challenges and he always has good advice...he is so smart...everybody loves him."

Jill

Forty-eight-year-old Jill has been married to Mathew for 28 years, and still calls him her hero. "I just gaze at the way he interacts with our grandchildren...just like he did with our children when they were being raised...he is a wonderful man," she smiles. "Mat grew up on a farm in the Midwest, and had a wonderful family experience. He talks all the time about how his father taught him to take care of his family, to work hard, to be honest, and to learn as much as he could. Although, he was a farm boy, his father really encouraged him to pursue formal education; which he did. I met Mat in college and we seem to fall in love at first sight. It did not take long for us to be married, but we continued our educational path. After I graduated, a couple of years and one child after Mat, we moved to Portland [OR] where Mat had landed a job as a high school mathematics teacher. Not long after that, another child, then another. Mat really loved the idea of having a big family, and I understood that from the beginning. I love him so much, and our children have been nothing short of a blessing to both of us." The sincerity and warmth in Jill's face was breathtaking and inspiring.

"I will never forget how Mat reacted when Mat, Jr., was born...boy you could not wipe the smile from his face, from that point on...it was something to behold. But, then, when our daughter Sarah was born... same humongous grin on his face...Sarah came a little over a year after Mat, Jr. Our other daughter Kathy was then born a couple of years later. Mat really wanted to have more children, but it was just not to be...but, boy, looky here; we are blessed with five wonderful grandchildren, and he is absolutely fanatic about them. Two of them don't live here...they live in Seattle, which, thank God, is not that far, so we get to visit a lot. But, the other rascals are all in the Portland area, and Mat does not get enough of them. 'Grandpa this and Grandpa that,' is all that goes on, and he loves it."

Jill is quite the talker. I had no problem getting her to share. "You mentioned his family in the Midwest, did Mat have siblings? "Oh my, did he?" She chuckled. "You should hear Mat talk on and on about what his life was like when he was growing up. That's where he got the idea that he wanted a lot of children...he grew up right in the middle of nine children...I mean children...they were not adults. And, they are still as close as you can imagine a family could be. Thick as thieves. Mat says that his mother and father were much loving parents...worked hard, and really showed their children how to love and be loved with commitment. As I had said, his father pretty much knew just about farming, but he really encouraged all of his children to go to college. His mother is also very supportive of all her children, grandchildren, and great-grandchildren...they are a family and everyone could see how close they still are."

"What about your family?" I took the opportunity. "I think that is why Mat and I connected so easily and have been so in love for so long. My family is very much similar to Mat's. We didn't grow up on a farm, but I am the middle child of seven children and my family is very close knit...just like Mat's father, my father was an extremely hardworking, proud man, who cared not just about our financial well being, but had the wisdom to pay attention to our social and emotional well being....he too, really encouraged all of his children to attend college, which actually happened. Both of our fathers had very strong family values and instilled those values into their children...and we can see even the adult grandchildren have adopted those same values, on both sides of the family...it is almost like we were all raised in the same household...we all have a tremendous sense of togetherness and family.

"What are we supposed to be talking about?" She asked with a laugh. "Why you admire Mat." I said with a knowing smile. I was so enjoying her enthusiasm. "Oh yea," she continued. "Well, he is such a manly man and so fatherly to everyone he runs into...and, as I said, the way he communicates with these wonderful grandchildren we have is so marvelous. The kids are wanting to know and understand things...they love showing him what they have learned in school...he lets them read to him all of the time...and, even the older ones...they just love talking with him...and I notice, it is always a conversation...he has this ability to get them to talk and share with him....I don't know how he does that, but that is what they all do...our children were like that with him. He is able to get them to think the way he wants them to think...act the way he wants, and do the things he wants...with them coming up with it on their own. They all have these very strong leadership qualities, and I know they got it from him...but he never has to push it on them...they love all of the sharing with him. I Love that about him. That is why I admire him so much. He makes the children and the grandchildren want to be like him. I can't wait to tell him tonight, that he is my admired man."

Others Who Admire Their Husband for Being Fatherly

A 58-year-old woman, who partially had her father in her life, from Los Angeles, California, shared, "Men are fundamental to a balanced life! They should be prepped for their responsibilities as men very early in life through their exposure to great male role models—and, hopefully, their own fathers. Men (like everyone else) need a script for life. Who is teaching them the script? What is the content of the script? How is the script manifested in their lives as children through adulthood? I am so well-treated by other cultures as a woman, we fall short of this in our own communities. It is a complicated issue, but simple things help: open doors for women, allow them off the elevator first, offer to give up your seat for a woman and her children and see the wondrous response you will receive from the women and others who are watching...very simple. I admire my husband because of his sound Midwestern principles, steady, extremely supportive of me and my personal endeavors, magnificent father to my children."

A 29-year-old man, who said that he did not have his father in his life, also said that he admires his husband because of his ability to be man enough to stand up to the principles of their love for one another and be proud of who they are. He shared, "At first it was a little scary coming out...but my husband is willing and very adamant about us being who we are and not being afraid to let others know about our love and our life together. He suggested to me that we should get married, invite all of our friends and family, and share this fabulous life with others who care about us, and not worry about those who may have a problem. How could I not admire such a man?"

Finally, a 47-year-old woman who indicated that she did grow up with her father in her life wrote, "I could have listed my brother and my father, my uncle, my pastor, and friends I know because I am surrounded by African American men who have overcome challenges and barriers and against all odds...have become successful husbands, fathers, and working responsible God-fearing, law-abiding citizens. In the media, this is not what you see. But it is mine and my sons' reality and I am glad my sons are seeing positive examples of African American men since it isn't being modeled on television. I chose my husband because he had the most challenges in becoming the man he is. He had no help from even his family and I am just proud of the man he is today...with no gang affiliation although he lived in a gang-infested area, no drug habit, although he grew up in a drug-infested area, and no criminal record although most of the young men he grew up with have at least one arrest or some other blemish on their criminal record."

2

Honesty Counts

*"I am beyond lucky to have had my dad in my life. He showed
me what it really means to be responsible for my actions and to
hold on. That life-long lesson of patience and staying committed shaped me into the man I am now."*

—A 33-YEAR-OLD MAN WHO GREW UP WITH AND ADMIRES HIS FATHER

*"Tell me who admires you and loves you, and I will tell you
who you are."*

— CHARLES AUGUSTIN

T HE FOURTH MOST frequently identified Quality/Behavior/Characteristics
(QBC) of an admired man is *honesty*. The men most selected as embodying *honest* Quality/Behavior/Characteristics (QBC) are fathers (34%), followed by husbands (27%), friends, (23%), pastor (9%), uncle (7%).

Data Facts: Every one of the respondents (100%) who selected
their *father* as possessing the *honest* Quality/Behavior/Characteristics

(QBC) indicated that they at least partially had their father in their life. Five-out-of-every six (83%) of the women who selected their *husband* in this category indicated that they had their father in their life. Only two-out-of-every-five (40%) of those who list *pastor* as having *honest* Quality/Behavior/Characteristics (QBC) indicate that they had their father in their life. All (100%) of these respondents are men. All (100%) of the women who listed *pastor* as having *honest* Quality/Behavior/ Characteristics (QBC) also indicated that they <u>did not</u> have their father in their life growing up.

Friend for Being Honest

Yong

Yong came to the shores of America with his parents at the age of 12. He is now a 21-year-old sophomore, majoring in software engineering at the University of Southern California. Conversations about his father centered on his father's high expectations of him, particularly with respect to his academic achievements. Additionally, Yong showed a consistent expression of respect and honor for his father, however, to the question about an admired man, Yong, after a bit of deliberation, shared, "I really admire my friend Julio. We have really been good friends since I started the engineering program here at USC. One of the problems I have had since I came to this county, once I caught on, is that it is hard to trust people. When I was 13 and 14-years-old I was always getting taken advantage of and told untruths. The thing that I really appreciate about Julio is that I can trust him. He tells me the truth; even if it may be something that is uncomfortable…he is like that with our other friends as well. He is dependable and truthful."

Jeff

"Man, I love thinking about my ole friend. We have been friends now for about 46 years…and, we are still hanging in there as good buddies.

I met Charles when I was about 13-years-old and we hit it off immediately. We don't see each other as much as I would like, you know we are old now and settled into our own situations in life, but believe me, we can feel each other all the time. If I call him right now, we would pick up right at the last time we talked, and you would think we have been talking every day...we are so connected." Jeff is a 59-year-old man who currently resides in Bellflower, California. He is a father of three girls, two of which are adults, and one 12-year-old son. He has one grandchild from his oldest daughter. He has been married twice and is currently separated from his second wife. He lives with his young son.

"I met Charles through a mutual friend while growing up in a Los Angeles housing project. We became so close so fast that our mutual friend became a bit jealous and started to avoid both of us...that was really too bad. Anyway, Charles became very good friends of me and my older brother, who was the same age as Charles. I'm not realty sure what it was that made us become such close friends so fast. I really admired how smart he was. He was the oldest of five brothers and sisters, lived with his mother and grandmother, read a lot and loved talking about things like sociology and stuff. It is really funny...we were all poor, living without fathers in our lives, but he was always talking about our sociological situation and for some reason it was interesting."

"While my brothers and I did have a father, who lived with his other family in Pomona [California], Charles had no real male role model to speak of at all. Our father would pick me and my brothers up each summer for us to visit him on his sort of farm for about two weeks. After a couple of years knowing Charles he started going with us. We were used to it, but Charles was amazed at the relationship we had with our dad, and he joined in just like another one of the sons, and my dad treated him as such. My dad had a slaughtering business and I can't tell you Charles' reaction to the first time he witnessed my dad killing and slaughtering a cow for sale. I mean I don't think he eat meat again for at least a week," Jeff chuckled. "He really loved these summer visits. It was not until we became adults and had a chance to talk about our past that I realized how these trips and the exposure to my father had such a profound affect on Charles and his ideas about family."

"There are so many things I admire about Charles. If I had to select just a few it would be his intelligence and his honesty. He has always been very honest in terms of how he feels about things. He shared with me and my brothers his affection for us and how much he learned from us. To make money, my brother and I started a lawn cutting business where we went around the neighborhood (outside of the housing project) offering to cut lawns for money. We probably got these values as a result of the exposure to our father who demonstrated such things to us. Charles did not have this type of exposure until he started going with us to our father's during the summer. While he was more of a reader, he started working with us...it was not at all his nature, but we were friends and he didn't mind doing what we were doing. He shared with us how he appreciated us for exposing him to this type of work habit."

"As we grew up, Charles was always willing to share his perspective about everything with me and my brother...I mean, you name it; education, sports, politics...he was considerably opinionated about politics, sociology and psychology. He always had a lot to share, and loved talking with me about such things. Once we started having families, I admired how much attention he paid to his children and the family, and he was always honest with me about certain situations both of us found ourselves in, trying to be good husbands and fathers. It was a struggle for both of us, but Charles is always willing to talk honestly about either of our situations. He has only been married one time. Like most of us, he had challenges with his marriage, but has managed to stay married and is currently with his one and only wife...it has made a difference in the well being of his children, who of course are now adults. The point is, he really tries to be true to himself and will be honest about his feelings and his thoughts. The thing about Charles is that he is not afraid to tell you what he is thinking...even about you as his friend. Whenever I hear from him, to this day, he will not end our conversation without saying, 'I love you man.' He is still very honest about what he considers as the value of our friendship. He has always been honest with me about what he thought I might do different...but, always shares his love for me and my children and my wives. He is always there for me, and, as much as I admire him, I am sure he would probably say that he admires me. We really helped each other cope with life...we have been through everything with each other...and I can always count on him to be there if and when I need him, and to bring the truth with him. I love Charles...I admire him as a friend and as a man who takes care of his family and friends."

Pamela

A 32-year-old woman from Flint, Michigan, who spoke fondly of the father she had in her life shares, "I am so glad you asked me that... I remember a friend of mine when I was in high school that I really admired. I remember how honest and friendly he was. He was not the most popular boy in school...you know, he was pretty smart, did not play sports or anything, really didn't talk to girls very much...but, I really enjoyed conversations with him. He would talk about just about anything, but I always thought that he had much more on his mind. The thing that really impressed me about him was his confidence, at least with me. He didn't really talk a lot with many of the others, particularly the girls. On my way to my classes I would see him waiting to walk me, and he would talk all the way...he would talk about things that came up in class, or things that he and his dad would talk about at home. He really loved talking about his dad...how his dad would talk with him about his school work, and how his dad really expected him to go to college and study something serious...something like engineering or math."

"So, why do you think he liked talking with you?" my curiosity inspired me to probe. "I was a pretty popular girl, and I realized that he did not have a lot of popular friends. I think that he felt that he could talk to me about things he rarely had a chance to talk about outside of his home, with his father. He did not have brothers and sisters so he was pretty lonely most of the time, I think. A lot of the things he talked about were similar to the things my father talked about...you know...

going to a good college, getting a good job, and being able to take care of your family. These were the things he would share with me and I would talk to him about. I would share with him my plans to attend Michigan State University and he would always say that we would be friends there…I didn't take that part too serious, but I knew he believe it…that was the thing about him, whatever he said, he believed and he was consistent."

"Did you have many classes together?" I asked. "Actually, we didn't. He was in the more advanced classes…I was pretty much a regular student, and I don't think the other advanced student really interested him, and he didn't know many of the other regular students." "Have you remained friends?" "No. I think I may have broken his heart. He never approached me in a way that he thought we could date or anything, but, after I had a chance to think about it later in life, I realized that it was probably on his mind, particularly after the way he acted after the high school Senior Prom. I didn't really have a boyfriend in high school…I was very popular with the popular boys, but they were not going to deal with my dad…at all," she smirked. "But, the senior prom was a really big deal. I supposed that I would not have minded going with him… it would have been a bit strange…if he had asked, but he didn't…and I didn't bring it up. Finally, I did accept an invitation from, of course, one of the good athletes at the school. Well, about a week later, while I was talking with him, one of my girlfriends interrupted us and said in front of him, 'Hey Girl, who you going to the prom with?' Just then, I realized this was very awkward. I saw the look on his face change instantly. It was like he wanted to hear my reply, but didn't want to hear it. Both of our expressions changed, and it was like the girlfriend that asked me that didn't have a clue what was happening…she was smiling from ear-to-ear. I told her that we would talk about it later and she danced off saying 'Okay girlfriend.' He searched for something to say, but I could hear the choking of his voice. After that moment he rarely even acknowledged me when he saw me. We never acted like we were an item, but he was hurt…so was I."

"So, what happened? Did you see him at the prom?" "No." "I am pretty sure he didn't attend the prom. The last I saw of him was on graduation day. They announced that he had received a scholarship to attend UCLA and was going to study some sort of engineering; I think it was mechanical engineering or something. His family was still in Flint years ago, and when I visited I did hear that he had done quite well for himself…when I look at the school yearbook from time to time I am somehow compelled to look at his picture…he did not sign my yearbook. I think about the great times I had talking with him. And, I get a little sad at the thought that the prom thing really broke his heart…he was really sweet to me…I wish he had been honest about his feelings for me…well, I guess he actually was…he would look for me every day…until I broke his heart."

Others Who Admire their Friend for Being Honest

A 52-year-old woman from Inglewood, California, shared, "He is honest, hardworking, and well intended. He has learned to consider the impact of his life choices on his family and others. He is a committed father to three sons." It was reported that she grew up with her father in her life.

Another woman, 56-years-old from Ashville, North Carolina, reporting that her father was only partially in her life, wrote, "The majority of men I have met in my life do not exemplify good behavior. I know they are out there but feel we have a great deal to do before we can say every man is like my friend."

A 57-year-old woman who said that her father was also partially in her life shared, "I had to really think about that question, it is unfortunate that I could not name my own father or even a close relative. The man I named is a friend I've known for the last three years. That is not a good commentary for 'men' in my life anyway. There is another one and I've only known him a few months; some of the same characteristics. He is a man of integrity, honest, spiritual-kind-always, tried to do the right thing, faithful to his wife; and tries to make a difference. Self-aware!"

Finally, a 38-year-old man from Germantown, Maryland, who only partially had his father in his life pondered, "I do not know why I am answering, truthfully."

Husband for Being Honest

Claudia

Claudia, 31-years-old, shared with me that she loves to bask along the sunny beach shores of Santa Monica, California, where she and her husband of three years reside. "My husband and I met when we were attending Santa Monica High School. It was a bit awkward considering I was a year ahead of him, but people accepted that we were a couple. He was just so nice to me, smart, a bit shy, but a sense of kindness that was unavoidably magnetic. He also really knew how to get along with different types of people. Although he was shy, don't at all be confused, he was really brave. Here was a 16-year-old black boy showing interest in being with a 17-year-old white girl...wanting to be her boyfriend...how brave is that?" She grinned. "His confidence in himself was really evident...he even won over my big brothers, who really acted like they were my father. Our father did not live with us, and would visit from time to time. He moved away from us when I was in elementary school, so my brothers were the men of the house...and sometimes they were not really easy to get along with." "Why is that?" I interrupted. "I'm not really sure, but I do know they both have quite a bit of resentment toward my father. They were both very good athletes when they were in high school, and they resented that our father was not around, like so many of the other fathers, to see them play. Anyway, they really seemed to like Bobby and showed a lot of respect toward him, when they met him." How old are your brothers?" I asked. "They are twins...35." "Younger siblings?" "No."

"So, tell me about Bobby and why you admire him," I offered. "From the time I met him I was attracted by how honest and genuine he was... still is. He has always been able to confront any issues...he is straight about his position on things and his feelings. I have never had to guess what he is thinking or feeling…he freely offers what is on his mind, whether he agrees with me or not. But, he is not argumentative at all…everything is open for discussion." I chimed in again. "Okay, so you were dating in high school, how is it that you got married?" "We just seem to develop this intense desire to always be with each other…we were never interested in anyone else. He told me not long after we started seeing each other that he wanted me to be his wife. The funny thing is, I was feeling the same way. After I left high school he was never worried about me getting interested in anyone else. I went on to SMCC [Santa Monica Community College], and he never felt threatened or different about me being his wife. After he graduated, he joined me at SMCC."

"Tell me about his family," I leaned in to listen. "I can't tell you how much I love his mother. She is one of the kindest and gentlest women you ever want to meet. Of course I was worried, you know, about how she would take the race thing. WOW!!! You would have never known we were of different races. She embraced me with so much love I knew I was with the right man. Our mothers met and loved each other…she even had a chance to meet my father before our wedding, and she hugged him like they were best friends." She paused to smile. "He has an older sister who also embraced and supported our being together…and now, after three years everyone still acts the same. Our mothers talk all the time like old friends."

"What about his father?" I finally got to the point. "Well that is another story all together. My husband is very, very torn, and has been for most of his life, about not having a father. If you get an opportunity to talk with him, you will discover just what I mean. The very subject of his father use to really bring out a different person in him. He talks about how life would have been so much better…how not having a positive role model, which was his father, in his life really caused him to struggle with things that he felt he would not have, if he had his father. I remember that even as an adult he would start to talk about how he wished his father would just show up once…then his voice would soften, and he would end up crying. I have had to spend some nights having to help him feel better. And, don't let him and my brothers start to talk about it...oh boy, look out. These men are hurt by not having a father to talk with them about anything. That is what they would say to each other, and sometimes my husband would say to me...he just wanted his father to talk to about anything. Like I said, my husband is brutally honest about things, and he will stand up in a crowd of hundreds of people and cry about how much he feels violated by not having his father in his life...even today, and he is 30-years-old."

Suddenly, she started laughing. "What? I said." She giggled, "I had to talk him out of adding things to our wedding vows about how a father should support his children. He wanted to add some sort of a manifesto about what kind of father he would be," she laughed some more. "From the time he insisted that we get married, he was continuously wanting to assure me that he would never leave me alone to raise our children. And, he would make it a point to say that he doesn't mean from outside of the home...that he would live with us forever...I believe him. But, I didn't think it needed to be in our wedding vows," she continued, laughing. "But, I know that he means it...I believe in him."

"So, what about it?" I smirked. "What about what?" She knowingly returned the serve. "What about children?" I admitted. She replied, "Well, that is something we have had several conversation about. I would love to have children now...he still has issues...I don't say that to him in that way, but I know that to be the case. I know that deep in the back of his mind he is still concerned about what type of father he will turn out to be...he is committed to our vows as husband and wife...I know that... but I also know that ultimately he is wanting to be sure not to be the type of father that either of us have...or, should I say, don't have. He says things like, he wants to make sure we are financially stable....he is still going to school and is thinking about transferring to maybe UCLA... he looks around and sees the challenges students have when they have children. I respect that, and I respect him. I guess it is just my womanly instincts that are in a hurry...I want to be a mother. I know I am going to be a fabulous mother, and I am ready. I have to respect him and his commitment to take care of his wife and children…and, I guess part of that commitment means being ready…that is what he says…that is the honesty that I so admire in my husband…In my man. I believe in my man. Our children will have a wonderful father…an admired man."

Caroline

Another lover of her husband is Caroline, a New York, New York transplant from Lexington, Massachusetts, who has been married for what she characterizes as, "Fifteen glorious and wonderful years." Thirty-nine-years-old, Caroline and her husband have two boys, ages nine and thirteen. Both are employed as modestly successful stockbrokers and live what many would consider a life of privilege—their boys both attend pricey private schools. Additionally, both Caroline and her husband are products of loving two parent families with a strong sense of family tradition and legacy. Talking with Caroline was very inspiring. Her engagement in the conversation is captivating.

"I know we have been blessed with affluence, and I recognize the influence both of our families have had on this almost inevitable blessing. We have both worked very hard to ensure that we maintain the legacy and expectation of our family lineage. These expectations include how we raise our children: Their values; resilience; fortitude; determination; accomplishment; and commitment to family. I am so blessed to have met a man that shares these values and is man enough to instill these values into his sons. My father was very proud of the man I told him I would make his son-in-law. It was extremely important to me to be considerate of my future children—with respect to who their father would be, and I am not at all disappointed." I listened intently.

"We were acquainted back in Lexington over 20 years ago. Our fathers were business acquaintances, and my father invited him to a family event. We almost instantly fell in love and of course had the resounding approval of our families to date. There are so many similarities between our families—the expectation for success and family values. We were married about five years after we were introduced with the full blessing of our entire families. We were almost like the model our younger siblings were to follow. I admired him before we were married I presume because of how well he got along with my father, who always had my heart. If he was good enough for my father's adulation he was certainly the man for me...and he has never let me down. Since our marriage I have grown to love and admire him for his honesty. Not, just his integrity as a successful entrepreneur, but, primarily because of his honesty and ways of communicating with his sons. Over the last few years I have marveled at how he engages and encourages them, even at their very young age, to pay attention to their character, and aspire to be successful at education, business, and family...to be prepared to carry on the tradition and legacy of both his paternal family and mine." I was mesmerized by many of her comments.

"Our sons already, at their young age, understand the science of the stock market. Their father plays games with them...predicting stock prices and the rise and fall of the market. They have saving accounts that they are very serious about...I mean they pay attention to the interest rates." She smiled. "They started an investment club at their school, and all of their teachers are very impressed with their leadership behavior and attentive personalities...they get this from their father and grandfathers," she said proudly. "The honesty in which my husband communicates with his children is extraordinary. And, they are responding to his loving influence. I am so reminded of how my father was with my brothers when I was growing up...and how he was with me. My father was honest about the challenges of being successful...the fortitude and resilience required to be committed to success. My husband has the same message for our children, and I admire that. He cares about the well-being and sustainability of our family...for our children, their children, and their children's children. How could you not admire a man for caring so much for his family and for being brave enough to always be honest with them about what will be required of them to maintain the legacy of their family?" WOW!!! I still reflect upon her declaration about, "...the fortitude and resilience required to be committed to success."

Alma

"I have to admit, I still have to say that the only man I can say that I ever admired was my ex. I mean after 34 years of marriage, he decides that he don't want to be married to me no more. Our children are just about all out the house, and he decides to vamanos. But, at least he was honest enough to tell me face-to-face. He tell me that I no longer made him feel like the man he is; I am not pretty enough for him; I gain too much around the waist; he can do better. I mean, it is pretty sad that this is the only man I can come up with to say I admire—at least he is honest. He decided that he can hang with some young filly that make him feel like a man again. He is a 56-year-old fool, but I can't stop him from doing what he want."

Alma, is a 51-year-old woman from San Jose, California. She grew up with her father rarely in her life and shares that her husband's experience with his father was even less. Alma and husband have three children, two of which have already left the home. She added, "It is really sad when the only man in your life you can think of to say you admire is your husband who no longer want to live with you and decides he wants to be eighteen again. I mean, I can't say I admire my papa, my brothers, any uncles, nobody. I really loved my husband...I want him to stay with me, but he don't care how much I cry, he don't bend...he make it very clear I am not pretty enough, and I'm too fat for him to be happy anymore."

This is a story worth really trying to understand. "Tell me more about your family," I requested. "Humm, I don't know much to say about it. We lived with our momma...I have three brothers and a good-for-nothing papa. He did the same thing to my momma...he left us when we were very young and only came by from time-to-time to beat up our momma...and to beat up my brothers who try to stop him. I stayed out of the way, too scared to even cry, until he finally leave. He come over drinking...and when momma try to get him to leave cause he is yelling at her for nothing, he start to hit her...then hit my brothers. I am really lucky I married a man that never hit me. He don't see his father hit his mother...cause he don't see his father at all. His mother had boyfriends, he say, when he was growing up...he never talk to them and da don't talk to him, so he left his home when he git 16 and learn to live on his own. He was so nice to me...I was so pretty...he say he never thought he would have such a pretty wife." Her face frowns. I am not sure whether she is about to laugh or cry. She catches herself, and gathers her emotions.

"We started having some problems about five years ago...I started gaining weight. He is a very hard worker, and I admired that about him too. He has been a very good provider...he bring money home and let me handle everything we need at home...he always work hard and come home. About five years ago he start to think more about how he look... started leaving me less money...getting home later. I didn't think about it...I was really busy trying to get these kids to act right...he did not spend much time with them at all...he really worked very hard."

"Tell me about your children." I followed up. "Da should be doing better." I see the frown return. This time I am positive of the source. "I want so much for them to be good kids, but da don't really have any good examples. No man from my family spends any time with them, and that is actually a good thing. My brothers and everyone else is really no good...not a good example for any children. Their papa work hard all the time and he don't really know what to do with them...he had no good papa either. Da have to figure out how to be good people on their own...I do my best, but I cannot teach the boys how to be men...and I am not really a good example for my daughter...I do the best I can." There is no shortage of tears flowing at this point.

"I am so scared that my children are going to make a mistake and bring a child into this messed up family...no grandpa...no great grandpa. I tell my husband that his children need him and dat duh grandbabies will need him. He seemed to listen for a long time, but I don't know what happen to him now." I can hardly understand her words through the crying that is now uninhibited. "Okay," I said reaching out to her. "Let's not talk about this." "No," she spoke clearly. "I need to talk...I been holding it in and I don't have anybody to talk with...I don't have friends…I don't have family…my kids don't care…I need to talk to some-body….I'm okay…just a few tears…it hurts a little bit, but I am okay." The Kleenex was already at the ready. I offered them to her, but she rubbed her face with her arm.

"So, what is going to happen now?" I asked cautiously. "Honestly, I hope that my husband comes back to me…I need him…I still love him. I want to be a family…I will forgive him. I know that a man can't help it when you get old and fat." The tears reappear. "He don't know what he is doing…I think he will figure out where he belong…the young girl will get tired of an ole man and he will have to come home." At this point I believe we were both crying. I felt so bad for her, and tried to stop her again, but she seemed to really appreciate me listening. I started to wonder who was hurting the most, me or her. We began to cry together. I felt like he had left me. "When I have grandbabies da gonna need da grandpa. I pray dat he understand dat and come home. I want to live a happy life again. I am very happy with my husband for over 34 years." She declared again through the tears. "I still love him… I never love any other man…not even my father…he is better to me than any man I ever know. The young girl cannot be a real woman for him…she will not be there to be with his grandbabies…he will miss his family and come home to me…I believe that he will remember how much I love him…I know he will remember how I took care of him for 34 loving years." She looked me straight in my eyes, her eyes filled with tears, and predicted, "My husband will return to me, and I will love him again…forever."

Others Who Admire Their Husband for Being Honest

A 41-year-old woman, from Fort Collins, Colorado, who had her father in her life shares, "He is very honest and a kind person. He truly thinks about others and does nice things for them."

A 56-year-old woman from Orlando, Florida, who also stated that she had her father in her life writes, "There is so much more I can say about my husband. He is the best thing that ever happened to me. Without him, I wouldn't have such joy and happiness in my life. He has taken on the duty of stay'in home with our son...so I was able to pursue my doctorate and begin teaching in higher education."

Another 56-year-old woman, this one from Chapel Hill, North Carolina, who also partially lived with her father in her life states that she admires her husband because of his honesty among other qualities. She also shares, "I adored my dad. My parents divorced when I was 12. I saw my dad weekly for the next four-and-a-half-years; then he moved half a world away. When he returned five years later, he lived several states away."

Finally, a 45-year-old woman who had her father in her life offered, "I appreciate a survey such as this one." Why, thank you.

Father for Being Honest

Michael

"My mother made my pops move out of the house about six years ago, but we seem to be doing okay. I mean, he still comes around a lot... checks on me and my sister...has really been encouraging to me about going to college and bettering myself...all the things he did when he lived with us." These are the words from Michael, a 19-year-old senior from Granada Hills High School, located in Granada Hills, California. I had the pleasure of meeting Michael at the California Science Center where he was chaperoning a group of middle school students on a field trip as part of a summer science program at their school. I found him to be an extremely intelligent young man that seemed very balanced. He shared, "I really admire the man my pops is primarily based on his honesty and hard work. He and my mom were having some financial issues, and he was trying very hard to work them out. I like that all along he was doing his best...would talk to me about the pressure...and was honest with me about the likelihood of he and my mom separating. It was really strange having my pops talk with me and start crying, but he really wanted me to understand as best as I could, and he wanted me and my sister to forgive him for not being more of a provider...he was doing his best." The sobering emotions that were flowing through Michael are evident in his facial expressions.

"What type of relationship have you had with your father?" I shifted. "My pops and I, and my sister, always had a great relationship. My pop loved doing things with us...talking with us about what we are going through...how we are doing in school...and he cares about the things that make us happy. The family really doesn't have a whole lot of money...my mother always makes sure that things are taken care of...we don't get lights turned off, or stuff like that, but my pops would all the time spend money, that maybe he should not spend, making sure that me and my sister have opportunities and have a good time.

"I remember one time that my mother didn't know, cause she was working all day, that pops, just out of the blue, took my sister and I to Magic Mountain...he didn't say a word, just told us to get in the car, we were going somewhere. He didn't make us get dressed in other clothes or nothing. WOW!!!! We were so surprised when we saw the park...that's the kind of stuff my pops likes to do. You should have heard my mother that night when she found out that he spent so much money...he never argue back about that kind of stuff...he just looks at her like he is one of the kids...that makes her so mad...but later she is okay. She sees how he just wants his kids to be happy and do some of the things other kids do to have some fun in our life...man, we had a lot of fun that day...he always did things like that. Sometimes small things like, taking us to lunch at a restaurant or something."

"Tell me some things you have learned from your father." "Aww, man. My pops really is a smart man...he don't have a whole lot of school education but he knows how to survive and he tells me lots of stories about how he and his brothers learned to survive when they first came to America. My father still is very proud of how he learned to survive when his father brought his family here, and how hard they learned to work to survive. I have learned a lot about how committed you have to be with your family…work hard…do well in school, so that it can be better for your kids…stay out of trouble…and take care of the family. My pops, and my uncles, sit around and tell stories about how they were able to do very well here, way better than where they were born and raised. Pops talks a lot about how hard his pop worked and taught him so many things. He didn't go to much school, cause the family needed him to work, but he makes sure me and Sarah are doing well in school… that is the first thing he says, 'Tell me what you are leaning in school.' When he comes over he still sits down with me for me to show him the mathematics I am doing in school. I know he doesn't understand it, but he makes sure that I understand it. He does the same thing with Sarah… he makes sure that she understands what she is supposed to be learning in the school."

"What do you know about your mother's family?" "My mother also tells lots of stories about her family, which is very similar to my father's family. They also came to America…wanting a better life…worked very hard…she grew up with her father for a long time, before he got into some trouble, and after going to jail awhile, was deported. He tried, but was never able to get back to America…so my mother's sisters and bothers were raised by their mother, some aunties and uncles…everybody chipped in to see that the family survived. She talked about going to see her father, but was too scared that she may not be able to come back… she talks about what a good man…hard worker…honest…good provider he is…she has always said that she hopes that I am like him when I have a family…put nothing, not even my own self, ahead of the well-being of the family. My mother is a very proud woman…she has lots of sisters… they are all very proud…and they put a lot of demands of everyone in the family…I know that she makes my pops feel bad…he does the best he can, but in her mind he does not measure up to her father…he tries… but, she does not see him like she sees her father."

I was really appreciating this story. I asked, "So how does your mother feel about your admiration of your father. You say that she wants you to be like her father." He starts to laugh a little. "Oh, whenever she says,

'You are just like your poppa' I see a little smile on her face. She can't hide it, she love my pops…she wants him to be different, but she really loves him. She try to act like she is not looking at him when he comes over to see me and Sarah, but I see her…he sees her too. Sometimes he will say very softly, 'I love momma, and one day she is going to marry me again.' Sometimes I think he say it just loud enough for momma to hear…I see a little smile on her face when she hears that…she wants him to be different but she still love him. We all still love him…he is my pops."

Samantha

"I don't know what I would do if I didn't have my father in my life," says Samantha. "He knows everything…takes care of me…makes sure I am doing what I should do without bugging on me. I love my father so much…he is everything." Sam, an only child, is a very high spirited high school senior who lives with her mother and father in suburban Lincoln Park, Chicago, Illinois. She is an avid volleyball player, on the debate team, in student government, and expected to be accepted into the likes of Princeton, Yale, Georgetown, and the University of Chicago. Eventually, she plans to go on to medical school to become a physician, like her mother, who is a pediatrician at a well-known hospital in the Chicago area. Her father, a software engineer, is her biggest fan, always traveling with her to her sporting and debating events. She speaks of him not only as a parent, but a good friend.

"I would not be who I am, were it not for the support and admiration of my father. I admire him so much and always have. He is the most loving and honest man I can imagine. I know I am very competitive, and my father is always there to give me constructive advice about everything that I pursue. He is almost brutally honest when he tells me how to sharpen up on my debate arguments, or even on my games…he is my best critic. But, he knows how to help me in the most loving way imaginable. He even gives me advice about my friends, particularly the ones that are male of course…also, sometimes how to deal with my mother…

and particularly my grandmas. The grandpas are all cool, like my father...but I have some real winners when it comes to my two grandmas." She rolls her eyes with a smile.

"Tell me about your father's father." I considered. "Oh, don't take it the wrong way. I really and truly love all my grandparents. I am very fortunate to have them in my life, and for how they raised my parents... I love them dearly and I know how much they love me. I know that my father's father was very strict with his children...my dad tells me stories about growing up. I realize that my father, as proud as he is about his own accomplishments, may be overcompensating with me...being so sweet and nice about what I do. When my father grew up he played sports and did a lot of the extra curricular things I do now in school, but when he talks about it, it is not always with the perspective of it being fun. Grandpapa was pretty rough on his children, and insisted on them being the very best at whatever they participated in. It's not all bad, I guess, because to this day my father is very good and precise at everything he does, which is a very good thing, in my opinion. However, he is always emphasizing to me that it is important that I have fun doing what I do. He is my biggest critic, but he makes sure that he doesn't take the fun out of my experiences."

"What about your academics? You have some mighty big shoes to fill," I smiled. "Even that," she responded. "Both of my parents, my grandparents, and just about everybody else in the family are very accomplished...went to the best universities, and have been extremely financially successful. But, my father has always been able to make a game out of everything. Right now, I am plowing through college acceptance letters with him and he makes a game out of it. I say, 'Dad, this is serious...this is my future we are deciding on.' And, he replies with comments like, 'It is nothing to stress over...if you flunk out of school you can always get paid washing the family cars.' Then, he would laugh out loud. I would say, 'Come on dad, please be serious.' Then, he would mock me by putting on what he calls, 'his serious face.' But, as usual, we would get done what is needed without the stress that I sometimes seem to want to bring." She smiles. "He would eventually get me to answer questions about the different options, and he would share very honest comments and perspectives about my personality, skills, and work habits that would help me really understand what I am embarking on. Not just about what university I am to attend, but anything that I need to talk about...I mean, he would first make fun of any and every boy that shows any interest in me, then I would eventually get a very honest opinion from him about his thoughts." She laughed, "If you are interested in me, you better be able to handle my father, cause he is going to be in your face...always and unapologetic."

Terrell

A native of Inglewood, California, now a resident of Rancho Cucamonga, Terrell credits his father for teaching him to be a forward thinking man with the highest level of "honesty and integrity." Now, 34-years-old, Terrell works as a pharmacy technician at a very large hospital not far from where he and his recently married bride reside. His bride of one year is a registered nurse at the same hospital.

"My dad was the pillar of honesty and integrity. He grew up in a housing project in South Central Los Angeles and worked very hard to, what he referred as, 'make something of himself,' and be able to provide for his family. He was actually very smart both streetwise and academically. He made the very best of whatever opportunities were available, and he did everything he could to instill those qualities in my brother and I. Hardly a day went by that my dad did not get into a sermon with us about being honest and working hard for what you want in life. I mean for him there were no excuses." I detected a smirk of reminiscence. "He did not want to hear it. If something happened to us that should not have – that was not at all our fault – he would respond, 'You shouldn't have been there for that to happen,' and then he wanted us to explain what we would do different next time for that not to happen, or anything like it to happen."

"A day didn't pass that our dad did not share a story with us about his growing up. He would tell us about how much it changed his life when his father left the family...how not long afterwards they moved from a nice home to the housing projects in Watts. Being so young at the time, about seven or eight-years-old, he would explain that he was not even ready, or understood the culture...how the kids were so rough... and how they would beat him up for no reason...he would say he just didn't understand it. Of course," he laughed, "It didn't take him long to catch on and figure out ways to adapt. As much as my father eventually appreciated where he lived and the people he grew up with, he also explained he never really became it. He explained to us that he learned to fit in...not stick out...do what it took to not bring negative attention to himself, but never really adopted some of the negative characteristics that so many people exhibited. He learned about what things people were doing, and even thought a lot about the impact it had on the families and the community at-large, but did not allow himself to become a part...while still managing to fit it. Although, we were not really living in quite the same situation, these were the skills our father wanted his kids to adopt and appreciate.

"Our dad and mother met each other when they were in junior high school. According to their stories, he was very particular about the type of girl he wanted as a girlfriend. He still fantasized about having the life he had once had, before his father left him, and wanted to start a family with someone he felt he would live with forever. My mother was very much different than most of the girls he knew, so he stayed very close to her, as friends, until it was okay with her to have a boyfriend. He knew her mother and everyone in her family...they were very accustomed to him, and finally, at the age of 25, he managed to get her to marry him... a couple of years later I was born...three years after that my sister was born. As soon as I was born my dad's whole life became about instilling strong family values and togetherness. To do this he always told us brutally honest stories about his growing up experiences and how to avoid situations that would get you, in his words, 'caught-up.'"

"So, how did he do with you and your sister?" I asked. "So far, we have turned out just fine. We are both college educated, and more importantly, we have very strong values with respect to the type of people we want to be...how we represent our families and our community. Our father instilled in us the value that we have a responsibility to our family and our community. As he got older, he loved doing community work in Watts, particularly in the housing projects where he grew up. It's funny; that as hard as he worked to find a way to get out and not be of that situation, he ended up almost wearing the experience and his time growing up as a badge of honor...he actually started to show signs of pride in where he grew up."

"My father's biggest pride was in how he stayed together with his wife, for over 36 years, and how he raised his children. I cannot tell you how proud my father was when I told him that I was going to be married. I love my father so much, and I am looking forward to being the man he expects me to be...a man like he was."

Terrell's father passed away suddenly, just two weeks before his wedding.

Carlos

Fifty-six-year-old Carlos has worked for the telephone company for over 35 years. He has three daughters, two sons, and twelve grandchildren, who all love him dearly. Before our interview he insisted that I come to his home in Bell Garden, California, to meet his family. He wanted it to be a day where most of them would be present, so what do you know, there was no better day than Cinco-de-Mayo. Just about the whole family would be there, including all the grandchildren. I was honored.

I arrived at Carlos' home at about 1:00 in the afternoon as he had suggested. Most of the family was already there, about half of the grandchildren. He introduced me to everyone with pride, telling them that I was writing a story about him. Everyone was extremely friendly. His wife wanted me to eat all day. She kept saying, "Eat something...you gotta let me know how you like it...come on...taste this." There was a lot of pride in her cooking...a tradition of her making sure that everyone eats as much as they could possibly eat, and be able to take some home when they leave. At about 3:00 just about everyone was there...music... dancing...laughing...everyone celebrating and honoring the elder men, including yours truly. The grandchildren were all over Carlos...the affection they showed him was infectious. Even the teenage grandchildren exhibited sincere affection for all the men, particularly Carlos, who was undoubtedly the patriarch of this fabulous extended family. My interview was going to be with Carlos about his admiration of his father—his honesty—but, what I was witnessing on this festive day was an avalanche of Admiration for this man, Carlos...the husband, the father of five, and the grandfather of twelve; and of course now, a friend of mine.

I went back to interview Carlos about a week later. I made sure I was appropriately hungry because I knew the routine when you stepped into his home. You are gonna eat, and take some home with you when you leave. "Good morning, Carlos!!!" I bellowed when I stepped in his home to see him perched and comfortable in his recliner. "Cómo estás, mi amigo." He replied with a knowing yet welcoming smile. "Muy bien, gracias." I replied with a cautious smile. "Ohhhh," he bellowed out. "Welcome to my home my friend." He said. After I was sufficiently nourished we finally had space to ourselves to talk about the man in his life that he admires.

"No one stand above my father." He declared. "He represents the symbol for honesty, heritage, and pride for this entire family. My father set the standard of respectability and honesty. He instilled in all of his children that above all other things tell the truth...no matter how much it may seem to hurt at first, the family survival must be based and grounded in truth. Truth about our heritage, truth about our families, and truth about ourselves; without it, we have nothing....this was my father. He came to this country seeking an opportunity for his family. When he arrived of course he faced obstacles, but he told his children that we would only survive and be welcomed if we were honest. He was able to earn citizenship after several years of trying, and to this day this family is proud to be legal Americans. The real point is that my father understood the long term benefits and rewards for being honest...and

I have passed this value on to my children and grandchildren. I would like to see some of my children have more, take advantage of the opportunities...education...good jobs...but, the thing is, they know I am always going to let them know that.

"We are happy...I am very proud of how all of my children are making sure that their children are being well educated...you have to make them feel good and important...like my father did with his children...you have to show them and their school that you care about their education and that you will do whatever you have to do at home to make sure that your children are able to keep up in school and learn as much as they can. This is what my father did...he would come up to the school...he wanted to know how we're doing...not what we say...he wanted to hear it from the teachers...from the school administrators...that is what I learned to do when my children were in school...not have problems with the school, but work with them to help my children...that is how I teach my children to be with my grandchildren...we can all go up to the school and see how they are doing...and, help them where they need help.

"Do you tell your children the truth, amigo?" He asked me. "Of course...yes." "Okay, then you know what I mean. All problems can be resolved and worked out. There is so much to offer in this country and I tell my children and grandchildren to be brave and take advantage of the opportunities. I am getting older...I will be retiring soon, I hope." He chuckled. "My sons will be in full charge of how the family progresses...I will rest in the love of my grandchildren...someday I will have great-grandchildren...and I am going to live out my fabulous life in joy and love. Do you have grandchildren, Señor Hickey?" He asked. "Not yet." I replied. He gave me a warm smile and said with a laugh, "Would you like to take one of mine...they really loved you when you met." I laughed along with him and replied, "If I don't get some very soon, I may have to take you up on that offer." We laughed together. Of course, at the time of this interview I did not have a grandchild. Since then, my grandchild Kian has been born, so it looks like I will not need one of his grandchildren.

My conversation with Carlos about his family brings to mind another issue that I would like to briefly address, particularly in light of my own evolving relationship with my son, who is now a father. Practicing clinical psychologist and psychoanalyst Michael J. Diamond enlightened, "Oftentimes the most significant change in the father-son relationship occurs when the son becomes a father himself."[1] Carlos, the grandfather of twelve grandchildren, five of which are sons of his two sons, spoke affectionately lighthearted about how he sometimes "butts heads" with his sons about how they "deal with their sons." He smiled and confessed, "I know I ask them to be softer with their sons than I was with them. I'm an old man now, and I don't want to see my grandchildren unhappy. I tell them to wait until they get home before yelling at their kids." Diamond adds;

> Some older fathers and maturing sons find that their shared interaction with grandchildren allows them to address many of the thorny issues that previously divided them, even those that have passed from father to son. In this way, a grandchild's birth and consequent growth create opportunities for reworking the father-son relationship.[2]

As you learn of the Admired Man Skills later in the book, be mindful of the change in the father-son relationship once the son becomes a father. "For many men, grandfatherhood represents their last chance to create a tenderer, even 'idealized' parental role, as this marks a chance to do it again the 'right' way."[3] I will clearly keep this in mind as I enjoy my son raising his son. I will stay cognitive of my son's desire to represent the admired man in his son's life, without interference from his father. He will not need me to tell him how to be a father—hopefully, I have already shown him that. I read an eloquent passage from http://grandparents.com, which I find to be awesomely prophetic. It reads, "A baby boy has a way of making a man out of his father, and a little boy out of his grandfather." I am already experiencing this transformation. If you are the grandfather, while you revel in the joy of your grandchildren, do not overlook or dismiss the other part of the equation. The child is also making a man out of your son—let him be the man. I am learning how to be happy about the fact that my grandson's father has a father; which is not the case for my son. The hope is that a new tradition has been set in motion.

This was one of the most delightful interviews that I conducted. Carlos and I became very good friends. I sincerely appreciated how candid and open he was, with his answers, with his thoughts, with his emotions, and of course, with his family. Thank you, Carlos.

Others Who Admire Their Father for Being Honest

A 40-year-old woman from Riverside, California, shares about her father who was in her life, "He loves teaching; is always giving. Also taught me to be strong and have boundaries. Honest, selfless, god fearing, and community oriented."

A 51-year-old woman who also had her father in her life, writes, "I just miss my dad. Honest and straight; love and caring; hard worker, always supporting our projects and advises us. Participated in all activities at school, involved us in social activities, provided us anything, and, never counted what he did for us. He was always there for us and for others. He made us laugh and smile. He gives us strength and took school very seriously."

A 45-year-old woman, who had her father in her life pondered, "I wish men of today were more like him."

Finally, a 33-year-old man who grew up with his father wrote, "I am beyond lucky to have had my dad in my life. He showed me what it really means to be responsible for my actions and to hold on. That life-long lesson of patience and staying committed shaped me into the man I am now."

3

Loving Is So Admirable

"I strive to be like him in every way."

—A 40-YEAR-OLD MAN WHO GREW UP WITH HIS FATHER AND ADMIRES HIS GRANDFA-
THER

*"To love is to admire with the heart; to admire is to love with
the mind"*

— THEOPHILE GAUTIER

⌇

THE THIRD MOST frequently identified Quality / Behavior / Characteristics of an Admired Man is *loving*. The men most selected as embodying *loving* Quality/Behavior/Characteristics (QBC) are fathers (45%),
followed by husbands (27%), friends, (12%), brothers (8%), and grandfathers (8%). I have decided to share stories about Brothers and Grandfathers who are Admired for their *Loving* Qualities rather that Friends,
who were actually identified with more frequency than Brothers and

Grandfathers. I decided this on the bases of the number of stories already shared about friends (for being *fatherly* and *honest*), and I sort of wanted to share some of the stories about the other roles an Admired Man embody.

Data Facts: Every one of the respondents (100%) who selected their *father, friend,* or *grandfather* as possessing the *loving* Quality/Behavior/Characteristics (QBC), indicate that they at least partially had their father in their life. Of the respondents, who select their *husband* or *brother* as possessing the *loving* Quality/Behavior/Characteristics (QBC), five-out-of-every-six (83%) indicates that they had their father in their life.

"In its essence, the ability of one mind to perceive and then experience elements of another person's mind is a profoundly important dimension of human experience."[1] At the core of the accounts offered relevant to the admiration of a man for their *loving* Quality/Behavior/Characteristics (QBC) lay this ability of the mind to experience elements of another's love.

Brother and Grandfather for being Loving

Allison

"Wow!!! What a great question," Allison pondered. "Let me see," she said as she gazed into her thoughts. "I am going to say my big brother. Yea, that is a good answer, my big brother." "So, why him?" I reminded her. "Well, he is probably the most loving person anyone would ever want to know," said the 27-year-old girl from Long Beach, California. She continued, "My whole life, I have always been able to depend on my brother to make me feel better about anything...and I mean anything. I could always confide in him...if I did something that maybe I should have known better...when we were kids...he would always look out for me and do anything to help me out...we are only two years apart in age, but he has always been like this huge hero for me. Of course, our father left the family while we were toddlers…at first he would visit us…maybe bring us things…then zappo…he stopped coming. I learned that you can't trust a man…except for my brother…he shows me what it feels like for someone to really love you…not just say it, but really mean it and show it."

"You hesitated when I asked you about the man you admire. Was there someone else you are considering?" I asked. "No, not really. I thought of him pretty fast, but I wasn't sure that he would be what you are really talking about. I was thinking more along the lines of a romantic sort of situation. But, I could not think of anyone else…I mean I am pretty skeptical of men in general." She started to laugh and said, "Somebody better step up to the standards my brother has set, as far has his expression of love for me, or I may not ever get married." Although, I got the humor, I asked her anyway, "What do you mean?" "I mean, my brother has not only looked out for me my whole life, but he is very expressive. When we were children he would tell me that he loves me. Even now, he has a girl friend, and he does not let that keep him from wanting me to hang out with them sometimes. And, he will tell her in a minute, 'I love my little sister, and I would do anything to make her happy.' She seems pretty cool with that. I never get any negative vibes from her…that's cool."

"What about your romantic interest? How does your brother react to other men who show interest in you?" "Oh, he is really a father figure. There can be no man in my life without my brother being knowledgeable. He is going to meet the guy and have a conversation. You would think that a woman of my age would not have her brother all in her business like this, but I am actually fine with it. He is my protector… he has been for a very long time in my life…and I really appreciate it." She smiled again and said, "It is really going to be interesting when either one of us gets married…I am sure he will be married first, cause his relationship seem to be much more stable than mine." She giggled. "Anyway, that's the story. I admired my big brother because he loves me so much, and he is not afraid to let everyone know, all the time."

John

An 18-year-old man from San Jose, California, who reported that he partially had his father in his life, said that his grandfather is the man he admires. "My grandpa was the most loving man everyone knew in our community. He loved everyone, and everyone knew it, because he would tell them. My grandfather lived just two blocks away from our home, so we could go see him whenever we wanted. My father left us for another woman when I was about 11-years-old…he got caught up in some things illegal, and now he is serving time in prison. My grandfather is his father, and he has always been very close to us, even after my father left us. My grandfather died at the age of 93 and everyone in the community came out to his funeral to pay respect. That is the kind of man my grandfather was…he respected everyone, and everyone respected him. I know people have a certain respect for me because I am his grandson.

"I have only seen my grandpa sad three times that I can remember. The first time is when our father left us. When my grandfather found out that our father had run off with another woman, and we went to his home he wept like a child. He was more broken-hearted than my mom. He kept saying, 'I can't believe that boy…I know I raised him better than that…you don't leave your family…ever…what in Heaven is wrong with him….he know better'. He kept saying he was sorry to all of us, between his crying. He made us all cry, cause it hurt him so much.

"The second time I saw my grandpa sad and crying was when granny died about six years ago now. They had been together for over 62 years, and he loved the life she breathed. He would tell us stories about when they met, somewhere in Louisiana, how he courted her, when he had to ask her father could he marry her, how her father made him do a lot of work on his farm before he gave his approval, and how she taught him how to love others the way God loves him. Grandpa would talk about Granny for hours without repeating a single story…oh, next time he talked about her you would hear some of the stories again," he laughed, "but, during storytelling time, he didn't repeat not one story.

"The third time, about two years ago, my grandpa cried in court, when my father was sentenced to go to prison for selling drugs. A lot of the family was at the courthouse that day, and grandpa was really shaken up by the reading of our father's sentence. He cried again about not understanding where he had gone wrong with his boy. 'I show him so much love in his life…we give him everything…why did the devil get his soul…why he leave his family to only get in trouble?', my grandpa cried. I guess we were not as broken-hearted about it, cause we had already suffered by him leaving us…we had already seen our mother cry her eyes out about him leaving her and leaving his kids…we were all cried out, but grandpa was broken.

"I miss my grandpa very much. He taught us all the power of expressing your emotions and loving each other. I am trying to find it in my heart to forgive my father for how he treated our mother and his children. I know in my heart that my grandpa would want me to find a way to forgive my father. My grandpa had countless stories about how important it is to forgive and to ask for forgiveness if you have done harm to another. I am going to work on that for the next few years…I believe my father will be released from prison. I don't know whether he intends to come around us at all, but I have to be ready to be the man my grandpa was before he joined grandma in Heaven. I am going to have to work on being the man my grandpa would expect me to be. I am going to have to work on forgiving my father, as I am sure my grandpa already has. I love you grandpa."

Kevin

"I admire my brother," Kevin shared without hesitation. "For all the accolades my brother has received over the years, he has always shown an extreme amount of love and gratitude toward his family and specifically toward me." Kevin is a 19-year-old high school senior from Trenton, New Jersey. He has always had his father in his life, and the brother he admires is his father's son from a prior relationship, his stepbrother, who is only a years-and-a-half older than Kevin. Both families have always lived in the same community and the relations are more than cordial. Kevin's father and the mothers do all they can to make both families feel attached. Over the years the mothers have watched out for all the children, and babysat for each other when needed. The children have always referred to one another as brothers and sisters. They just have different mothers and live in different homes.

"My brother was really a big high school athlete. He was very popular at the high school we attended. His name was always in the papers about how many points he scored in basketball, football and lacrosse. I was not at all like him, but no matter how much attention he received he would always talk about his little brother. He would always make people recognized me as his brother, who is very smart. He always treated me like I was special. We never called each other stepbrothers, and if anyone else said that he would correct them; 'He is my brother.'"

"Tell me about your relationship with your father," I suggested. "It is very good. My father is the reason we all love each other so much…it is modeled by our father. It has never been discussed, nor has it ever really seemed relevant, what happened with the other mother, but my father shows nothing but love for all of the children and has taught us to have the same feelings about each other. Even our mothers get along like sisters. My father is really a very good man, and he is modeling how a man should be for all of his children." In Kevin's home there is also a younger sister with the same father and mother. There are also two younger children (a boy and a girl) in the other family with a different, and missing, father. Again, they are all treated as brothers and sisters and look up to Kevin's father as the head of the family.

"Tell me what sort of things you and your older brother talk about." I inquired. "He loves to talk about everything. Everywhere we go people want to talk to him and he usually makes people feel good. When we have time by ourselves to talk he really tries to encourage me to do good things with my life. It is sort of strange because it looks like he has everything…everyone likes him, but he will sometimes tell me to not be like him. I admire him and what he does…he works at the supermarket and everyone knows and remembers him, but he is always telling me to be real smart. He tells me, 'Kevin, you are better than this. Work hard at your schoolwork and get out of here. Go see the world...go to college and be something...these people around here don't wannna do nothing but stay here...reminiscing about the past, that really ain't all of that.' When he talks like that I don't know what to think. He is so great to me, and it seems like he is putting himself down. He tells me that he wish he had done better...that he wish his dad would have encouraged him to be smarter in school. He says that he should have gone to college and been able to get a better job than just working at the local market. He says, 'Yea, I know it seems like people like me, cause I was a big athlete in high school, but look at me now...I should be better than this.' As much as I admire him for how he loves me, I can't help but feel sorry for him when he gets like this, but I always want to hear it. It always makes me see just how much he does love me...he puts himself down to encourage me to do good things."

"Does your father encourage you to do the kinds of things your brother talks about?" He pondered for a moment. "Not really. My father works very hard to keep our families together and to provide for us. He really doesn't spend a lot of casual time with us. Even when my brother was playing at the school, our father rarely came to see him...he is working all of the time. As long as we don't get into trouble...he is always saying, 'You boys be respectful of people, and don't get into any trouble...I am working too hard to have to run down there to get you out of jail.'" Kevin smiled. "That's all my dad cares about....don't make him have to come and get you out of jail."

"Do you and your brother talk about your father?" "No, not much. I realize that my brother thinks that our father should have been a better father for him. He loves being at our house and being a family, but sometimes I use to see the hurt in his eyes, when my father would come home while he was there. I can see that he doesn't talk to him as much as he does me. He talks with him a little bit, but it is different.

Everybody was so excited about how well my brother did in sports, and our father just didn't seem to care that much...I know that he would care, he was just so busy working all the time that he didn't make a big deal about it...I don't know why." "Did your brother seem to be affected by this?" I asked. "I am not really sure. He would always speak to our dad; ask him how he was doing; tell him about something going on at his house, and laugh about it. But, when my dad didn't respond too much, he would just start talking with me and our younger brothers and sisters...I can imagine now that it probably hurt him a little bit... how could it not?"

"So, what are your plans?" "Well, I am planning to go to a community college and learn computer science. I want to be able to make the type of living that allows me to give my children the things they need, and still be able to show them love and support. I know that children need to feel loved, that is how my big brother makes me feel. I know that my brother does not feel a lot of love from our father...I didn't really feel that much myself. And, I know my father is doing the best he can...he is trying to take care of both his families and I love him for that. But, I also know that children need to feel the love...we need you to have some time to sit down and talk with us about what our day is like...talk with us about what we are thinking and what we are feeling. I am thinking that I will make sure that I make enough money so that our needs are taken care of and I have time to spend showing my children and my wife how much I love them. I feel really special that I have a big brother that does everything he can to make sure all of his little bothers and sisters know how much he loves them. He takes whatever time it takes to make us feel loved. That is very special."

Others Who Admire Their Grandfather or Brother for Being Loving

A 53-year-old man from Lexington, Kentucky, who reported to have grown up with his father in his life shared, "My brother was the greatest. He really knew how to show the entire family how to love each other. No matter what else was going on in his life...and he had some challenges...

he always had a smile on his face and love in his heart. God bless him. He has joined Jesus, and I know he is smiling."

A 28-year-old woman from Richfield, Connecticut, who also reported that she grew up with her father in her life wrote about her grandfather's love. "He overcame many obstacles, made a crap load of money and is the nicest, most compassionate and loving man I know."

Others Who Admire Their Friend for Being Loving

Since there were several who responded that they admired a friend for being loving, I will share some of those comments as well.

A 53-year-old woman from Cleveland, Ohio, who reported that she partially had her father in her life wrote, "I lost my dad at 12 years of age and I often wonder what it may have been like to share a little more time with him. I admire a friend who works with me. He is such a caring and loving man."

An 18-year-old man from Hollywood, California, who reported having his father in his life shared, "I don't know how I would survive without my homeboy. My family life is messed up, and my friend is always there. He has literally wiped the tears off of my face, after I have had a confrontation at home with my mom and my father...they don't understand what I am trying to do with my life...my friend is always there to support me...I love this dude...he is always showing me much love."

A 46-year-old woman from Grand Rapids, Michigan, who reported having her father in her life, shared, "WOW!! This really brings me back. I remember a friend of mine when I was in college, who I really loved. We were just friends, but he was always there supporting me when I had trouble with anything. We stayed close friends for several years after college, but once I got married that pretty much had to stop." She laughed. "I wonder what happened to him...I miss him."

Finally, a 17-year-old man from Los Angeles, California who said he did not have his father in his life growing up wrote, "My best friend told me that he is gay...but that don't matter. We have been friends since we were six-years-old, and I love him. I know that he loves me...we will be friends forever."

Husband for Being Loving

Isabella

"My hubby is the love of my life," Isabella declared. "He is always man enough to show the world that he loves me...he has been doing that for over eight years now, and I love him so much." Throughout my entire interview with Isabella she would not stop smiling. Thirty-one-year-old Isabella, her husband of eight years and their three children reside in Boyle Heights, California. She explained to me that they both she and her husband grew up with very loving and engaged fathers in their homes. She shared, "I am used to being loved and cared for. There was not a day that went by, when I was growing up, that my papa did not tell all of his hijos that he loves us. My hubby's life was the same. He would always tell me how much his mother and father were in love...how he wants a life like that...how much his father told him that he loves him... that is what I love so much about my hubby, he knows how to express his love for me and his children.

"You should see it when we have a big family celebration...Ohhhh the love is all over the place. See that's the thing...both of our families are so use to expressing our thanks...for everything...that we all get along so well...my brothers are like his brothers...his sisters are like my sisters... our parents are all so happy seeing us when we are all together...a really big family with lots of little ninos running around the place." I could barely get a question in; she is so enthusiastic. "All the kids love playing with each other, and there is never any fighting, or mad at each other, or nothing. They see how the parents are acting toward each other and they are learning how to act toward each other...and other people they see. We have all learned that all we have to do is respect other people...

treat them the way we like to be treated…and nothing but blessings will come your way. All of our husbands know how to show their wife love and appreciation, and all of the wives in our families know how to take care of their man, and take care of things in the home, and take care of the children. We all know how important it is that the children feel that they are getting all the love…then they know how to have a family… that is how we know how to be a family…we learn from our momma and papa…how to show love and caring for everyone."

"WOW," I responded to Isabella. "You are really excited about your family." I hardly knew what questions to ask her. "Oh, I am sorry. I know I talk a lot…they always say to me, 'Isabella, slow down when you talk.' I can't help it, particularly when I talk about my hubby and my family…I get really excited and happy. My girlfriends…you know, my chicas…they are all wanting to get to know my brother-in-law…I say 'naw girls'…he is so much like my hubby. He works very hard…I tell them, '…he is too young for you.' He is only 18-years-old, just about to leave high school and go to college…I love it that he has also learned to show affection…he is such a loving uncle to our children…they really love him…he comes and picks them up…takes them to McDonalds and stuff…really treating them like his uncles treat him…the whole family knows how to show love…my kids are so lucky to have the uncles they have, on both sides of the family…I mean this is just one family…you know what I mean." "I guess I do," I thought to myself. She is all over the place.

"So Isabella," I interrupted, "What do you like doing?" Not knowing at all where this question was coming from, just probing for her reaction. "Oh, I love going to see movies…going out to dinner and stuff. I love hanging out with my friends sometimes…but not too much time. I gotta have things ready and happy for my hubby when he gets home. We mostly go out together." I jumped in, "Do you take kids out with you?" "Oh, yes…my hubby loves being out with our ninos…he says it all the time…how much fun he had as a child…his papa always taking the kids everywhere…he talks about his papa taking them to Disneyland every year...his papa taking them to movies...out to dinner and stuff... he says all the time that he was always thinking when he was growing up that he was going to make his ninos happy like he was happy as a little boy...they are very happy...he shows them so much love...at home, and everywhere....that is what I love so much about my hubby...he knows how to show his love to his family...he don't care who may be looking... he always shows us love."

I started laughing to myself as the interview was winding down. I thought of asking her "Is there anything you would like to add?" WOW!! Right!! Love makes her Happy!!!

Amani

Twenty-five-year-old Amani and her husband Samaad reside in Chicago, Illinois, with their two daughters, ages two and five. They have been married for six years, and have been very close acquaintances for about 10 years. While Amani shares that she has lived with her father during childhood, Samaad has not. This was actually one of my most unique interviewing experiences, for this book, in that Samaad sat in while the interview took place. I have done several group interviews, including an interview I will share later with a family. The thing that is unique about this particular experience is that Samaad is not officially included as one of the interviewees; however, he does chime in from time-to-time.

"Good afternoon Mr. and Mrs. Jackson. Thank you very much for allowing me this time with you. I appreciate you sharing with me your thoughts and selection of an admired man, and you're reasoning why." "You are very welcome my brother," Samaad responded, while Amani acknowledged me with a slight nodding gesture. "So, Amani, lets talk about the man you admire and why," I opened.

"Thank you, Dr. Hickey, for allowing me the space to share in your research. Of course the man I admire is my husband; primarily on the bases of the consistent and unshakable love that he exhibits for his wife and children. I understand, Dr. Hickey, the extraordinary power that a man has and how that power is manifested when a man finds that place in his heart, where he can openly and uncompromisingly express affection and love toward his wife and their children. My husband has mastered the embodied spirituality of that power...and, he shares that power with his family. Together, he and I have learned to channel our energies and wisdom toward positivity and emergence for our two daughters...providing the foundation for their discovery of the powers I have spoken of...the power of love in the household...which manifest itself in your total existence.

"As I have mentioned to you in our previous talk, I have learned to appreciate the blessing of a loving man in my life. My father demonstrated to his family what a man is supposed to bring to his family. My father's attention to his children was consistent...and remains so to this day. I dreamed of someday having a husband that could match what I saw between my father and mother. Daily, daily, daily my father would make the whole family listen to him express his love for our mother...daily...every day...he still does. My mother and father met when they were teens growing up in Macon, Georgia. They fell in love instantly, and he worked his fingers to the bones to get enough money to move to Chicago with his new bride. They were married after only six months of meeting, but it was true love that continues to this day...forty-one-years and still going strong. My father never let the glamour of the big city change who he is, and he always told his children, 'I ain't nutt'in without this little lady here.' And, that is the way he lives.

"When I introduced this man," she gestured toward Samaad, "to my father, he stared him in the eyes and demanded to talk with him, one-on-one. I didn't...none of us...had to hear what he was going to say to him...the same thing that my mother's father said to my father before he ran off with my mother...we all knew what he was going to say." She shared an ever-so-slight knowing smile. My curiosity got the best of me. "So, what did he say?" I looked toward Samaad.

Mr. Jackson smiled and added, "Mr. Moore is a very wise man, Dr. Hickey. He shared with me the very secrets my wife is sharing with you about the power a man possesses when he allows himself to manifest love toward all that are in his presence, particularly, as my wife has said, his family...starting with his wife...where his children receive the benefit of observing the love and respect for their mother...then allowing the children to feel and experience his direct love for them. In this way they learn to love and respect themselves, and to accept nothing short of love and respect from others. Our children have been the benefactors of experiencing a family legacy of this type of loving expression."

Directing my attention back to Amani, I said, "Mrs. Jackson, if you don't mind, I would like to get your words on what you know about your husband's experience with his father, and how it affects your family today." In an almost imperceptible manner she waited for his unspoken approval. She kept her eyes on me, but I could feel a sort of spiritual communication between them as a few seconds passed before she spoke. Finally, an assuring smile appeared on both of their faces which seemed simultaneously. I almost thought I heard violins.

"Dr. Hickey," she asked me, "Did you grow up with your father in your home?" Of course, I was almost caught off guard. However, given that I am never shy about discussing my family history and the affects of not having my father in my life has had on who I am today, I was happy to answer her question, although I was not sure of the context...not yet at least. "No, I did not." I replied with brevity. "Much like yourself, Dr. Hickey," she picked up, "my husband has found, through some guidance of others, and through the honest exploration of his own pain, a beacon of enlightenment that has guided him to salvation. His honesty and pain provided the ingredients of commitment and fortitude, to provide for himself the family experience he hungered for as a child. My husband, like yourself Dr. Hickey, was able to see through the entrapment of conformity and familiarity and find within himself an affirmation of his true value, one that is entrusted in love: The true love of his wife and soul mate; a true commitment to his children." I was simply, in a word, "mesmerized."

Linda

"Way too much throughout high school and college I would find myself crying…I had suffered seeing my friends' fathers attend the father/daughter dances; cheer for them during softball and basketball games; greet and sometimes scare their boyfriends; and, walk them down the aisle during their weddings." Her eyes began to redden, but there were no drops of tears. "Finally, at 32-years-old I had another man's love. I admire my husband."

Linda is a 43-year-old woman from Chicago, Illinois. I was introduced to Linda by a teacher I met at a middle school parent engagement workshop in Chicago during one of my trips, where I managed to get in a few interviews. Linda is a former 8th grade teacher at the school.

She continued, "I was a very smart girl in school…rather shy…had a few friends that I really enjoyed most of the time. What I really enjoyed was the time I spent with my father, specifically when he lived with my mother and I. We were a very happy, middle class family…at least I was happy. My father was a physician and my mother a school teacher…that is probably how I ended up being a teacher. Don't get me wrong, I really enjoy the profession…it is quite rewarding to me. I really enjoy doing what I felt was a righteous thing, helping children who were not afforded so many of the luxuries of life that others take for granted. Anyway, I really enjoyed my childhood until my father was killed in an automobile accident. I was nine-years-old and really didn't understand the gravity of his death until I started attending high school. I had really handled not having a father pretty well. My mother had three brothers, my uncles, who did everything they could to fill the void; including me with their children on the things they did, and I felt a lot of love. But, when I hit high school it was a big difference. I started to see just how much a father could mean to a young lady. My friends were wallowing in the love from their fathers and I was finding myself very jealous and wanting."

"Were there any other girls that didn't have fathers, among your friends?" I asked. "Oh no. I made it a point not to be seen as the pathetic no daddy girl. I did all that I could to act like the popular girls…

the ones who had the cool fathers…and, for the most part, at least I thought, I pulled it off okay. My conversations about my dad were always happy, and related to growing up. I am sure most of them knew I didn't have a dad, it really wasn't anything that they seem to think about…I mean, why would they? They all had their happy little lives and probably didn't think much about what was going on in my home. You know, they were casual friends that didn't pry into my life. However, it became very obvious as the time passed. Their fathers were showing up at their school events. I remember purposely not signing up for any afterschool programs like sports or drama because I knew I would not have a father to show up. I was always a big fan of them at events, masking my pain, cheering along with the other students, while watching how loved the girls felt, performing before their fathers."

"So, tell me about your husband," I distracted. "Oh, yes, that is what this is supposed to be about, isn't it?" She laughed. "I met my husband when I was 25-years-old. I had just completed college, and when I realized that he really liked me, it was like magic. I had not really had boyfriends growing up…I was too smart," she smirked. "But, we started talking…he was genuinely interested in me…he was very affectionate…and we were married less than a year after we met. He loved me so well. He made me feel special all of the time and I always felt special, even when he was not around. He always said very kind things to me…brought me gifts all the time and put a lot of effort into making me happy."

"What do you know about his family background?" "He grew up in Seattle with his family. He always seemed to have fond memories of growing up…he had both parents he lived with, and a couple of sisters. He left Seattle to attend college in Michigan, and from there moved to Chicago. He didn't really talk a whole lot about growing up, but the little he did talk about, it seemed that he had a normal and happy life. He was very stable." At this point I observed that her voice was softening and her attention was wavering. Although, I already knew about the eventuality of her happy marriage, I was committed to giving her space. She had so much enjoyed talking about how much her husband loved her and how special it made her feel. Yes, she does get distracted with the experiences of her youth; how she felt growing up without her dad, and the pain of having to cope with not experiencing the things that she so admired in the experience of other girls, throughout high school and college. But, today I watched and experienced with her the recollection of a happy, beautiful, yet short marriage.

After a few minutes of quiet reflection, some smiling, and some tears, Linda spoke. Clearing her throat and wiping away a few tears she reengaged with me. She looked directly into my eyes and said clearly, "After two of the most wonderful years of my life, my husband was killed in an automobile accident, just like my father had left me. The two most wonderful men I have ever had both left me in the same manner. I have not given even a thought of being in love again. Yes...as I said, I admire my husband. He found me and brought me the joy I so much missed after my father was killed. He made me feel like a little girl, and like a woman...a woman that deserves to be loved. He kissed and touched me every day of our wonderful life together. And, then he left me. I love you baby...and I will never love another."

Sue

Sue and her husband of 12 years reside in a quiet community near San Diego, California. They do not have any children, but say they are planning to expand the family next year. Sue is a university professor of sociology. Her husband Dan, who Sue says she dearly admires, is an insurance broker. They met in college and were married four years later. Sue is 34-years-old.

"Well, I know it is the same old story, love at first sight, right?" she laughs. "But, that is what it seemed like. I was a young freshman, and he was just a sophomore. We had a lot of mutual friends, who, you know, hung out doing the things college students do. That's right," She laughed again, "we were your typical group of Asian students that clung to each other everywhere we went. I started liking Dan pretty quickly. While the group was always having fun and trying to figure our way around…with the assistance of the experienced Asians on campus," laughing again, "Dan always found a way to look at me in a way that indicated that he was interested in being more than a tour guide…I liked the way he would look at me." So, after my freshmen year, we got brave enough to actually kiss each other…then it was on… we were in love," she laughed again.

"After 12 years of marriage Dan is still every bit of the charmer he was when we met. He still looks at me with a gleam in his eyes, and I am still very gitty about his sexy stare. He still makes me feel like the young freshman college student trying to figure things out."

"How did your family react to you dating in college?" "Oh boy," she responded. "My mother was not at all happy when I told her over the telephone that I had a boyfriend. She lives in Los Angeles, where I was raised, and I thought she was going to jump in her car and come and get me out of here. She was very concerned about me being distracted from my studies and getting my heart broken. This is what she started talking about, 'Sue, you cannot let yourself become venerable to a boy…he will take your attention away from your school work, only to find someone else when you are not good enough anymore.' I say, 'Mother please don't worry about that, you will like him when you meet him.' I knew exactly why my mother was feeling that way…she was broken-hearted when my father left her for another woman. I remember her doing nothing but crying for months when he left. He did not come over to even visit and check on us but a few times, and she was devastated."

"What about you?" I asked. "How did you take his leaving the family in that way? How old were you?" "Ummm, I was about 13-years-old I think. My father was really not a very affectionate man…he never really talked much to me or my mother…he had friends that would come over and they would talk a lot…he would have my mother act as some sort of servant for his friends of course, and I was just to stay in my room…that's pretty much how he was with me all the time…the quieter I was the better. Once, when I was a teenager, my father leaving came up in a talk my mother and I was having. I told her that I felt that we were actually better off without him, and she lost it. I told her that I never missed him…he never really acted like a father to me…not like I saw some other fathers being with their children. My mother came up with all sorts of excuses for him…mind you, she had not seen his ass in over four or five years, but she still wanted me to honor him…bullshit! Anyway, I guest the point is I didn't know him as a child well enough to miss him. I have to admit, I guess I still get a little upset about how he made my mother feel about herself. Just like she makes excuses for his sorry ass, she blamed herself for him finding another woman…she felt like she was not good enough anymore…anyway, lets move on, I don't want to be upset." I was thinking the same thing.

"So, let's talk about Dan again." I said, as she laughed and reached over to slap me five. We both laughed, and the tension was released. "That's a good idea," she laughed. "Anyway, I wanted to tell you about my mother meeting Dan. That weekend when I told her about Dan, we had been dating for well over six months, I knew I needed to take him to meet my mother very, very soon, or she was gonna be up here. Oh my God, you would not believe it. We walked into the house…I did not tell her I was coming…I said, 'Mother…mother.' And she came out of the family room. She look at me and Dan, and her eyes were as wide open as she could get them. I said, 'Mother, this is my friend Dan.' I was not brave enough to say boyfriend." My mother covered her wide open mouth and walked slowly to Dan, removing her apron that she always wears, and gave him the biggest hug you can ever imagine. I mean you would have thought Dan was her long lost son. She hugged him like she knew him. She led him by the hand into the family room, sat him on the couch and sat right next to him, never letting his hand go. He and I were dumbfounded. I started telling her things about him…what he is studying in college, where he is from, I may have even told her his favorite color," she joked. "But, all she did was look at him like she already knew everything about him. I was totally surprised and was searching for something to say that would break the spell she was in. I finally said, 'Mother, Dan has been my boyfriend for six months now.' Then, she broke out crying and hugging him again. I almost got jealous…she was acting like she was more proud of him than me. Then, Dan returned her embrace…they were just hugging each other and starting to talk with each other. My mother had a marvelous day. She finally started paying a little attention to me…she was in love with Dan.

"To this day my mother loves my admired man. She also admires him as much as I do. Our getting married seems to have changed my mother's life. She is so much happier than before she met Dan, even after all of this time. I don't recall her ever again being down on herself about my father, at least in my presents. It is almost as if having Dan in our lives, and the way he treats her, changed her whole perspective about her own value.

"Dan and I have worked very hard at our careers and were somehow slow at trying to have children. But, we both agree that it is about time. We want to share our love for each other with little ones of our own. We have a few nieces and nephews on his side of the family, but it is time for us to have our own children. Dan is such a good man to me…he always has been. He is going to be a fabulous father, as he is a husband. I am such a fortunate woman to have met Dan. He is pretty fortunate as well…there ain't a whole lot of women running around out there as awesome as I am," she closed with a big smile. I smiled along with her. I think she is right-on.

Others Who Admire Their Husband for Being Loving

A 32-year-old woman from Knoxville, Tennessee, who had her father in her life shares about her husband, "His strength of character and his love for myself and our children makes me admire him beyond anyone."

A 22-year-old woman from San Luis Obispo, California, wrote, "I grew up with an adoptive father and my biological father was in the picture as well."

Finally, a 44-year-old woman from Seattle, Washington, shared, "Neither of us had the best fathers and yet we chose to break the cycle."

Father for Being Loving

Sarina

"My dad has always meant the world to me, my mother, and my brother and sister. There is nothing in the world that my dad would not do to take care of our family, and the love that pours from his heart is ever flowing. He dedicates his life to making sure we get the best life has to offer, and that no harm comes our way. As a Baptist preacher with a large congregation, my dad is always in the spotlight. He is committed to offering prayer and salvation to countless families. It is his work to listen to the problems of others; to help feed those who are hungry; to pray for those who are lost, but at the end of the day, my dad makes sure that his family feels not only his blessing, but we are covered in his love."

Sarina is a 20-year-old community college student who resides with her family in Portland, Oregon. She is the middle child of three children in the family. She has an older sister and a younger brother. "I should be so lucky to meet a man with my dad's loving personality. My dad grew up in a Christian family and has dedicated his life to Christian beliefs, and inspiring his family to embrace the Bible. Beyond that he also encourages his family, including our mother, to be life-long learners as well. Both he and our mother take college courses. My dad is working on a master's degree. That is the thing, he practices what he preaches. Not only in church but in life. Sometimes, his sermons have a message about the members continuing their education. He makes it a point to clarify that, 'It doesn't matter what age you are, God wants all of his children to be educated to the fullest extent of the powerful brain God has gifted us with.' My father is very well liked and appreciated by everyone at our church as well as in the community. Everyone also knows what kind of man he is as well.

"He has always talked with his children about how we present our-selves at church, school and in the neighborhood. We have all lived un-der the spotlight of living up to the expectations and reputation of our father…sometimes that can be difficult, but most of the time it is pretty much like we are anyway…we have been raised to be pretty much the way people see us." "How do you feel about that?" I inquired. "Well, as I said, we are use to it. Most of the time I am honored by the way people react to me and speak to me. You should see how people look at us whenever our dad delivers a sermon that features his children…the love and respect that comes our way is awesome. People cannot help but feel the love our dad has for his family. It makes others want to not only love us, but show more love and appreciation for their own children and families…I have been told that several times in my life by some of the other children who have attended our church over the years.

"One of my best friends once shared with me, 'Your father has had such a positive influence on my family. My mom and dad had been having a lot of problems…we were so afraid that they were going to break-up, but they continued to talk. It was my dad's idea that they start attending church, and they heard your father talking about your family. When they left they were very happy, and whenever they have challenges they refer to your father and your family…they attend the service just about twice a month now…and, I often see them referring to the Bible…some of the verses that your father preaches on at church. My family is so blessed, and saved because of your father.'" "Have you shared those testimonies with your father?" I asked Sarina. "Of course I have," she responded. "What does he say about it?" "Well, you know, he is the Reverend. He acts all nonchalant about it, but I know that he is moved by stories like that. He takes a great deal of pride in helping people with personal problems…especially marriage problems. And, whenever he hears about one of his sermons helping someone person-ally it really inspires him…we will hear about it until next Sunday." She laughed. "But, it's cool. We love it when our dad is inspired; he works so hard and does so much to inspire others…he deserves to feel some of the love coming back at him. He is so loving of others. It is just his nature."

D'Ante

D'Ante, a resident of Dallas, Texas, is the father of two sons, ages thirteen and nine. He is a 34-year-old freight operator who has experienced very unstable employment opportunities. He grew up in a very stable family in New Orleans, Louisiana, and moved to Dallas less than a year ago, hoping to find more stable employment. He has an older brother that still resides in New Orleans and an older sister who lives with her husband and children in Houston, Texas. His parents, who are still married, also reside in New Orleans, the place of their birth.

"I can still remember the love that my daddy shows all his children back home…when we was grow'in up. One thing us kids knew every day was that our daddy loved us…he made sure that we heard it a lot and that we felt it. He treat my momma like a queen and he treat my sister like a queen. He teach me and my brother how to work hard and try to tell us to be good family man. Yes, dat's the man I admire…my daddy… I still admire him cause of the love he shown me all my life…and how he treat us and our momma. When I was grow'in up I wanted to be just like my daddy. Everybody from all over love my daddy cause he was so giving…and he is a Christian. I remember when he was sick and in the hospital…I was just a young boy then…everybody came over to our home to check on my momma and us kids. Everybody bring food and stuff so that we would be okay. My daddy was the one that works and my momma most of the time stay home and keep the kids and make sure the house is clean, that my daddy have a good meal, that his work clothes are always clean, and that everything would be just the way he like it at home. When he git home he would always play wit us kids and tell my momma how much he love her. Dat's the thing, he make sure we all know how much he love us. I grew up wanting to be just like my daddy. I would think about it when I was growin' up that I wanted a momma for my children just like my momma and I would be just like my daddy…

my kids would know I love them and da momma all the time...I guess I didn't do so good." He uttered with shame.

"What do you mean?" I leaned in. "Well, you know." He replied. "Let's hear it from you." I said. "I don't know," he uttered. "I tried to be a good daddy. I love my wife and kids, I just couldn't keep it together... I should have been more education so that I could have a good job. I was doing okay for a while, but, after Katrina things really got bad and I did not have any work...I'm looking at my kids all duh time, and they depending on me to be the man...my wife look sad all duh time...my daddy and momma have to help us...my brother have to help. When we lose our place we have to move in with my daddy...and, I was not feeling like a man at all. I wish I had more education but I don't and I could not keep a job...like before...to keep my family strong...to keep my children from looking sad...I mean da was happy...da is kids...but I know that da deserve better...and I did not feel good.

"When I couldn't take it any more I finally move out of my daddy house about a year ago...I leave my wife and kids there. I could not look at my children face anymore...my wife will do better finding another man to take care of my children...I gotta leave so that I can feel better. I didn't really have no place to go...so I lived on the street a little...then my friend let me stay some time with him...I find odd things to do for money and survive." "Did you think you would go back to get your family after you started getting it together?" I offered. "I am too shame of myself...I don't want to see da faces after I ran off...I don't want to see my daddy and momma either...I am shame. Finally, somebody tell me I should come to Texas...lot of men come here to do better. I was lucky enough to get a ride here from a trucker friend I know...and, I was able to get some work...I don't know how long I will have it...but for now it is good."

"So, what about your family?" I offered again. "I don't know," he uttered. I could feel his pain as well as his tears beginning to roll down his face. "I love my kids...I am so sorry I left them the way I did...I haven't gone back to see them at all and I am so shame of myself...I didn't think

I was selfish…I just couldn't stand to have them see me not a man. I started thinking that da were better off without me…my wife would find a good daddy for them…people do that all the time, and I was thinking that is what she is going to do…I don't know…maybe she did find another man…da don't know where I am." "Do you feel better now?" I asked, probing for his self talk about how he had left his children. "Naw, I don't." The tears flowing stronger. I hated putting him through this, but I could feel that it was in some way making him reflect on some much needed suppressed emotions, shrouded in excuses. He started to cry out loud while reaching for me to provide physical comfort. I could feel my own emotions starting to erupt. I knew that was enough. I hugged him and whispered in his ear, "Find out how your wife and children are doing. Call them and let them know that you are trying to do better, that you love them, and that you want to see them. They are probably worried sick about you, and they need to know." I don't know whether this was the right advice or not, but it sure seems like a start.

Daniel

I met Daniel through one of the other individuals I interviewed while traveling in the Midwest for a round of interviews. He resides with his family in the suburbs of Midland, Michigan. Daniel is 18-years-old and has been accepted and plans to attend California State University Pomona. He eventually intends to go to medical school to become a physician. He states that he is primarily interested in cardiology, like his father. "My father is really a fabulous individual who has saved hundred of lives, as a cardiologist. He has been such an inspiration to me and my older brother, who is also a physician, and I have always wanted to follow in their footsteps. Aside from inspiring his sons to be servants, he has shown us so much love…love for our mother and so much attention to us while we are developing into men. This is such an important thing to our father…the type of men we develop into and the quality of service we contribute to society. Our father spends considerable time giving his time to causes, visiting schools, mentoring other young men through community organizations, and volunteering for organizations that service needy families. He has shown me and my brother the path to such service by allowing us to be with him as often as it is feasible...of course our studies and preparedness is a priority. I think the most powerful attributes that our father has instilled in us is the value of self-discipline and determination. For as long as I can remember during my life our father has preached that love starts with those two attributes. He would always remind us that 'Love for others starts with the love of yourself. The love you have of yourself is demonstrated through discipline and determination. To love others is to love yourself,' and we believed our father, because he demonstrated so much love for his family."

Of course, desiring a deeper understanding, I asked Daniel about his father's life. "My father came to this country, when he was just four-years-old, with his family from Kyoto, Japan. Our grandparents were very young and wanted to take advantages of the opportunities available in America. Of course, they were specifically seeking the educational opportunities and wanted to ensure that their children could benefit from such. My father has older sisters who are also very well educated, here in America of course. Our grandparents are also very loving and supportive. They are very proud people and love so very much all of their grandchildren. They look upon us with an abundance of pride, and they look upon our parents with so much respect. I hear my grandfather talking with my father sometimes about his pride in how my father followed through with his education, how much he demonstrates love for his family, and how he has encouraged his children to pursue high standards and goals."

"What did your grandfather do for a living?" I inquired. "I don't really know what he did in Kyoto, but they settled around Trenton, New Jersey, for a few years after they arrived. My grandfather worked very diligently to earn citizenship in America that was very important to him. He wanted his children to have all the benefits of citizenship and did not want to worry about having to leave this country. I am not sure what my grandfather did for a living in Trenton, but he ended up in Detroit, not too long after being in America, working at a hospital as an orderly. Obviously, this experience inspired him to encourage his children to pursue careers as physicians. My grandfather was very impressed with the responsibilities of physicians and made friends with several while he worked at the hospital; that's the story we are told.", he said, with a rare change of expression—a mild smirk. "Anyway, he managed to encourage and inspire all of his children to be exceptional in school, and to pursue medical professions. Now, it is his grandchildren who are in the profession and he could not be more proud."

"Do you think this tradition will carry over to his great-grandchildren?" I said in a lighthearted tone. "Oh you better believe it," he smiled.

Adriana

"My poppa would say every night, 'Poppa loves his little babies tonight, and poppa is going to love you in the morning.' We lived to hear our poppa say that to us every night. The funny thing is that we were getting older and would have friends spend the night and he would still say that to us, and we still loved it. I loved my poppa so much, and I miss him."

Two years ago Adriana, her two sisters, her three brothers, her mother, nine grandchildren, and a host of cousins suffered the loss of their beloved poppa, as his body succumbed to liver cancer. He had been hospitalized for over four months which allowed friends and relatives to come by and share their love and kind gestures with poppa and the family. He fell into a coma for his final two day, and then his life ended. Tears consumed her eyes throughout our conversation; some of joy and some of sorrow.

Residing in Bellflower, California, 22-year-old Adriana and her five-year-old son reside with her momma together with one of her older sisters and her three children, one of which is a teenager. Adriana and her sister are charged with taking care of momma, who is now an aging 86-years-old and is starting to have signs of dementia. Everyone, including momma, still talks about how much they miss poppa and the love he shared with the family.

"My poppa was the best man in the world. Out of all the men you can run across in your life, he knew how to make everyone feel very, very special. He was such a lover of life, all the time…he never let anything get him down…and he would not let you have a sad face. He knew how to talk to all the children…even when I was a child…and make them feel good about themselves. He loved to make everyone laugh…he made sure you felt good about yourself no matter what. I remembered that he wanted me to do very good in school, and go to college…he wanted me to study law in school…he would say to me, 'Anna, you gotta learn law school and be a big time lawyer.' He loved watching *Law and Order* on television. He would say, 'Anna, look at those women lawyers on TV and judges…you can do that…you have the mind for that…you go to the college where they let you be a lawyer when you finish. Our family is so proud of you and you can do it.' I would always say to him that I was going to be a lawyer and make him very proud of me, and he would remind me, 'I am already proud of you, Anna. I am always proud of you and all my children…sometimes they stray a little bit, but I know they are good and they are going to do great things…I know that my Anna is going to do great things too…my Anna is going to be a big time lawyer…maybe a judge some day.'

"You can just imagine how I could have felt about myself, when I found out that I was going to have a baby, and I had not even finished high school yet. I had done the same thing that both my older sisters had done, gotten pregnant without being married. At least they had graduated high school already." She laughed. "But, I didn't feel bad, because I had already seen how my poppa acted with my sisters…and he acted the same way with me. Not one let down of encouragement…all I could feel was his love and excitement about having another grandchild. He never, ever, ever made his children feel bad about their mistakes. He never even made you feel like it was a mistake as far as he felt. He just loved you and encouraged you to love our children. And, he still encouraged you to get more education…we all try to go to school and learn something when we can.

"When one of my brothers got in some serious trouble, and spend some time in jail, my poppa still stood by him like he loves him. I will never forget that in my whole life. We were disappointed that my brother started hanging out with the wrong people, and started getting in trouble. My poppa knew that my brother was getting into trouble because once the police came to the house looking for him. But, poppa always showed my brother his love…he always told us that he would be okay and that he would get back into school and do good things. Even though we knew our brother was headed in the wrong path, our poppa somehow made us feel better. My brother ended up spending a couple of years in jail, and when he came out there was nothing but love coming from poppa. Our poppa pick right up where he left off," she laughed, "telling my brother how special he is '…he gonna go back to school…and he gonna be great…no problem, he just had a little set-back.' Oh, my poppa was always thinking of the best."

"So, what happened with your brother after his release?" I could not help but ponder. "Actually, my brother did start getting his act together. He met a very nice girl, who my poppa of course adored, and he stopped getting into trouble. He learned how to do plumbing and started making money for himself. My poppa had a way of making you come around to what is good for you, and this is what happened to my brother. He started helping my other brother learn plumbing and they talk about starting their own business. They would sit around and talk with poppa and momma about when they plan to own their business, and my poppa would not act surprised at all. We were like, 'Yea right, you are going to start your own business, in what life?' But, our poppa would not act surprised at all. He acted like he knew they would do that and it was what he expected. He talked with them like they already had the business. He would talk with them about what the business name is, what city it would be in…he wanted it to be in Hollywood, '…where you can work on the rich folk houses' he would say. He was confident that my brothers were going to have their own business. Even in the hospital, before he got really sick", the tears starting to flow along with her voice starting to choke up, "...even in the hospital he asked my brother how the business was going...he asked him how he was getting business in Hollywood," she cried. I had to give her a minute. I also had to give myself a minute.

"Okay, I'm sorry." She uttered. "I miss my poppa so much," she paused briefly. "So, anyway," she continued, while wiping her eyes. "That is how our poppa was. He was always encouraging us all to be great...and he always acted like we were already great, no matter what the situation was, he was showing us love." The tears reappeared. "I miss our poppa and I love him so much." The tears pouring again. It was pretty clear to me that I needed to end this one, like so many others. I didn't want her to suffer from the conversation. As I tried to bring the conversation to an end, she demanded, "No, no, no...I love talking about my poppa. I'm okay, something got in my eye," she laughed. I could not help but laugh with her.

For the balance of our conversation she shared very similar stories with me about how poppa encouraged his children to go beyond what it seemed they could achieve. I eventually asked Alaina what she expected from herself." She replied, "Every morning I still hear my poppa saying, 'Poppa loves his little babies tonight, and poppa is going to love you in the morning.' I have made up my mind. I don't know what it is going to take, or how long it is going to take, but I am going to be a lawyer and then I am going to be a judge, just like my poppa expects of me. And what I expect of myself." We smiled together.

Others Who Admire Their Father for Being Loving
(all reporting that they had their fathers in their lives as children)
A 56-year-old woman from Compton, California, shared, "My father continues to provide guidance to his grandchildren."

A 34-year-old woman from Antelope Valley, California wrote, "The most amazing thing of a man is the love for their children and they are there no matter what."

A 50-year-old man from Los Angeles, California, stated, "When I think of both of my parents, the word that comes to mind is 'good!'"

Another man from Los Angeles, 33-years-old, shared, "I am beyond lucky to have had my dad in my life. He showed me what it really means to be responsible for my actions and to hold on. That life-long lesson of patience and staying committed shaped me into the man I am now."

A 25-year-old woman from Chicago, Illinois, shares, "My father is the most important person in my life. My most admired qualities come from him. I couldn't bear to be without my mother and father."

A 33-year-old man from Cedar Falls, Iowa, said that he admires his father, "Because he's my father and he loved me and raised me."

A 27-year-old woman from Chicago wrote, "Lost my mother when I was young—my dad is my best friend and my hero."

A 51-year-old woman from Los Angeles shared, "I just miss my dad. honest and straight; love and caring; hard worker; always supporting our projects and advises us. Participated in all activities at school; involved us in social activities; provide us anything, never count what he did for us. He was always there for us and for others. He made us laugh and smile. He gave us strength and took school very seriously."

Finally, a 54-year-old man from Los Angeles declared, "I look at myself and feel I pale in comparison to my father. He's been dead for more than 17 years and he still comes up in conversation with family and friends. My father was never a grandstander and never sought attention, yet people remember him because of his character and devotion to family. Even on his deathbed, the family's welfare took precedence over his fight against stomach cancer. He thought himself half a man because he was very weak and confined to a bed, unable to support his family the way he felt that he should. That could not have been further from the truth."

4

Hardworking Men

"I've witnessed my brother working hard to support his family in racist America. I've witnessed my brother struggling against the odds in a country which both hates and fears him. I've witnessed my brother's pain after being denied employment by lesser males who feared his abilities."

— A 62-YEAR-OLD WOMAN WHO DID NOT HAVE HER FATHER IN HER LIVE, AND ADMIRES HER BROTHER.

"The love of family and the admiration of friends is much more important than wealth and privilege."

— CHARLES KURALT

‿⁓

THE SECOND MOST frequently identified Quality/Behavior/Characteristics (QBC) of an Admired Man is *hardworking*. The men most selected as embodying *hardworking* Quality / Behavior / Characteristics (QBC) are

Fathers (67%), followed by husband/brother (9%), friends, (8%), grand-fathers (7%).

Data Facts: Of the respondents, who select their *father* as possessing the *hardworking* Quality/Behavior/Characteristics (QBC), 96% indicate that they at least partially had their father in their life. Comparatively, of those who list a *friend* in this category, five-out-of-every-six (83%) in-dicate that they had their father in their life. Similarly, of those who select their *brother* or *husband* with the *hardworking* Quality/Behavior/Characteristics (QBC), four-out-of-every-six (67%) indicate that they had their father in their life. All of those who list their *grandfather* in this category (100%) did at least partially have their father in their life.

Friend for Being Hardworking

Rebecca

Thirty-three-year-old Rebecca lives with her two children in Denver, Colorado, where she attended college, and says that she admires her friend Rob. She has a nine-year-old son, and a six-year-old daughter. After an eight year marriage, she has been divorced for two years from her husband who she met in college. Originally from St. Paul, Minnesota, she is employed as a staff accountant at a popular amusement park in the Denver area.

"Hello, Dr. Hickey," she greeted me. "It's so nice to see you again." We had briefly met and discussed the nature of this project two days ago, when I was interviewing another potential participant, that didn't work out. "Hi, Rebecca," I replied. "It is a pleasure seeing you again. How was your son's baseball game?" On the day we met she told me about her son being on a baseball team and being really excited about it. "Oh, thank you for asking. He had a fabulous time. He's got to get a little better, but you can't tell him that. He thought he was awesome. You have to love his enthusiasm." She smiled.

"Okay, so Rebecca, name a man that you admire, and tell me why?" She replied instantly, "At this point in my life I would have to say my friend Rob, who lives in this apartment. I have to admit, I would have loved to say my ex; at one time he was just that, but now, I would have to say Rob...my ex has really disappointed me over the last few years. I mean, you would think that he would at least come and see his children. I know that he has a problem with me, but don't take it out on your children, you know what I mean? Since our divorce, he refuses to come by, even to see his kids." "You said that he has a problem with you?" I could not help it. "Since we got married, he has always had a problem with how I relate to others...he was always very possessive and jealous...always thinking that I had something going on with other men. I have a lot of guy friends...I always have...that doesn't mean I am sleeping with'em. Anyway, it finally got to be too many problems. He was always very unhappy with me being out too late at night...I just like having fun...sometimes there are guys there...I am just having fun. Well, he could not get over this one situation, that I admit, may have gotten a little out of hand; and, he could not forgive me, so he filed for divorce. But, I don't know why he takes it out on his kids...just like my father treated his kids."

"So, what is it about Rob that you admire?" I changed the subject. She smiled and replied, "He is so sweet, and such a hard worker. I see him getting up so early and coming in so late from work. He's a construction worker and always wants to help with things around here. He also always wants to help me with problems with my car as well." "Does he help others in the apartment?" "I don't really know, but I don't think so. He's a very quiet man...lives by himself...I never really see him talking with other people, or people visiting him. He likes to talk with my kids, particularly my son...showing him things...when he fixes things in my apartment he shows my son...I tell him that he doesn't have to fix some of these things, the manager is responsible...but, I don't want to hurt his feelings, so I let him do things for me."

"So, why do you think he wants to help you so much?" "Oh, I don't know...we met about a year ago, when I moved here, and he just seemed to want to help me with things." "Does, he ever suggests being more than friends?" My curiosity getting the best of me. "I don't really think that he is interested in anything else...I did let him kiss me once, after we had a couple of glasses of wine." she blushes. "Just once?" I replied with a tone of skepticism. "We've kissed a few times I guest, but we're just friends."

Others Who Admire Their Friend for Being Hardworking

A 27-year-old woman, who did not have a father in her life, from Lancaster, California, writes, "I saw different roles of different men growing up. It was a little confusing knowing which one was a great role model, as a dad, to look at. So I took all good traits from all. I have a friend that I really admire."

A 52-year-old woman from Inglewood, California, talks about a friend she admires. "He is honest, hardworking and well intended. He has learned to consider the impact of his life choices on his family and others. He is a committed father to three sons." She did not have her father in her life.

Finally, a 53-year-old woman from Los Angeles, California, who grew up with her father in her life, shared her thoughts about a friend she admires. "He is extremely intelligent, creative, hardworking, and independent."

Husband/Brother for Being Hardworking

Brenda

"I have the most hardworking, loving man in my life I could ever want. My husband is the model of admiration; for me, our children; our many nieces and nephews; even our parents admire him. You will not find another man that gives so much of himself for the well-being, joy, and benefit of others. He works tirelessly at his job, where he mentors other young men to be committed to their work and their families, and it makes a difference. The thing is, I am used to that and so is he. I am so fortunate to have married a man that has so many of the values I grew up with." Brenda and her husband of 14 years live and work in Indianapolis, Indiana, with their four children; two boys and two girls. They met in college during their freshmen year, and were married just weeks after graduating college. Not long after being married they started their family.

I asked her to explain what she meant by them having the same values before they were married. "I grew up on the south side of Chicago with my family. I have four brothers and two sisters. The sisters are both older than me, and one of my brothers is older than me. We watched our father work hard during his entire life. Our father watched his father work hard...there is a strong work ethic that is generational in my family, among the men. All of my brothers work very hard and take care of their families...just like my father showed them. Our father left us about six-years ago, but he left a legacy of love, commitment, determination and hard work to get the things you need in your life. My father would not subscribe to any excuses. He believed that any man or woman could put themselves in a position to gain and achieve the things they need for their family to do better than the last generation. He preached this obsessively and all of his children got it. We are all college educated, and those who are married and have children are committed parents. This came from the example set by our parents...from the almost daily preaching of our father...and it made a difference...and he never wavered. He was a happy man when he passed away, and it was because he knew that his message about family and hard work had made a difference in his family...passed along from his father.

"Now, the real interesting and blessing is the similarities with my husband's background. He grew up in Detroit, with almost the same family size as my family in Chicago. He has four brothers and three sisters, and he is just about in the middle like I am. When we met in college, and got interested in each other, we would talk all the time about the similar values our parents had about hardwork, family, education, and everything. I think that is what made us so attracted to one another, we had so much in common. I mean really? At first we didn't just cling to each other romantically, we really got to know each other as friends who enjoyed sharing our family stories, and that seemed to evolve into an attraction...that is the way it should be always. Anyway, oh my God, after we had been dating for about five months, it was summer break and I was going to drive back home, to Chicago. Since Detroit was not far off the route we decided that he would ride with me and I would drop him off, and I would get to meet some of his family. We were already pretty serious about our relationship and really thought it had a good chance. I mean, given the overwhelming similarity of values and background.

"Oh my God, I tell you. When I started talking with his parents," She illuminated the brightest smile, "I was sitting there talking with my parents. I could not believe them...I mean they even looked like them," she laughed. "His father? Oh my God. I may have been sitting right there talking to my father. He started talking about all the things, in almost the same manner with the same words that I had heard all of my life...I was hypnotized. He started talking about how, particularly men, had to be committed to working hard, taking care of their families, always working to do better, loving their wife, caring for their communities.... Oh my God, he was my father. I was thinking, these too men must have been brothers. And, his mother...she acted just like my mother when my father starts...she agrees, goes back and forth to the kitchen getting more things for us to eat, and chiming in from time-to-time about how a woman is suppose to support her husband, work hard herself, and make sure the home is a place of peace for the entire family. She, just like my mother, believes that her role as a mother taking care of the children was not at all diminished by seeing that her man is comfortable when he gets home. I mean, both his mother and my mother are college educated and have had some professional experience during the early times in their marriages. But, for both of them, once they had children, that became the focus...taking care of the children, lots of them mind you; taking care of the home; and taking care of their man...letting him know how much he is loved and cared for…supporting him. I had to tear myself away to get back on the road, to get home. I'll tell you, it seemed that I was already home. I could not wait to share this with my family.

"This was such an exciting experience that when I got home, I called him and told him that he must come to Chicago to visit my parents before the summer was up, and he agreed. We knew that there was something special with our love for each other…he smiled throughout the entire time I was talking with his parents, because he knew that they were being all the things he had already told me about…he was cracking up at times at my expressions and the way I was able to talk with his parents as if I had known them all of my life…I had. So, I think he wanted to have the same experience with my parents…I could not wait.

"Well, I am sure I don't have to tell you what happened." She laughed, trying to hold back tears. "I could not stop laughing at him. You should have seen the look in his eyes when my father was talking to him. I knew exactly how he was feeling….the exact way I felt when I met his parents… there was so much love flowing through us…it was spiritual…while he talked with my father, there was an energy flowing between us…an energy that almost seem to confirm and cement our love for each other… a feeling of destiny being manifested…we were raised in two different households…with two different generational paths…that were so much alike…it seemed that we were raised to be with each other…his parents, my parents, his grandparents, and my grandparents were all contributors to this heavenly created conspiracy to bring us together. There is so much love that permeates the lives of this wonderful extended family…I can still feel my father's hands in it daily, rest his soul. Our children are being modeled for what it means to be a loving family…our sons are seeing on a daily bases how a man is suppose to make his wife feel… and our daughters are being modeled on how to support your family and work hard to see that home is a place of love…a place of peace…a place of togetherness. Our daughters are also learning what to expect from the father of their children and husband. How a man is suppose to care about your feelings and well being; how to take care of your heart.

Hardwork and commitment is the key. I love and admire my husband for his commitment and hardwork."

James

James is a 41-year-old man who lives with his family in Houston, Texas. He has been married for 16 years and has six children; four daughters and two sons. He shared with me that it is his younger brother who he admires. "My brother Chris is actually the man I would have to say I admire. I have watched him really work hard at constructing a life for himself that is very promising. I know how devastating it was for him when our father left him and our mother, when he was about 12-years-old…I had just started college. I had the opportunity to grow up with our father with me while I was growing up, but for some reason he decided he wanted to change his life and left Chris and our mother. Chris has always been a very sensitive and likable kid. He absolutely loved having fun as a child and really loved family things with our father. He also really seemed to enjoy having a bigger brother…somewhat not in his age range, but he loved trying to hang around with me. Talk about a talker…he would talk my ear off about something he had done with our father. I totally understood because I knew how our father was, and he did take me places to have fun when I was growing up. Our father seemed to want to experience what he did not experience as a young boy, so he may have overindulged us a little bit. Anyway, Chris ate it up. Well, my father leaving him was overwhelmingly devastating to him for years.

"Up until this, he was doing very well in school, academically. He loved playing sports and had a very good head on his shoulders. He was so looking forward to getting into high school, and even talked about wanting to someday be a Longhorn, at the University of Texas, where my father and I attended. But, after my father left home, he seemed to change dramatically…I guess I can understand why…his world had changed. My father would come back to visit, but Chris seemed disinterested. He was actually pretty angry and felt betrayed. I would come over, at our mother's suggestion, to talk with him, and honestly, all he really did was cry…he was very hurt and angry.

"Anyway, despite the best efforts of our mom and me, for a long time he really slumped into a depression…he became very withdrawn. I had started a family and really didn't have a lot of time with him, but I put in a lot of effort. I let him spend time at my house, but that really didn't seem to help much. I was at a loss. He did not at all have the sort of high school experience we expected of him. He played on the basketball team, but really didn't seem to be trying to be the athlete we knew he could be…he was very disinterested in just about everything during high school. When he graduated he went on to a community college to study psychology. That was a total surprise to me and my mother. We were thinking, 'When did he get interested in psychology?' So, I asked him about it, and he said he was interested in children and family psychology. He had done some reading about it, and really thought it was an interesting profession to go into. Who would have known?

"Anyway, at the community college he started taking course that were related to the topics of child development, sociology and psychology and became very interested and engaged. Suddenly, this was all he wanted to talk about. We thought he would play basketball at the school, because they had a pretty good team, but he said he was not interested. Whenever he would visit, he would try to give me advice on what kinds of things I should involve my kids in. He was really working very hard to understand these things. I started to see the old Chris…very inspired, excited and hardworking. At first, he got an internship at a day care facility, then he managed to get a very impressive internship at a major hospital, where he worked with some psychologist.

"After just two years at the community college he managed to transfer to the University of Texas into the Department of Psychology, where he earned a degree. He is now working on a doctorate degree in Family Psychology. The thing that is so awesome is that he really worked hard to understand this subject and to put himself in a position to help other children who he feels suffers from the type of feelings he was having. I am so very impressed with the work he has done...the research papers he has written, and the trajectory of his life. He really turned things around for himself. Over the years he managed to contact our dad. He has made our mother the proudest lady in the city...she is proud of him...I am proud of him. I am not sure about what the relationship is between he and our father...it is the one thing he does not talk about much...but, he is clearly a recovered man. He is very passionate about the work he does and about making a difference in the lives of children."

"Wow," I responded. Do you know of any plans he has to start a family?" "Yea, we have asked him about that...and, so far he is pretty non-responsive to our probing," he smiled. "He always says things like, '...in due time,' or 'I have hundreds of children.' In our conversations about his work, he always refers to the children and families he works with as his family and his children. He loves what he does, and I so admire him for it."

Others Who Admire their Husband/Brother for Being Hardworking

A 56-year-old woman from Chapel Hill, North Carolina, who had her father partially in her life shares, "I adored my dad. My parents divorced when I was 12. Saw my dad weekly for the next four-and-a-half years; then he moved half a world away. When he returned five years later, he lived several states away." She shared that she admires her husband.

A 45-year-old woman from Decatur, Georgia, who had her father in her life, and admires her brother writes, "If people would take the time to communicate, teach and help we would not have so many young people, and grown people who disrespect themselves and others. Work, motivation, and education never hurt anyone. Men young and old need to learn respect!!"

A 44-year-old woman from Baltimore, Maryland, who did not grow up with her father writes, "I grew up in foster care. My foster father was amazing! He passed away from cancer when I was seven-years-old. He was the last positive male role model in the house, other than my brother. There were other positive men around, like teachers, but not as constant, with day-to-day interaction."

Finally, a 32-year-old woman from San Francisco, California, who also grew up with her father in her life and admires her brother, warmed my heart by writing, "Good luck with your research!

Fathers for Being Hardworking

Roderick

"I have just really learned to appreciate how hard my dad works to make sure my brothers and I have all the necessities in life, and are able to enjoy so many of the extras. I mean, what did I know about what it takes to be the father and mother of three boys...work hard to provide private schooling, and still manage to be around for us to connect with. I have managed to do well enough in school to be accepted to attend USC next year, and I know I owe it all to my dad's hard work and determination to keep our family thriving after the death of our mother six years ago. Our lives were so perfect when my mother was alive. We had the perfect loving family. Both our parents worked very hard to provide all the things we needed. They kept us going to church on Sunday and working hard in school during the week. We have always attended private schools, and our parents managed to be actively engaged in our schools...they knew all of our teachers...and talked with the principals. After our mother's death, it almost seemed like nothing changed. My father started working a part-time job in addition to his day job, and still managed to spend a lot of time with us, stay connected with our school, and even attend some of our afterschool events...just like he did when our mother was alive. Hardly, anything changed with him. He just had to work much harder."

Roderick, a 19-year-old graduating senior from high school this year, on his way to the University of Southern California, with a partial scholarship and lots of grants, to study computer science and engineering lives in Culver City, California, with his father, 16-year-old brother and 12-year-old brother. "Our father is constantly encouraging us...telling us that we can have anything in this world we want as long as we are willing to work hard for it...never give up. I have watched my father demonstrate this during our lives. He has always been hardworking, and we recognized it. He took such good care of us and our mother, yet it was like he was never tired...a ball of energy our dad. Our mother would love to get him into a conversation about why he was so committed to being a good father...and I am telling you, he is very committed.

"Our mother would share with us, while he just listened, how when they were dating all he talked about was how he missed having a father in his life growing up...and, how much he thought he would have so much more...education and other advantages if he had his father. He was almost obsessed with how the other kids in his community were always so happy...always doing things with their father...and, how he sort of envied it. Our mother would laugh at him and say that she could not help but love a man that was so determined to be a good father. She did grow up with her father in her life, and sort of understood how important it would be for her children to have their father. Wow, little did she know...or maybe she did.

"Our father has lived up to every word our mother said he promised her. What they didn't know was that he was going to have to be every bit of that father, and our mother. As far as working hard, he would have to get a part-time job working at a warehouse on some evenings to keep up the standard of living he and our mother provided. He was going to have to take up the slack with respect to keeping us in line and making sure that we kept up the high standards of achievement he and our mother had instilled in us. I'll tell you, when it came to education, our mother was no joke. She was on us from the git-go...preschool," he laughed. "To our mother, nothing in the world was more important than us being well educated....our dad didn't really talk about it nearly as much as our mother. Well, he did after she passed away...I mean he picked it up just like she was giving it to us...having another job did not slow him up a bit. We are still getting all the attention we want," he laughed again. "And, still going to church on Sundays...our father is no joke."

"So, how do you feel about the demands put upon you to do all the things he requires: Achieving at a high level in school, furthering your education at such a high level, and attending church services regularly?" " Oh, we are used to it, and we owe it to our parents to at least work as hard at preparing to provide for our families as they have for their family. When my mother would talk about how my father dreamed of having a family where he could be the type of father he did not have, sometimes I would take a glance at his face. Sometimes I could almost feel a sort of suppressed anguish brewing up inside his soul. I know that my father is very proud of his sons and the work he has done to get us where we are, but I also know now that he is still tormented with thoughts about how his life would have been different if his father had been like he is with us. Although he would laugh along with our mother when she talked about such things, he would eventually, in a joking manner, break up the conversation. He would laugh, 'Okay, that's enough...no more talk about the pitiful boy with no daddy,' but, I realize now that there was actually pain behind the laughter. I realize that as much as my father enjoys being a father, he wishes he had experienced what his boys are experiencing. Sometimes, I sit down and just talk to him about how he is doing, you know, how he is feeling?"

"What does he say?" "He talks about how much he misses his wife. He talks about how much he loves her, and how much she means to him. The tears swell up in both of our eyes when he talks like that." The tears began to appear now in Roderick's eyes. He uttered, "I miss my mother as well; very much. My brothers and I are so fortunate to have her in our lives. We are also extremely blessed to have the father that we have. I pray that someday I will find a woman to be the mother of my children in the manner that our mother was for us. I will have the same vow and promise that my father had with our mother. I will always love her and will always be at her side with our children. I will be the man they admire."

Peter

"I am the man I am today because of the man my father is," declared Peter, a 43-year-old insurance broker who resides with his wife in upper Manhattan, New York. "Talking about an admired man, that was my father. He was, until he retired a few years now, a very successful mortgage broker here in New York, for most of his adult life. He was the pillar of hard work and he made sure both me and my sister understood the value and requirements of hard work. He would encourage us, 'When others leave work, you are still working; when others are asleep, you are still working.' That is how you make it in the world, my friend. You have to out work your competitors. You have to grind until they blink, then you will taste the fruit juice of success. These are the values that were instilled in me by my father."

"Do you see much of him now?" "Yes, from time-to-time we get an opportunity to take time off, and I visit him and mother. His mind is still sharp as a bat. He loves talking about business, how I or my sister are doing, sharing strategic plans for the future, how to leverage opportunities…he loves this stuff, and I am so blessed that as a lad he shared this type of wisdom with me…he kept us in the right kinds of schools where this sort of thinking was not only encouraged but supported through our academic requirements and overall social interaction. The schools were for children with likeminded parents who understood the value of building legacy wealth and well-being.

"Trust me, my parents and many of the parents of the community and school were very giving. We support lot of charities through not only our financial contributions but our engagement as well. I had the most fabulous time last year visiting a shelter in the city during the holidays. It is so marvelous to watch young children opening Christmas presents that they would surely not have been able to acquire if not for the generosity of so many giving families. It is truly a blessing to have the good fortune to be able to put such bright smiles on so many faces. These are the values that my father made sure my sister and I share. Making such contributions is very important in this country. We must give to those in need."

"Do you and your wife have plans for expanding your family?" "A few years back we considered the option of having children of our own. So far, we have decided that there is so much we are still accomplishing and we are not really sure it would be to our best interest right now; or, to the children we would be bring into the family. We are crazy busy and are actually very happy with our lifestyle and our freedom to really explore the range of opportunities that we are presented with. We decided that children just may not be in our future. We really want to leverage the opportunities we have before us at the present. And, I suppose this is one of the joys we get from giving to others. We don't have children of our own, but you can imagine the joy of knowing you can bring such happiness to the children of the less fortunate; oh the smile on a little boy or girl's face when you hand them a gift. They smile so brightly when you take pictures with them, to hang upon the walls of the shelter.

"Anyway, I so much appreciate you taking an interest, Dr. Hickey, in such a provocative topic. I am delighted to have had this time thinking about my dear father as an admired man, a credit that he is so much deserving of. I also want to wish you the greatest of good fortune. I look forward to learning of the publication of your book, and having an opportunity to talk with you again. Thank you again ever-so-much for our conversation."

Patrice

Fifty-three-year-old Patrice, from Carson, California, loves to talk about how much she loves and admires her father. "I have always adored my father. He was very hardworking and an inspiration to his children." Patrice has no children and has never been married. She does spend some time with her younger brother's children. She loves being Auntie Pat, and trying to spoil them. When they visit her she gives them all the things their parents don't want them to have. "I know you have probably heard this a hundred times interviewing people, but I truly love my father. It seemed that he always knew my thoughts and what I needed to hear to feel better when something didn't go the way I would like. He paid so much attention to his children...he always knew just what to say or do. I remember when I was in the seventh or eighth grade and I wanted to be in this play. My father rehearsed with me for hours as I prepared for my audition. I was so excited about being in the school play I knew that I would be very popular and more of the other kids would like me...I wasn't the most popular girl in school...I was very plain Jane, as they say. Anyway, rehearsing with my father was such a fun experience for me...he really made me feel like I was a good actress."

"Well?" I asked. "Did you get the part?" "Well, that was the thing that was so odd. I didn't get the part and I thought I was going to be devastated if I didn't get it, but I wasn't. My father was so good working with me, it was like I had already performed the part with the person that meant the most to me, my dad. As he was rehearsing with me, he really made me feel like I was the best actress there was. He was able to say his lines and admire and cheer for me as I said my lines. He had already made me feel accomplished before I tried out, and I was already satisfied with my performance, in front of my dad. That is how he made me feel all the time."

"Did you grow up giving much thought to having a family and some children of your own?" I inquired. "Not really. For some reason getting married and having children never really appealed to me. I don't know why, I was just always pretty content with living a pretty simple life. I went straight to college after graduating high school. After getting my bachelor's degree in English literature I decided to continue and received a teacher's credential and master's degree in education. I am pretty satisfied with being an English teacher and college counselor. I have all the nieces and nephews I need when I feel like playing with children. They are so loving and happy, I have a ball when I am with them. In the interim, I really enjoy my work. That is the thing that I valued about my father. He had a work ethic that was laudable, and he seemed to enjoy working."

"What did your father do for a living?" "Oh," she laughed. "I guess I should have mentioned that. He was an English professor at a community college. He just retired a couple of years ago. Now, he is trying his hand at writing. When you have an opportunity I would love to introduce you. He would be extremely interested in your writing and ideas. This is the type of stuff he really enjoys. He loves to read and write about odd subjects... not your run-of-the-mill ordinary politics or things like that. He really appreciates subjects that are rarely talked about. He would really get into a topic like how fathers are admired. I am sure he believes that he is one of the best, cause that is what he always seemed to be striving for...wanting his children to feel special. He worked very hard...taught as many courses as he could...which I know he enjoyed doing...to make sure his family was well provided for. It is such a pleasure talking about him, and I hope you have an opportunity to meet him. You and he will really enjoy your discussion. He is a great man, and I love him greatly. I always get the impression that he realizes how much I adore him, by the big smile he delivers to me each and every time I see him. He is so very special to me. Thank you again for allowing me this space to talk about my daddy."

Cheryl

"I'll tell you this. Since I started going to high school and boys started showing interest in me, they were catching hell when they came to my home and met my daddy," Cheryl laughed with pride. In her freshman year at the University of Michigan, where she is studying nursing, Cheryl happily reflected on her admired man. "My daddy, of course." She continued, "My daddy makes sure that I always feel special and good. He is a very gentle giant...quiet most of the time, but is crazy about his 'Earl;' a nickname I acquired from my little brother before he could pronounce Cheryl. Somehow my daddy picked it up and no matter how grown I become, I am always going to be my daddy's Earl. I guess whenever I get a husband he is going to have to get used to his wife being Earl," she giggled.

"My daddy is one of the hardest working men you would ever want to know. I believe that at one time he had three jobs. He was one of the typical men," she giggled again, "that put a lot of value, and will judge your character, by the number of jobs you have." Still giggling, and making me laugh a little. "The first thing he would say to any man I introduce is, 'What kind of work do you do?' I'm like thinking, 'Dang, daddy. Give the boy a chance to at least tell you his name.' And, if the boy does have a job, he wants to know what other jobs he has. But, I really think I know what was really going on with that, the older I got and the more consistent he was with the routine. As I got older, particularly as I started preparing to go to college, I realized how special I felt...how self reliant, self confident and how much self respect I have. I started to understand that my expectations of myself and of any man that may be interested in me were very, very high.

"My daddy worked very hard and he did all that he could to make me, my brother, and my momma feel very special. I realize now that what he was doing, by sending these boys through the ringer about how many jobs they had, and the boys were still in high school, was in a way telling me to expect the very, very best for myself. I now realize that whenever I see a man that I might be interested in, and they show interest in me, my mind starts to think about just how hard they are willing to work? Not just for my attention, but how hard will they work for their family? What evidence of that do I see in them now? My daddy demonstrated through-out my life that a man is suppose to provide not just material things but a sense of well-being and security, and that takes work; hard work; many hours of work. I finally got it.

"I can't tell you how proud my daddy was when I told him that I was accepted to go to college. It didn't really matter to him what college it was, just to have a member of his family in college means the world to my daddy. He grew up pretty much without. His mother had nine children, raising them by herself. He had to drop out of school to help provide for the family. He says that it was a dream of his to be more educated and be different than the typical men he saw in his community, but it just wasn't the circumstances for that to happen. Eventually, he found a woman that he married, my momma, and they moved away from the country to Lancing, where my daddy was able to find factory work.

"Well, you already know, once he had the opportunity to work; that is what he did. My momma worked in a factory as well, until I was born. Then, he wanted my momma to stay home and take care of his baby, I wasn't Earl yet," she rolled her eye playfully. "Reluctantly, my mother complied. All this meant, however, was that my daddy had to have more jobs. When I was growing up, as far back as I can remember my daddy was doing nothing but sleeping and going to work. He always managed to get in a little time with me, telling me how special I am. He still does that. But, I remember he was always tired and always getting ready to go to work. He never ever looked like he didn't want to go. I believe that for him the factory work was not a mere job, but an obligation to his children and his family.

"I am looking forward to the day that my daddy can rest. I am obligated to be successful in my nursing and whatever else I have to do, so that my daddy can finally rest. Before I left for college I told him that. I said to him that I would do a good job in college, and that I was going to come back home and take care of him and momma." "How did he react to that?" I asked. "Just like I figured he would," she replied. "He said, 'Earl, we are doing just fine. You ain't gotta take care of us, we are taking good care of ourselves.' Daddy, I say, I want you to rest and have time to not have to get up and work so hard. You deserve to relax. You have taken such good care of me, momma, and Jacob for a long time and you deserve to relax and enjoy. 'I'm good,' he repeated. 'That is just the type of man I am. I am supposed to be the one that takes good care of my family. Don't ever forget that baby, a man is supposed to take GOOD CARE of his family.' I left him alone after he said that. I get the message loud and clear. My daddy is the man I admire, and he was telling me to accept in my life, no less than an admired man who is willing to work hard to deserve having Earl as his loving wife."

Others Who Admire Their Father for Being Hardworking

A 24-year-old woman who reported only partially having her father in her life spoke about her father, "Regardless of whether he liked it or not, he worked hard to make sure I had everything I could possibly need, and he served our country in the US Air Force."

A 47-year-old man who partially had his father in his life wrote, "I think forthright, honest, principled are undervalued male traits."

A 35-year-old man who did grow up with his father in his life offered, "I study social psychology and would love to talk about the outcome of this survey."

A 32-year-old woman who reported growing up with her father stated simply, "My dad is cool."

A 28-year-old man who grew up with his father in his life shared, "My father is the greatest man on the face of the Earth. That is not an opinion. His strength, kindness, knowledge, and sense of humor are second to none. He has the physical prowess of Chuck Norris and the ingenuity of MacGyver. His ability to reason rivals that of Spock, but his ability to connect with others surpasses the most popular person you know. He is a hardworking, everyday American with a heart of gold-plated steel." I shared this one in the introduction. It is well worth repeating.

Another 28-year-old man who grew up with his father in his life wrote, "Dads are important!"

A 27-year-old woman who was raised by her father shares, "I lost my mother when I was young – my dad is my best friend and my hero."

A 40-year-old woman who had her father in her life writes of her father, "He is no longer with me and I miss him very much."

A 46-year-old man who also had his father in his life states proudly, "My father lived a life of service: service member and city firefighter."

A 56-year-old man who had his father compliments, "I appreciate this survey as it has given me one more opportunity to think of my father who I truly love."

5

Nothing More Important than Family

"I would love to see more men, who spend more time working, take a more proactive role in their children's lives. And for those who are absent fathers, they should challenge themselves to be 'real' men instead of thinking their absence doesn't have a negative impact on their children."

— A 63-YEAR-OLD WOMAN WHO GREW UP WITH HER FATHER WHO SHE ADMIRES

"I hurt my wife, my kids, my mother, my wife's family, my friends, my foundation and kids all around the world who admired me."

— TIGER WOODS

⌒

THE FIRST MOST frequently identified Quality/Behavior/Characteristics (QBC) of an admired man is *family*. The men most selected as embodying *family* Quality/Behavior/Characteristics (QBC) are fathers

(41%), followed by brother (19%), friends, (17%), husband (14%), and uncle (9%).

Data Facts: Every one of the respondents (100%) who select their *father* as possessing the *family* Quality/Behavior/Characteristics (QBC) also indicate that they at least partially had their father in their life. Comparatively, of those who select their *brother* with the *family* Quality/Behavior/Characteristics (QBC), five-out-of-every-six (83%) indicate that they had their father in their life. Additionally, those who list a *friend* in this category, five-out-of-every-seven (71%) indicate that they had their father in their life. As we move down the role hierarchy, from *father* to *friend* in the *family* Quality/Behavior/Characteristics (QBC) category, it is less likely the respondent had their father in their life growing up. However, for those women who indicate their *husband*, in the *family* category, the percentage jumps back up to 100%, for at least partially having their father in their life. This suggests an interesting correlation between how women feel about their husband, at least in the *family* Quality/Behavior/Characteristics (QBC) category, when they have had their father in their life. I am compelled to propose a closer examination of the subconscious mate selection process/experience between women who admired their father, or at least had him partially in their life while growing up, in contrast to those who did not admire their father, or have him in their life. Clearly, there is something to learn about the similarities between the Quality/Behavior/Characteristics (QBC) of an admired man (or not) in the beginning and early years of a girl's life, and the Quality / Behavior / Characteristics (QBC) of an admired man (or not) they choose (or not) to start a *family* (or have children) with. Moreover, what might this say about the selection of mates for women who did not have an admired man, or father in their early years of life?

Of the respondents who indicated that there was no man they admired, 68% are men, with a somewhat surprisingly low one-out-of-every-five (20%) of them indicating that they did not have their father in their life, meaning 80% of these men did have their father at least partially in their life.

We are now at the final chapter with respect to the Quality/ Behavior/Characteristics of an admired man—the most frequent being *family*. Clearly, given the uniformity of conscious reflection in the flowing metanarratives throughout Chapters I through IV—the frequent sharing of embodied emotions—there is clarion evidence of a discernibly descriptive spiritual/emotional fabric, a stream of consciousness, that adjoins collectively shared and expressed feelings around the phenomenology of family. Affectively, the previously mentioned categorical reasons offered for why a man is admired, namely, being; *fatherly, honest, loving*, and *hardworking*, intensify to a crescendo of affirmation around how important family is to the spiritual/emotional fabric of humanity.

Consider the case of Beverly in Chapter I who reflected back on an old friend she admired for being *fatherly*. She recalled, "He talked a lot about his *family* and I really got the impression he had a great relationship with his own father...he was always talking about his father, and the things his father taught him about caring for others. His stories always reminded me of my father and older brother. I reflect back on how much my brother turned out to be just like my father. Both of them put nothing before their *family*." Jen, in her question to me about not considering admired women in the research, stated, "...there are many women around me that dedicate their life for their *family*, education, society."

Raul also reflected on his admiration for his father for being *fatherly* as well as his meaning to the *family*, stating, "Nothing in the world could distract my dad from *working hard* and giving his *family* all that he can get his hands on for us...I know that I have a responsibility to my *family* to be the greatest I can be." Referring to her husband, Yolanda boasted, "My husband also fit right into my *family* in a way you would not imagine. My mother, father and brothers and sisters fell in love with him from the start," thus pointing out the importance of extended *families*. She added, "My father lived a glorious young life, as his father was so *loving* with his *family*." Jill similarly spoke of her husband, "He talks all the time about how his father taught him to take care of his *family*...Mat really loved the idea of having a big *family*."

In Chapter II, Jeff talks about his admiration for his friend Charles on the basis of *honesty*. In addition he mentions his friend in the context of *family*. "Once we started having *families*, I admired how much attention he paid to his children and the *family*. I love Charles. I admire him as a friend and as a man who takes care of his *family* and friends." Pamela, speaking of a friend she admires, is reminded of her father. She shared, "A lot of the things he talked about were similar to the things my father talked about, you know, going to a good college, getting a good job, and being able to take care of your *family*." In a different sort of twist, Caroline spoke about the significance of *family* tradition and lineage. Of their affluence she shares proudly, "I know we have been blessed with affluence, and I recognize the influence both of our *families* have had on this almost inevitable blessing. We have both worked very hard to ensure that we maintain the legacy and expectation of our *family* lineage. These expectations include how we raise our children: Their values, resilience, fortitude, determination, accomplishment, and commitment to *family*. I am so blessed to have met a man that shared these values and is man enough to instill these values into his sons." I believe the real relevant point in Caroline's comment centers on the issue of *family* expectations, shared values, and commitment that is handed down to the next generation.

Unfortunately, Alma shares the adverse effect that *family* can have. She speaks sadly about her concerns regarding the modeling and influences surrounding her children. "I want so much for them to be good kids, but they don't really have any good examples. No man from my *family* spends any time with them, and that is actually a good thing. My brothers and everyone else is really no good...not a good example for any children. Their papa work hard all the time and he don't really know what to do with them...he had no good papa either." However, Michael talks about *family* survival, sharing, "My father still is very proud of how he learned to survive when his father brought his *family* here, and how hard they learned to work to survive. I have learned a lot about how committed you have to be with your *family*...work hard...do well in school, so that it can be better for your kids...stay out of trouble...and take care of the *family*."

And, of course we cannot forget from Chapter III, Isabella's enthusiastic account of the *loving* relationship that her *Family* shares with her husband's *family*, to form one big happy *family*. She shared, "You should see it when we have a big *family* celebration...Ohhhh the love is all over the place. See that's the thing...both of our *families* are so use to expressing our thanks...for everything...that we all get along so well...my brothers are like his brothers...his sisters are like my sisters...our parents are all so happy seeing us when we are all together...a really big *family* with lots of little ninos running around the place."

Story after story illustrates personal affirmations that reflect the overarching value of *family* in the context of assessing the Quality/Behavior/Characteristics (QBC) of an admired man. I need to start out by sharing the accounts of a person discussed in Chapter I.

Friend for Being Family

Ben

Recall Alison, the 26-year-old young lady from Newport Beach, California. In the *fatherly* category, she selected her childhood friend Ben, who is now 27-year-old, as the man she admires. Having grown up as a single child in a very loving and supporting family; and, having a tremendous amount of affection and admiration for her father, she wants to honor her friend Ben, as he so much reminds her of her father. Ben, a single child who did not grow up with his father, and had very little relationship with him, instead spent a significant amount of time with Alison's father. As a result of my interview with Alison, she arranged for me to interview Ben about his choice of an admired man, and why. Not too surprising his choice was Jerry, Alison's father.

"So Ben, how did you feel when you heard that Alison selected you as the man she admires," I asked. "I was really surprised. I have known her all of my life...we are friends...I would have never thought that I would be someone admired. I don't know if I really do anything for someone to say that about me." I followed up, "How do you feel about it?" "I don't know" he said, smiling from ear-to-ear. "It's really embarrassing a bit. I mean why would she admire me?" "Do you like being admired?" I asked. "I don't know...I guess it is okay." He replied, maintaining a shy smile.

"Tell me a man that you know, and who knows you, that you admire." I asked directly. I intentionally and suddenly changed the focus and demeanor of our engagement. I was curious about how Ben would react to this sudden seriousness in my voice. I could see that it did affect him a bit. His eye brows rose slightly and he removed the smile on his face instantly. As he paused to contemplate the question, he slowly raised his hand to his forehead, slightly rubbing it. Then, he spoke almost simultaneously with his smile reappearing. "I really admire Alison's father." I stayed silent, allowing him the space to contemplate on his own words, and what they meant to him. I had a sense of his thoughts and emotions swirling around in his mind and body—consciousness and subconscious. I said nothing, wanting him to speak first. "Yes." He uttered. "I really admire how he is with his family." Silence again. He began looking around toward the floor as he thought about what to say. I gave him the time. He started breathing a little deeper. I resisted interrupting. "A man takes care of his family...he should always be there...he doesn't come around sometime...he is always there when you need him...not when he feels like it, or it is his day to come by...he cares about you always." The tone of his voice started to change. I could sense his emotions beginning to speak for him. A slight tremble began to regulate his voice. The volume began to rise. I could tell he was reflecting on more than his admiration for Alison's father. He was clearly beginning to reflect on his own father hunger. Child and adolescent psychiatrist and author Dr. James M. Herzog discusses what he has coined as father hunger. "Despite the fact that many children today grow up without their father in their life, there is much clinical evidence to support the idea that children need a father."[1] He goes on to define father hunger as, "...an affective state experienced when the father is felt to be absent."[2] I gave Ben space to express his thoughts and emotions.

"I wish my father would have been like Alison's dad during my life.... growing up. He came by after he and my mom divorced but it ain't the same as how Alison's dad is. I admire how he is always with them. Making sure everything is okay...making sure Alison is okay and that she feels good about herself." I found this to be a great place to intervene. "What do you mean?" I asked. He responded, "Well, Alison is always happy. No matter what, I never see her lacking confidence—she believes she can accomplish anything...she has always been that way. Her dad makes sure she feels good." "So, what is your relationship like with Alison's father?" I asked. As the smile reemerged he replied, "I love spending time with him. He lets me help him do things around their home. He has shown me things I can do at my home...he treats me like I am his son...like he loves me." Again, I see his eyes drifting; his voice changing; and, the emotions rising. "I wish my father would have been this way with me....I love my father...I wish he loved me like Alison's dad loves her...the way he takes care of the family...my mother and I deserve better...to be a real family." I see his eyes reddening. Tears start to emerge. "A loving together family is what a man makes sure his son experiences...that is what I needed in my life...that is the kind of man I know I am going to be...I will always make sure my family knows that I care, and that I am taking care of them...Alison's dad models that for me...I want to be a man like he is." The tears are now flowing. "I am not going to be like my father. I am going to love my family." I let the conversation end with that. I reached over and held Ben until he finished crying—until both of us felt better.

Richard

"I have known my friend Kenneth forever. We went to elementary school, middle school, and high school together. I have to admit, I have always admired him, and I still admire him." Richard is a 24-year-old University of Maryland master's student who grew up in Edgewood, Maryland, with an alcoholic father in his life. During our conversation he managed to speak fondly about his father, but there was clear evidence that he harbored significant pain related to his relationship with his father. "I am very grateful that my father has been in our lives. In spite of some issues, my sister and brothers and I at least have our father to be proud of us and to show that he cares for us. Our mother really has to struggle... my father has a pretty bad drinking problem...it prevents him from really being able to maintain a job...we know he loves us...he just has this problem. We could not figure out why he could not stop the drinking... he would try...he would tell the family that he was going to be better... he realizes that he could be a better provider so he tries, but he just can't seem to get better...I have seen my father cry during his worst times... when he has been so taken out from drinking that he could hardly stand up...he hurts when he is drunk...he just can't help it...at least so far." I could see and feel the hurt Richard experiences...I could see his chest starting to rise and fall with deliberate intention. For most of our conversation I managed to keep him focused on his friend Kenneth; his admired man.

"I really appreciate my relationship with Kenneth. He is such a valuable role model to so many people. He always loved working with young people and wanting to inspire them to work hard in school. He did not have a father and really worked hard to help his mom manage their family and keep things together. He knew about the things I was going through in my family and he would always remind me of how fortunate I was to have my father at least in our home, and how he, as a child, fantasized about having a father." Again, notable expert on father research, Herzog suggests "father hunger" accounts for the need for fatherless boys to seek and fantasize about a "good enough man" in their lives.[3] "'I wish I had a father that I could talk to and could come and see me at school playing football' Kenneth would say after we had a really good football game.

"Just before we graduated high school, Kenneth's girlfriend became pregnant. I thought that this would devastate him; he had an opportunity to play college football, and I know how much football meant to Kenneth. I was really worried about how he would handle this. He really loved his girlfriend, and spent a lot of time with her. He had gotten to know her mother and sisters and brother as well. He spend a lot of time with them…it was like he was wanting to be the father figure at her home as well as his home. He enjoyed being around her family." "She didn't have a father in the home?" I wanted to be clear. "No, their father did not live with them…he came by there from time-to-time, and he knew Kenneth, but he didn't live with them. He didn't really seem to have a problem with Kenneth.

"Anyway, I was really surprised at how Kenneth responded to finding out that he was going to be a father…he was more happy than I had seen him in his whole life. He was excited and proud…only 18-years-old, and he was happy about it. I asked him what he was going to do about playing football at one of the colleges that were extremely interested in him. His response was, 'I am going to be a child's father,' he said. 'My first responsibility is to make sure that when this child enters the world they know and feel that they are loved by their mother and father. I am going to see to it that my child knows what it is to be in a full loving family. This child will feel the love of his mother, his mother's family, his father's family, and his father.' When I asked him about school he said that he wasn't going to go right now, and would take at least a year off, then they would both try to go to school. He said that they may have to go to a community college, but he wanted to give full attention to his child. He insisted that they were going to get married before the baby was born, because it was important to him that his baby had, what he called, 'a father that is legit.'" I could not help but laugh at that comment.

Richard continued, "I have been blown away every since Kenneth and I had those conversations about his future and how important his child was to him…he is all about family. I mean, I thought I understood some of his comments about my father and family before. I thought I understood why he liked working with kids, and why he worked so hard to help his mother. But, I did not really get the full understanding of his feelings until he shared with me his plans to have a loving and caring family, with his soon to be wife and child. I have never seen such commitment in the eyes of a person as I did Kenneth. I could not help but admire the kind of family man Kenneth was already showing. I mean, for real. It was all over him and the baby was not even born yet."

"So, what happened," The anxiety already built up in me. Richard gave a huge grin as he leaned back in the chair. "I'm going to tell you Dr. Hickey," he started, "I thought I admired Kenneth when he told me about his plans. That was nothing. Kenneth and Jessica were married in less than two months after he talked to me about her being pregnant. I was the best man at their wedding. Kenny Jr. was born four months later. Of course, I am the Godfather" Suddenly, I could see tears forming in Richard's eyes again. He started to get very choked up in his voice. He continued, with a struggle, "Kenneth has done every single thing he said he would do. Six months after Kenny, Jr., was born, Kenneth started taking classes at night at the community college. He worked hard all day at a hospital while he was going to school. Jessica was also able to attend college where she studied to be a teacher. Both of their mothers and sisters and brothers helped them out with babysitting as they were working very hard to stay in school." Richard could hardly contain his emotions. His tears flowed harder and harder. "Kenneth worked so hard to make sure Jessica was able to do what she needed in school, and he stayed in school as well. Jessica finished college and got her teaching credentials and now teaches at an elementary school near them." He paused to sip from bottle water, and wiped his eyes, but the tears were relentless. "Kenneth finished a nursing program and is now a registered nurse for a local hospital. Are you hearing me? And, with all of this happening, they also have another child, a little girl that is now a year old. I am also her godfather. Kenneth is the most admired man I know. His commitment to have a loving family is second to none. I listened to him when we were growing up. He always talked about how someday he would have a family and that he would do any and everything he could to make sure that his wife and children felt special and that they could depend on him forever. He has done just that.

He is my hero. I love Kenneth for the kind of man he said he would be, and the kind of man he is. He is one-of-a kind."

Others Who Admire Their Friend for Being Family

A 52-year-old woman from Corona, California, wrote, "I was raised by my stepfather. He was a great provider, but a horrible communicator. He never spent much time with us children. And, he was verbally abusive." She admires a friend.

Another 52-year-old woman from Inglewood, California, who grew up with her father in her life shared, "A man who follow God is a man who can and will lead his family right. God bless you."

Brother for Being Family

Luis

A transplant from San Antonio, Texas, Luis moved to Los Angeles to work as an aid for a popular Southern California politician after completing a master's degree from the University of California at Berkeley. He is already 31-years-old, and is beginning to contemplate starting a family. He grew up in San Antonio in a very loving family that included his mother and father; and a ten-year older brother, and two-year younger sister. He shares that they were a very close knit family, sharing a lot of love and support for each other. Both his father and mother were raised in two-parent households and have always stressed the importance of a man being committed to his family, no matter what. He emphatically announced that it is his older brother Carlos that he admires.

"Oh, it all starts with our dad, of course. I admire my dad. Carlos and I are our dad," he laughed. "But, I really want to give my big brother props for the kind of man and the example he is for me and any young man that pays attention to him. I know he is so much like our pops, and my pops has always talked a lot about his pop...this goes a long way back, and my brother is picking up right where he is expected to do, and he motivates me to be the kind of man he and my pop and my grandfather are. The men in this family put their family first, ahead of anything else. The family comes first, and everyone in the family had to know that they can depend on the head of the family, the big poppa.

"My brother Carlos started his family when he was 17-years-old. He stood up like a man and took on all the responsibility. He now has four children and they are doing so well in school and stuff...they are wonderful kids. His wife is always beautiful and he makes her feel beautiful...the kids are beautiful. I admire how he, even after having kids so young, he was able to make sure he worked hard enough to provide all the financial needs of his family. He continued to get his education and makes sure that all of his children are serious about their education. I think the thing that makes me so proud of my brother is how he continues the values of our father. He is the embodiment of the values and example that our father was to us on a daily basis. Our father would not only walk-the-walk, but he would tell us about the walk, and would sometimes have us walk-the-walk with him. He would take us with him to work sometimes, and if he had to negotiate with someone about the work he would contract to do, sometimes he would take us with him. He would explain to the people he was doing business with, '...these are my sons and they are here to learn about doing business. Some day they will be the head of a family and they will know how to take care of business.' We really got use to that speech. I can hear him saying that right now," he smiled.

"Now, my brother is just like him. He takes his 12-year-old son with him to business meetings, just like our dad did. Sometimes, he talks with his kids like they are adults, I mean the topics. He breaks it down so that they understand the concepts he wants them to grasp. I'll tell you, that is so much like our dad was with us. Our dad would say, 'Let me break it down so that you understand.' They are so much alike."

"You mentioned thinking about having a family. Tell me about those thoughts," I suggested. He shared, "Right now I am really working hard, and I really want to be sure that I am ready. My brother was very special and he was ready. I am not sure I am ready at this point in my life. I would like to have a family, like my brother's and like the family I was raised in. But, I know I have to be sure that I have the time and commitment to my wife and children. That is why I haven't pursued a relationship that would lead to a family right now. I guess that is also part of my admiration for my bother. He knew when he was ready, and he was ready to put in the amount of time and the level of commitment to have the type of family we are used to. I don't think I am quite there yet. I am very committed to the work I do right now and I have learned from both my father and my brother, you have to have the mental toughness to work as hard as they did, educate themselves, and be committed to spend quality time with your wife and family. Wow!!! I'll tell you, they are very special to be able to do all of that with the quality and energy they spend on their families. Someday, I'll be there as well. I look forward to living up to the standards of my grandfather, father, and brother. All admired men."

Others Who Admire Their Brother for Being Family

A 66-year-old woman from Philadelphia, Pennsylvania, who grew up with her father shared, "I'm very proud of my younger brother for the man he has become! He is bringing up two sons...and doing an excellent job at turning them into strong, principled men."

A 52-year-old woman from Los Angeles, California, who partially had her father in her life wrote, "As the saying goes, when a man loves and honors his mother, he is a great lover of womankind. I look for that characteristic in all men. It is most admirable." She admires her brother.

Finally, a 56-year-old woman from Los Angeles, who grew up with her father in her life and reported admiration for her bother shared, "It would take too long to write why I admire this man so, he is most of all a God-fearing man. Respecting others while sharing an agape love."

Father for Being Family

Rita

"I have been in the foster care system for over 11 years," Rita shared with me. "For the first seven years in the system I was placed in over nine homes. I was never able to stay connected with my older brother and sister at all. I don't know where they are. At first I was with a home that tried to make some sort of an effort to connect us, but, after leaving that home that was pretty much it. Nobody really tried to reconnect us, and finally it was like, what's the use? I was bounced around so much I started to not even care much for myself.

"At the age of 14, I was finally placed with a family that for some reason really cared for me. They had one other foster girl my age and they were treating us like they loved us. Since they called us sisters, I accepted that, and didn't dare think about troubling them with trying to locate my biological sister and brother. This woman and her husband treated us like they were our mother and father. That is what they told me when I was placed with them. They introduced themselves as my mom and dad. I was really blown away at first and it took me a little while to accept that they were being for real. I did not at all trust them. I had learned not to trust anyone to do anything but take advantage of what they can get for having you, and eventually break your heart. I knew it was just a matter of time before I would be too much trouble again and would be sent off somewhere else. I knew it was just a matter of time.

"Today, I admire my father. He is not my foster father, he is my father. From the day I became a part of this family I have felt nothing but love. It took me a little while to understand what I was feeling, but they continued to remind my sister and I that they love us. I finally began to recognize it. I began to understand that I was feeling the same way other children feel when they are loved at home by their mother and father. It was really weird at first; not knowing what love feels like. I know now, because my sister and I were getting it every day. For the first time in my life I was happy about going to school. I was happy because I knew I was just as good as anybody else at the school. I was happy because I begin to believe that I was not going to be checked out of the school to go to another one, to have to adjust to a whole new environment and group of kids at school and at home. I really love my mother and father, but my father was really very special to us. He always talked with us about how smart we are and how important it is that we do very well in school. No one had ever said anything about school. I had to attend schools, but they did not seem to care about what I was doing…it didn't matter anyway, because eventually I was leaving the school anyway. That is how it felt to me. Why should I really care myself what I did in school, since I knew I would not be there very long?

"My father was not having that. He made sure that we understood that he expected us to not only do well in school, but he made sure we understood what it means to have high expectation of ourselves. Over time, both my sister and I began to catch on. Since we were in the same grade we started helping and encouraging each other. It is an amazing thing to reflect back on the transformation in our lives, and how we began to feel better about ourselves. How our ability and willingness to trust had began to make a difference in how we thought of not only what was happening for us on a daily basis, but additionally how we began to think about our future. My sister and I started to laugh and talk a lot at night about what we were going to do when we grew up…you hear me? When we grow up? The more I began to feel better about myself and my future the more I seemed to witness myself go through this transformation of mind. It was really a strange but exciting experience for me. And, I was watching my sister go through the same thing. We talked and laughed about it all the time. At first, we were very scared because we didn't know when it would end, but over time the trust and belief kicked in and we were finding ourselves to be different people, and the experiences we were having began to be positive, fun, and inspiring. I owe this to how my father was able to make me think and feel about myself. He made sure I did not feel like a foster child. He made sure I felt like a child that is loved by her mother and her father."

"So, I understand that you have aged out of the system now. What does that mean for you?" Dr. Hickey, I aged out of the system a long time ago. I stopped being a part of that system after I started to believe and trust the love I was receiving from my sister, mother and father. When I turned 18, that was just a bureaucratic formality. I had almost forgotten that I was ever a foster child. I would wonder sometimes what happened to my biological sister and brother but I would not let that get me down. I was really enjoying my life and I knew I had a positive future ahead of me." "And, what is that future?" "Come on Dr. Hickey, you already know," she smiled. "Yes, but say it anyway," I returned her smile.

"I have been awarded several scholarships and will be a freshman at Stanford University after the summer. I had a choice of some of the most prestigious universities in the country, and I have chosen to be a Stanford Cardinal. Also, my sister will be attending Berkeley in the fall. You see what I mean. My father did this for us. He made us believe we were as good as any other person. It was not easy for him but he was persistent. He did whatever he had to do. You should have seen how he interacted with people at the different schools we attending. I am telling you, he not only made us believe, he made sure that it was reinforced at school. He had better not find out that we were being mistreated. Now, we are both on our way to prestigious universities with enough scholarships and grants to have our education paid for."

"What are you planning to study?" I inquired. "I am going to study psychology for my undergraduate degree. I will eventually obtain a law degree and practice children and family law. I am extremely interested in this field, obviously, and it is my expectation to someday be a judge in children court. There is a lot of work in that area that needs to be done, and I am committed to this endeavor. I owe it to myself, and furthermore, I owe it to my family, everyone in my family. I am going to put some real effort in the next few weeks to track down the other sister and brother that make up my family. They need to know who I am, and I need to know who they are. I owe this to my mother and father. They taught me how to love. They taught me what it means to have a family."

About two weeks after my interview with Rita she called me to share that she had made a lot of progress in almost tracking down the last place her sister and brother were placed. She said that, hopefully, if she found that out, it would help her locate where they may be living now.

Less than three days after the call about tracking down her siblings I receive another call from Rita. "Hello, Dr. Hickey," she said in a very monotone voice. I was hoping she didn't have disappointing news about the search for her siblings. "Yes, Rita, how are you doing?" I said with a supporting yet cautious reservation. "I'm not too good Dr. Hickey," she replied. "My father had a massive heart attack last night, and he has left me." My heart suddenly dropped. My stomach tightened. My eyes closed. I could not believe what I was hearing. "Ohhh," was all I was able to utter, and then I heard her crying on the other end of the phone. I felt helpless. "I am so sorry, Rita." I managed. I listened to her sobbing with anguish through the line. "Is there anything I can do?" I offered. She replied that she wanted me to know, and that she would like me to attend his funeral services. She said, "I know that he would appreciate you being there. On the day you interviewed me, I told him about your work and our interview and he was so excited. He was looking forward to reading your book and hopefully meeting you. I told him how inspiring it was for me to have the opportunity to share how much I love him and he smiled the rest of the day. I know that he would be honored if you were at his going home." I relied, "Yes, I will be there."

The Santini Family

The Santini family resides in Brooklyn, New York. I had the highest honor of getting an opportunity to talk with the whole family about their feelings on family and how the children, who are now adults, admire the patriarch of the family. I met the two sisters and one brother at their parent's home. Included in the discussion were their mother and their father, neither of whom spoke much, they mostly listened and laughed. Four grandbabies were also around climbing all over grandma and grandpa while their parents talked about their beloved pop. The daughters are: 18-year-old Gabriella and 23-year-old Elizabeth: Son, 32 -year-old Paul. Three of the grandchildren are Paul's while the youngest grandchild belongs to Elizabeth. The grandchildren are very close in age, ranging from four to seven-years-old.

"Hello, Dr. Hickey. It is so nice to see you again, Come on in and meet the family," I was warmly greeted by Elizabeth. "I have been telling them all about you, and your book, and they cannot wait to tell you things about our pop. He and our mother are here as well to make sure we don't say anything out of line, or embarrass him," she laughed, as I stepped into their home. I was warmly greeted and introduced to everyone. After our getting to know each other period, and of course being fed some of the most delicious pasta I have ever tasted, we were ready to go. I avoided the red wine they offered, but invited them to help themselves.

"Again, I really want to thank you all for giving me this time with you. I sincerely appreciate your time and gracious hospitality. So, Elizabeth suggested that you would all want to contribute to the conversation about why you all admire your father. She has already informed me that you are all so very happy about being raised in such a loving and supportive household with an unbreakable family bond and commitment to one another. She informs me that this comes primarily as a result of the influence and dedication of your father. Am I getting that right?" I smiled while perusing all of their welcoming faces.

"Oh sure," Paul laughed, butter him up good. We won't be able to stand him at all after this one." Everyone laughed, including me. "But seriously," Elizabeth chimed in, "Our pop is really an extremely admirable man. He really understands how to instill love and trust into a family unit. How to have his entire family, not just those that are here right now, but all of our cousins, our in-law families, everybody. Paul, do you remember when Auntie Clara got all angry at that family picnic and wanted to tell everybody off? Do you remember how pop handled her? Do you remember pop?" Pop nodded with a gentle smile and looked at his wife. Paul chimed in, "Of course I do. Our pop is always in control of things. Auntie Clara had sipped a little too much vino, and she was on a rampage. She was going to tell everybody off, and pop got up and started imitating her, you know exaggerating what she was saying and how she sounded. He cracked everybody up; even she had to start laughing. Nobody got mad. For the rest of the day, from time-to-time somebody, even the children, would start to imitate how she was acting, and she could not stop laughing." "Your aunt, was this his sister?" "No, that's what we are telling you, Auntie Clara is our uncle's wife, on our mother's side. But, with our pop it never matters we are all family, and everyone in the family understands that. He will not let you forget that or let you not be apart of the love this family shares with each member of the family."

"Oh, it's not just the blood member of the family, you guys know that," Gabriella spoke up. "Pop is going to bring all of your friends into the family. If you come to our home, you become part of the family. Pop is going to ask you questions and give you advice. He is going to be all in your business, and want to know why you are doing one thing or another. This is how he treats my friends when they visit, and they love coming over. They all call him pop, because that is how he treats them and makes them all feel. I even almost get jealous, like, wait a minute, pop, you are my daddy, why you all helping out my friends with their issues? Letting them tell him how they are doing at school, about their boyfriend issues and everything," she started laughing. "But, the thing is," she continued, they love it. They tell me it feels like they are in the family. They say that they feel an obligation to do the right thing after he talks to them about right and wrong, and how it doesn't matter whether someone is watching you…I mean, who does that? Who talks to their daughter's friends like that?" A couple of them shouted out together, "POP." We all laughed again. I felt this odd feeling, and I looked over at Pop, and he smiled and said, "I am going to have a few questions for you young man after you are done with this, what you call, research." "Oh boy," Paul laughed. "See, now you are a part of an Italian family in Brooklyn." More laughing.

"Okay, let's stay serious I said," still grinning. "We are serious," Elizabeth smirked. "When you leave this home you are going to be Dr. Chris Hickey Santini. And, don't think you have had all that you are going to eat today. And, pop is not letting you out of this home before he knows all of your business and gives you some good advice on some things." Paul chimed in again, "I remember I was having some problems with my math in high school. The teacher sent a note home suggesting that maybe a parent conference was in order." The family started laughing again. Mommy covered her face with the palms of her hand, trying to contain her laughing. "What happened?" I busted out. Paul continued, "I was like, you really inviting my pop to come up to the school to talk with you about me. I had to sit in on their discussion. I already knew what was going to happen. Momma had sent some cookies with him, not to give to the teacher, but to share with the teachers. We all sat up and eat home made raisin oatmeal cookies together. We are supposed to be talking about my not doing well in math, and we are sitting around passing each other napkins to wipe the cookie crumbs from our lips." Everyone was just laughing. I was trying my best to keep it together. I could not help but visualize this and it was making my gut hurt trying to not lose it. I almost had to tell him to stop; I could not take much more. Paul added, "I thought they were going to send me out to get some milk. Anyway, by the time pop finished with him the man was apologizing for not doing a better job assisting me with my understanding. He started question his overall teaching technique with the entire class.

"He and pop were discussing different ways the teacher could better communicate with the class and how the teacher could have a better relationship with the class. The man even wanted to plan another meeting with Pop to go over his progress. Now, mind you, pop ain't ever stepped one foot into a teacher education course, but he was mentoring the math teacher on how to teach high school math." At this point, I am in tears. "The real funny thing is that they planned their next talk to be at our home. Are you kidding me?" I had totally forgotten my research objectives. I can't remember laughing so much. Everyone in the room was laughing. Paul did not let up, "I was thinking, if that man comes to this home, that's it for him. When momma and pop finish with him I will have an A in that class for sure. Fortunately, he must have thought better of it later, because they never had another meeting, but I will say he took a lot of pop's suggestions and the instruction and most of the students' understanding improved dramatically, including mine."

Throughout all the laughing we were doing, what did not go unnoticed by me was the constant playful attention that pop had with the grandchildren. At no time during our time together were the grandchildren not physically engaged with momma and pop. While all the laughing was happening from time-to-time I could hear them saying, "I love you grandpa...I love you grandma. At times I detected a little game going on with the children, to get his attention when he started laughing at one of the stories. The love that this family openly displays is contagious. I had so much fun with them. And, yes. After the interview and laughing was done, pop did have a conversation between he and I, which is where it remains; between me and pop. I adore him. I also admire him.

Others Who Admire their Father for Being Family

A 56-year-old man from Baltimore, Maryland, writes, "With a third-grade education my father raised all of us to be professional, Christian, and strong parents and now grandparents. He was always there. When my mother left six kids ranging in age from four to fifteen, my father resisted splitting us up among relatives and decided to raise us by himself."

A 50-year-old woman from Rosewood, California writes, "My father's influence caused me to set my expectation bar really high, maybe to my detriment."

A 38-year-old woman from Wilmington, California, states, "I have been blessed to have, beside my father, three male best friends that I admire; that take care of their family, hard workers and each have individual qualities I admire and look for in a man. I admire a man for his strength and dedication to his faith and family: His loyalty and understanding."

Finally, a 27-year-old woman from Chicago, Illinois, shared, "I lost my mother when I was young - my dad is my best friend and my hero."

6

L(ife)eadership Development Principles

*"My father is, hands down, the most valuable person I have
in my life. Our mother passed away while my sister and I were
very young, and our father has been our salvation. Every day
he shares with us the skills we need to grow up and take care of
ourselves. We both love our father. I pray that someday I have
children, and they feel the same way about me."*

— AN 18-YEAR-OLD MAN WHO LIVES WITH AND ADMIRES HIS FATHER.

*"The function of education is to teach one to think intensively
and to think critically. Intelligence plus character—that is the
goal of true education."*

— DR. MARTIN LUTHER KING, JR.

AFTER REVIEWING THE work that has been done on this topic by others
(see Chapter VIII), along with the information I collected during
this research, I asked myself, "What's the point? Why does this matter?"

Traditionally, one might accept the position that the point of most research, particularly social science research, need not be much more than the data resulting from the research. Of course, we know that action research (research specifically intended to include action on the part of those doing the research) is traditionally designed to directly affect change as an element of the research process, however, this project is not intended to follow or meet the criteria of action research. Moreover, unlike research that is intended to only satisfy the qualification of answering the research question, it has always been my intent to use the results of my survey and interviews to suggest a set of life and leadership development principles that provide a foundation for change: particularly, a change in how men perceive and embody various concepts of leadership in the context of raising their Admired Man Quotient (AMQ); the nexus between what matters the most, emotionally, to the admired man's **M**ost **V**aluable **P**eople and what matters the most, emotionally, to himself, the admired man.

Whereas Chapters I through V illustrate more than sufficient testimonial evidence of the Quality/Behavior/Characteristics (QBC) that we collectively consider admirable in men, the purpose of this chapter is to a identify and explain a general set of L(ife)eadership skills that facilitate the physical/spiritual/emotional embodiment of life and leadership development. Although some of the voice of this text is directed toward men who desire to raise their Admired Man Quotient, it is equally intended for others who may be in the role of a mentor and/or those, including women, who desire to understand how they can help another raise their Admired Man Quotient. There is a specific section for parents, men and/or women, who are facilitating and/or responsible for, so to speak, the "making of an admired man."

Data Facts: The concept of leadership, in the more academic/formal sense of the practice, as a Quality/Behavior/Characteristics (QBC) for an admired man, is for all intents and purposes non-existent in the survey results. Although, just about all of the Quality/Behavior/Characteristics (QBC) illuminating from the survey as well as the interviews are clearly leadership traits, the participants rarely, if at all, use the term leadership, or identify the values they admire in men as leadership qualities. Corporate leadership consultants, Mark C. Thompson and Bonita S. Thompson had very similar results in their national survey of over a thousand participants. They shared, "We asked what traits participants admire in a leader, and then compared those traits with what they wanted to be admired for as a person. Turns out that they aren't the same thing…apparently there is a big difference between what we want to be valued [admired] for and what we say we value in our leaders."[1]

It is my belief that the intrinsic value in identifying the associative relationship between evidenced-based attributes of leadership and leadership development; and, the Quality/Behavior/Characteristics (QBC) in what we collectively and universally attribute to an admired man, affords us an opportunity to construct evidenced-based principles, skills, and practices that contribute to the making of an admired man. Leadership author Sally Helgesen reminds us that, "Scholarly and popular books that identify strong leaders and attempt to analyze the nature of their success have found a wide and hungry audience. Universities have initiated courses, or even whole departments, to study, teach, and encourage leadership."[2] Why shouldn't we take advantage of these efforts and resources in deepening our understanding of the nature and making of an admired man? In effect, what I am proposing is that if there are evidenced-based leadership development skills and practices that result in the making of a leader, then it follows that much of this same evidence can be consulted in the developmental skills and practices that result in the making of an admired man. Youth leadership experts, Susan R. Komives, professor emerita and former director of the College Student Personnel Graduate Program at the University of Maryland; Nance Lucas, associate dean and associate professor at New Century College at George Mason University; and, Timothy R. McMahon, faculty consultant in the Teaching Effectiveness Program at the University of Oregon suggest to college students, "Think about the leadership exhibited by the people you have admired in the national or international news, in your home community, on campus, at work, or in the career field you are choosing."[3] Wow!! That sounds familiar. Moreover, they suggest, "Think ahead to the places and relationships in which you could become more active—your classes, class projects, student employment position, residence hall, honor societies, student government, Greek organizations, athletic teams, PTA meetings, your family [another familiar concept], friendship groups, your off-campus work, community-service settings, your church or temple."[4] These experts are suggesting a synergy between the qualities students find in (other) leaders, and the types of activities they can engage themselves in, that exhibit the leadership qualities they see in others.

Accentuating the credibility of this point, Cashman insists there is a "…personal awakening needed to enhance our leadership effectiveness."[5] Moreover, "…our ability to grow as a leader is based on our ability to grow as a person."[6] Komives, Lucas, and McMahon add, "Leadership skills are life skills that can be applied to personal relationships as well as to work and organizational responsibilities. By redirecting your own life in the context of family, values and dreams, you can become a productive colleague with others."[7] Finding the connection and relationship between personal life/leadership and effective collegial business/organizational leadership is thus an essential aspect of leadership success.

I am particularly inspired by Cashman's discussion of the authentic nature of leadership being more relevant than the external description of what a leader does.[8] Likewise, I will "borrow" his insight to suggests that it is the internal nature of a man that rewards him the title of being an admired man; more so than just the things that he does. Why an admired man does what he does is an essential ingredient in our understanding of the admired man's nature. It is our deep-dive understanding of the nature of an admired man that provides the framework of our exploration into the skills and practices requisite for the making and development of an admired man. In a somewhat cyclical process, it is the manifestation of the skills and practices of an admired man that in turn loop back into the continuous transformation of an admired man's nature. Moreover, what an admired man does transforms who the admired man is by nature: An admired man does—who an admired man is. Modifying Cashman's, "essential questions to enhance...leadership effectiveness,"[9] I ask these questions in order to provide insight into the core nature of an admired man:

- How authentic are you as a man?
- How deep and broad is your self-expression?
- How much value are you creating?

Cashman credits a chairman and CEO of a large corporation for adding, "The missing link in leadership development is growing the person to grow the leader."[10] The goal of this chapter is to make this connection in the context of our having a functional understanding of the associative relationship between leadership development strategies and the development of a regular, common, everyday, admired man; be he a co-worker; stranger on the bus or subway; CEO of a Fortune 500 Corporation; employee; nephew; son-in-law; executive director of a non-profit corporation; professional athlete; grandson; boss or supervisor; entertainer; cousin; mentor; boyfriend; uncle; pastor; grandfather; brother; husband; friend; father; or, of course some combinations thereof.

With respect to my belief regarding the association between leadership development and admired man development, Thompson and Thompson note, "According to our research, people who find meaning and engagement in their work report eight common traits they admire most in their leaders. Those characteristics include being honest, supportive, cooperative, friendly, loyal, clear, hardworking, but also demonstrating a sense of fun and connection to family."[11] Clearly, not only does this list bear a resounding similarity to the list of Quality/Behavior/ Characteristics (QBC) my research identifies for an admired man, it also helps to make the case for my belief that evidenced-based leadership development strategies provide a solid foundation for an evidence-based approach to the development of an admired man. This chapter engages a phenomenological (the study of the development of human consciousness) approach in exploring detailed skills and practices commensurate with that belief. To harken back to my previous explanation of such an approach, Benz and Shapiro clarify, "…phenomenology attempts to take seriously the fact that we are conscious beings and that everything we know is something that we know only in and through consciousness… [it] makes us stop taking for granted the things that we normally take for granted, and that is part of mindfulness."[12] Merleau-Ponty asserts that "Self-consciousness is the very being of the mind at work. The act by which I am conscious of something must be itself apprehended in the moment in which it is accomplished, otherwise it would break apart."[13] Reference to mindfulness and consciousness research is important to setting the context for my discussion of the skills and practices that provide the foundation for the making of an admired man. Moreover, the acts and actions of an admired man, in the context of the skills and practices that exemplify an admired man, are apprehended and conscious at the time of the acts and continuous, holding the act and the admired man together. This embodies being an admired man. I would also like to make note of an overarching thread of commonality and consistency shared in each and every one of the accounts, surveys, and face-to-face interviews presented here, uniting the reasons given with respect to *why* a man is admired. Each and every one of the reasons given included some level of embodied reference to the indelible evidence that all of the reasons were for things that matter. Every one of the stories, accounts, testimonies, and comments were about things that mattered to the individual or group of individuals sharing.

As the reader; in your review of the "L(ife)eadership Skills and Practices for the Development of an Admired Man and Leader," it is significantly requisite that your subsequent actions and behavior be grounded and directed with respect to things that really matter to the individuals and groups whose admiration is being sought. You will be admired for how you affect the things that matter in the lives of others. Additionally, there must be a reciprocal relationship between the things that matter to others, and the things that matter to you; they need to be in alignment. This defines your Admired Man Quotient (AMQ);

the nexus between what matters the most, emotionally, to the admired man's **M**ost **V**aluable **P**eople and what matters the most, emotionally, to himself, the admired man. Cashman concludes, "We typically admire certain people not only because of their achievements, character, or personality, but because they connect with something inside of us which we regard as meaningful [and that matters]."[14] This requires the inordinate skill and ability to pay attention. Every one of the L(ife)eadership skills we will now discuss require that you first and foremost pay attention to the things that really matter to those whose space you share. Commitment, dedication, and attention are the keys to the embodiment of the skills and practices of an admired man.

L(ife)eadership Skills

The following L(ife)eadership skills are listed in the approximate order in which they would have the appropriate affect on an infant, school-age boy, adolescent, and young adult. Each of the skills requires an application and practice modification, dependent upon the age/stage of life of the learner. Most of the earlier skills are actually acquired by the modeling of a parent, preferably the father: The admired man in the family and in the home—fully present. This is not at all to mandate that women are not effective in teaching and supporting the acquisition of these L(ife)eadership skills by their sons, or daughters for that matter. While it is profoundly significant that these skills be modeled by a man, it is equally important that single mothers are proficiently secure in their understanding of the application of these skills; enabling them to not only be adroitly articulate in sharing these skills with their children, but also enabling them to be sufficiently selective about the men they expose their children to—men that are allowed "role modeling" access to their children. **NOTE TO SINGLE MOTHERS:** Please do not be naïve. When you bring any and all men (including relatives) around your children, you are giving these men "role modeling" access to your children. Herzog enlightens, "Men need to be with men in order to learn how to become men. This need requires careful and ongoing care and monitoring, often, but not only, provided by a woman if the need is to be optimally met."[15] Your son(s) will learn to be like the men they see, the men that have been given role-modeling access to them. Your daughter(s) will seek the attention of the type of men they see; who have been given role-modeling access to them. **NOTE TO FATHERS:** This admonishment applies to you as well. If you are not *fully present* in your children's daily lives, you risk someone else, other than their mother, having "role-modeling" access to your children. They will seek what they see.

While this list is not meant to represent all the possible L(ife)eadership skills a youth may need to mature into a productive parent, citizen, and community leader, I offer the following particular L(ife)eadership skills specifically aligned and required for being admired.

Happy – Fun Loving – Creativity	Well Groomed – Well Dressed – Appearance	Stress Management – Healthy – Safety	Self-Identity – Self Control – Self Discipline	Self-Respect – Respectful – Embracing – Inclusive
Listening – Active Listening	Communication – Verbal/Nonverbal – Self Disclosure	Negotiation – Partnering – Teamwork – Relationships – Adaptable	Assertiveness – Self-Confidence – Initiative – Leadership Development	Problem Solving – Critical Thinking – Follow Through
Decision Making – Risk Taking	Contemplation – Self Reflective/ Purpose – Emotional Awareness – Intentionality – Accountability	Reliable – Positive – Optimistic	Time Management – Organized – Dependable – Goal Setting – Planning – Routine	Personal Growth/ Achievement – Maturity – Financial Literacy/ Management

Just briefly, I will cover a description of each of the above L(ife)eadership skills:

Happy - Fun Loving - Creativity

When and how does a father influence the happy and fun-loving yet to be born future admired man? Before birth? Day one? While it may sound almost academic, so to speak, a father can profoundly influence the health and well-being of an unborn child in a number of ways; affecting the development of the unborn's neurological, spiritual, and physical development, which of course influences, to a large degree, their instinct for happiness upon birth. Common sense things like assisting and encouraging the mother to eat healthy food; not smoking; keeping the mother emotionally balanced; being present as she reads to the unborn child; and ensuring that her environment is peaceful and joyful, all contribute to the birth of a "happy baby."

Well Groomed - Well Dressed - Appearance

At the earliest stages of life children begin to recognize cleanliness and appearance. One of the most profound ways your son can be impacted with respect to their self-image and appearance is through the modeling of the men in their lives. Starting with you, infant boys gain a sense of acceptable appearances (including cleanliness) for a boy and a man.

Notable author and publicist, Gina Smith shares, "Several studies I have read state that people make a judgment of you within the first five minutes of meeting you. They take in your physical appearance, what you say, and then they render judgment on you."[16] Moreover, "While it isn't fair, it is a reality."[17]

Stress Management - Healthy/Fitness - Safety

Jawer and Micozzi help us understand the significance of a healthy mother on the future health and well-being of her children. They share factors that affect the mother during pregnancy that can contribute to the ability of their child's lifetime capacity for handling stress as well as their predisposition to a range of challenging conditions, including allergies. They explain how the onset of stress on the mother triggers her adrenal glands to produce copious amounts of stress hormones, particularly cortisol, which is passed through to the fetus. It does not take much imagination to understand how a volatile relationship with a mate, or the prospect of being a single mother, can undoubtedly generate stress in a pregnant woman.

Self-Identity - Self Control - Self Discipline - Self Responsibility

At the zero-to-five age range in your child's life the development of such representations are likely to have long-range and lasting affects on their evolving self-identity as well as their sense of self-value. The ramifications are profound when you consider the possibility of an alternative representation;   "self-with-any-man-who-will-show-me-any-attention," made plausible in your absence as a consistent positive male role model—an admired man—who is intentional and consistent; insistent; present; and, accessible. The stories shared in chapters I – V are replete with personal self-reflections that typify various self-with-other representations that invoked both joy and pain; always exemplified by accounts of how an "other" made a "self" feel, and its impact on their sense of self-identity.

Self-Respect - Respectful - Embracive - Inclusive

The admired man demonstrates to his children the ability and skill to genuinely applaud and appreciate the achievement and recognition of others. He understands that he can learn something from just about anyone, if he is willing to give others the space to share. The paradox again is that the admired man is very often admired and recognized for these very Quality / Behavior / Characteristics (QBC)—the confidence you show by not always looking for the spotlight.

Listening - Active Listening

Beginning before your child is born and continuing at the moment your child is born, talk, talk, talk, and talk some more to and with them. The more you talk with them the more they learn to listen and gain confidence in their communication skills. Recent research finds that your talking to your child in utero affects their cognitive development in a positive way. Larry and Debra, a couple from Seattle, Washington, talking about their new five-month-old son Michael, shared with me, "Our little man loves to talk with us. We started to talk with him while pregnant and it seemed he came out wanting to talk some more. Babble, babble, babble all day, and you better pay attention and talk back to him or he gets very upset," Debra smiled. "He seems to know if you are engaged with him...he expects you to listen to what he has to say" they both knowingly laughed.

Communication - Verbal/Nonverbal - Self Disclosure

Even at the young age of three-years-old your children need to become aware of situations that require learned actions on their part. They must be taught how to respond to situations that are unusual, and you, the adults in the family must have an ear open to their communication of something odd or unusual. I recall when my son was about three-years-old and was supposed to be playing with his toys in his room. He came into the family room where my wife and I were looking at TV and said, "Hot daddy hot." Of course, I had no idea what he was referring to, but it sounded cute. I probably said something like, "Yea, hot," and continued to look at the TV. But, after he said it a couple more times and seemed insistent, I thought he may be trying to tell me something I should look into. Duhh!!! Well, apparently he had decided to cook one of his toys. I followed him into the kitchen and found that his toy was flaming in the oven. He knew that this was something that he should probably report, but lacked the vocabulary to say, "Dad, I am sorry. But I have put my Go-Bot into the oven and now it is aflame. Please accept my apologies, and, I promise not to do this again, but in the meantime, you better come and put the fire out, otherwise we may need to evacuate and contact the fire department: This can't be a good thing." Instead, he was limited to, "Hot daddy, hot."

Negotiation - Partnering -Team Work - Relationships - Adaptable

The best friends for a zero-to-five-year-old future admired man are the members of his family: father, mother, and siblings. Then comes loving extended family members who help reinforce the values and skills being instilled at home. It is the role of the admired man to ensure this is the case. You are the protector of the values you and your wife initiate for the family. It is not always easy, but that is why you are the admired man. If your children will be exposed to a babysitter outside of the home, who has other children, be mindful of who the parents are of the other children. It is a delicate line, but it is one that helps you have confidence that your children are safe and that they are not getting exposed to values and behaviors that are inconsistent with those they experience at home—the values and behaviors that you and your family model.

Assertiveness - Self-Confidence - Self-Esteem - Initiative - Leadership Development

I almost want to say that these skills are at the center of the matter. All of the other skills discussed are predicated on how these personal skills: being assertive, having self-confidence, maintaining self-esteem, showing initiative, and, of course, continuous leadership development are embodied.

While there can be some positive things said about ambition and competitiveness, you do want to teach your children to frame these traits and skills in a manner that is consistent with what I call, negotiated leadership: leadership that is collaborative, collective, and shared. This is the most effective form of leadership and it can be taught at a very early age, as it is modeled by a child's parents and siblings.

Problem solving - Critical Thinking - Follow Through - Academic Achievement

Even on the topic of problem solving and critical thinking the admired man's influence on his children zero to five-years-old is profound. Very early in life your children explore their bodies, their voice, their surroundings, and their relationships. When and how you interact with your newborn helps to establish the foundation for how they process external and internal input, with respect to their relationships and their ever expanding world. Their learning right now seems random; you provide the order and emotional connection to their learning.

Decision Making - Risk Taking

Of course unavoidable attributes of leadership, problem solving, and critical thinking are risk taking and decision making. While there are conceivably very few decisions-making opportunities for a baby zero-to-five, starting at about six to seven-years-old is a good time to help your children understand the decision making process and how it relates to risk taking. This is a time to help them understand the concept of weighing options, and understanding that very often there are options.

Contemplation - Self Reflective/Purpose - Emotional Awareness - Intentionality- Accountability

Learning the skills of contemplation, self-reflective/purpose, emotional awareness, intentionality and accountability starts at birth. It starts with the parents embracing the practices of contemplation and responding with their newborn with intentionality. When parents reflect (interact) their child's emotions back to them through play, talking, and being physical, they are already teaching the infant self-reflection and purpose. The child already learns that it is okay to be who they are and to express themselves. You are teaching them that they can count on you engaging with them.

Reliable - Positive - Optimistic

Thinking positive and being optimistic is actually a very natural thing for young children, particularly when it is modeled by the parents. I recall enjoying the story about the advice my three-year-old daughter gave her five-year-old brother, after he shared that he had an unpleasant dream. She shares, "Just think about Disneyland when you go to bed." My daughter seemed to understand the power of high expectations, and that if you expected good things, your consciousness will follow. It is profoundly important and effective when the admired man has high expectations of himself and his children.

Time Management - Organized - Dependable - Goal Setting - Planning - Routine

Now, that you are more than well prepared to provide mentoring and guidance to your children about being reliable, positive, and optimistic, another very significant skillful characteristic you can indulge your children with is goal setting. Certainly, between the age of zero-to-five they are pretty much on their own agenda with respect to goals. You know: getting what they want, when they want it; playing with their toys; eating when they are hungry; etc. They pretty much have their own set of standards and goals, which parents have to acquiesce to. However, at just about the time your son reaches six-years-old, it is a great idea to introduce the concept of goal setting. This fits perfectly along with them understanding the values shared in the family. Values articulate not only how you perceive things should be done, but what things should be done is an important consideration. Determining, out of the myriad of possibilities, what things are done, in alignment with your core values and things that matter, is a derivative of the goal setting process.

Personal Growth/Achievement - Maturity - Financial Literacy/Management - Mentoring

Well, it won't be soon enough for your pre-teen to start getting an allowance from you. Surely, they will have plenty of things that they just gotta buy. Your responsibility is to make sure they understand the value of money beyond the things that they purchase. They need to have a perspective about responsible money management and some sense of financial literacy.

Needless to say, the art of saving money is not exactly easy for many adults. The good news is that the issue of money management for the common household is gaining in popularity and people are starting to understand and embrace the idea that financial literacy is not just for the "super rich." As people are starting to live more vibrant lives for longer periods the need to have saved and invested resources is gaining in understanding.

Companion Workbooks

The companion workbooks: The Making of an Admired Man: L(ife) eadership Skills Workbook – Parent's Gallery (for ages 0-12); and, The Making of an Admired Man: L(ife)eadership Skills Workbook – Take the Stage (for ages 13+) provide age/stage of life examples, projects, activities worksheets, and discussion topics that assist young men (and women), students, parents, counselors, mentors, teachers, etc., in developing and practicing Admired Man L(ife)eadership Skills. An important point that I will continue to reiterate is that men and/or mentors who work with boys and other men to develop these skills also advance their own Admired Man Quotient (AMQ) in the process. The workbooks also provide information on how to arrange a presentation and/or workshop for your group (of any size), conducted by a Certified Admired Man L(ife) eadership Skills Coach. There is also information in the workbooks on how to become a Certified Admired Man L(ife)eadership Skills Coach.

7

Things that Matter

*"My father is, hands down, the most valuable person I have
in my life. Our mother passed away while my sister and I were
very young, and our father has been our salvation. Every day
he shares with us the skills we need to grow up and take care of
ourselves. We both love our father. I pray that someday I have
children, and they feel the same way about me."*

— AN 18-YEAR-OLD MAN WHO LIVES WITH AND ADMIRES HIS FATHER.

*"The function of education is to teach one to think intensively
and to think critically. Intelligence plus character – that is the
goal of true education."*

— DR MARTIN LUTHER KING, JR.

THOMPSON AND THOMPSON discuss "How to Become an MVP" or Most
Valued Person. They eloquently point out that, "To be valued, respected, and admired, you must know what the important people in your

professional and personal life—your Most Valuable People or MVPs—value most."[1] This involves knowing what the people who mean the most to you really care about, and playing a significant part in fulfilling or meeting the needs most associated with the things they care about most. The skills I have outlined are significant with respect to being tooled to meet both of the requirements just mentioned: a) being aware of what your MVPs really care about (what really matters to them); and, b) being in position and knowing how to meet the requirements to fulfill the needs associated with what your MVPs care about. To really know what really matters to your MVPs is by no means an easy and frivolous undertaking. Most people give little deep dive, root level thought about the things that really matter the most to themselves, not less others. We are all so caught up in the day-to-day hustle bustle negotiations with everyone else who are also caught up in the same drive-by relationships that we rarely seek the space to entertain such a enterprise. (Point: mindful meditation is an excellent tool for slowing down and getting to know one's self.) If you don't know yourself, how can you really know another? Moreover, you may not know clearly what matters the most to you. The point is that if we don't know what people appreciate and value, we cannot know what really matters to them. Likewise, if you don't know what really matters to the people who mean the most to you, try as you might, you will not meet their needs.

The tricky part of this equation is that very often the things that matter the most to your MVPs may not be the things that you value the most, or that matter the most to you. How you negotiate this paradox is critical in being an admired man. Finding the intersection, or nexus, between what matters the most to your MVPs and what matters to you articulates the very essence of an admired man. It is at this intersection, or nexus, that it is defined, what your MVP appreciates most about you, and what you appreciate most about you. Here is where your values intersect and your Admired Man Quotient is maximized. It is my assertion that the maximization of this level of understanding and actualization requires an almost cosmic metaphysical stream of consciousness between men and women: This level of, what I will refer to as human spirituality, is not just about men, but rather, it is about the interrelationship between both men and women—humanistic leadership; conceptually, very much like Vail's "learning as a way of being" perspective – the whole person sharing common learning experiences with another whole person.

Work eloquently frames the overarching purpose and power of leadership and its outcome to society. He shares:

> Unlike other activities and efforts that may immediately have a single and realizable result or outcome, leadership is a dynamic and ongoing process that produces a stream of both intangible efforts and tangible results that are consistent with a socially meaningful vision. Less bounded by finite time constraints and one-time outcomes, the stream of leadership efforts and results rebounds not only to the benefit of those who are followers, but also of those who are not. In other words, the beneficial effects of true leadership cannot be limited, so to speak, to "the movement," whether it's civil rights, feminism, or another movement; rather, they must be felt by others and manifested in many of society's communities and institutions.[2]

Therefore, the admired man movement must not be simply about the uplifting of the Quality/Behavior/Characteristics (QBC) of men for the exiguous sake of their immediate and limited environment, but for the benefit of a larger sphere of humanity. Additionally, it is not just simply about men. The values, qualities, behaviors, characteristics, skills, practices, and things that matter are equally applicable to women in respect to their equal affect on this same sphere of humanity. I trust you realize by now, this book is not really, simply, just about being an admired man. It is all about humanity—humanistic leadership

Kouzes and Posner share a list of Seven Leadership Lessons for achieving extraordinary results. They are: (1) Leaders don't wait; (2)

Character counts; (3) Leaders have their hands in the clouds and their feet on the ground; (4) Shared values make a difference; (5) You can't do it alone; (6) The legacy you leave is the life you lead; and, finally (7) Leadership is everyone's business.[3]

Let's take another look at some of the things that really matter to the people that I had the privilege and honor of being touched by.

A 24-year-old man from Atlanta shared, "I really admire my 19-year-old brother. He always *knows what to do and say to make others feel important*...I want others to *feel about me as they feel about him*."

A 16-year-old girl from Detroit promised, "I am going to marry a man that *treats me like my father treats my mother*."

"Men have never done a damn thing for me *that did me any good*", said a 32-year-old woman.

A 53-year-old woman who did grow up with her father in her life, and shares that her boyfriend was the man she admires disclosed, "*worked hard, raised his children,* ...allowed me into his life...*not threatened* by my three advanced degrees...an *all-around good person*."

A 14-year-old girl who partially had her father in her life shares, "I admire my brother because he has *made the best out of nothing*."

A 52-year-old woman indicated that her friend is "*a committed father* to three sons."

A 53-year-old woman, said her father, "*made us laugh and smile*."

A 54-year-old man whose admired man was his father indicated, "people remember him because of his *character and devotion* to family."

A 28-year-old man who grow up with his father characterized his father as an "everyday American with a *heart of gold-plated steel*."

A 32-year-old woman explained, "What makes a man admirable is *selflessness*."

Alison, from Newport Beach, shared about her father, "I always felt *safe and happy*...all I can remember is *being happy*...I was *having fun*... if I was having trouble with a subject in school, he could help, but first he would make me feel good. He would *build up my confidence*...or distract me from feeling bad or feeling unsure. Then, after I felt better about myself we would talk about the trouble I was having…he always made sure *I felt good about me first.*"

Raul, a 28-year-old college student from San Diego, says of his father, "When people are around him they seem to understand that he will *look out for their best interest…they can count on him.*"

Twenty-one-year-old USC student, Yong, said of his friend Julio, who he admires, "He is *dependable and truthful.*"

Jeff says about his friend he admires, "he is *not afraid to tell you what he is thinking.*"

Claudia, an 31-year-old who lives with her husband of three years in Santa Monica, says of her husband, "I have never had to guess what he is *thinking or feeling…*we just seem to develop this *intense desire* to always be with each other."

Allison, of Long Beach, California, says that her brother, "shows me what it feels like for someone to really *love* you…not just say it, but *really mean it and show it…*he is *not afraid* to let everyone know, *all the time.*"

Roderick, a 19-year-old graduating senior from high school; on his way to study computer science and engineering at USC vowed, "someday I will find a woman to be the mother of my children in the manner that our mother was for us. I will have the same vow and promise that my father had with our mother. I will always *love her and will always be at her side with our children.* I will be their admired man.

Fifty-three-year-old Patrice stated that it seemed that her father, "always *knew my thoughts* and *what I need to hear to feel better.*"

A 24-year-old woman proudly boasts that her father, "*served our country* in the US Air Force."

Rita said about her foster father, "he made sure we understood what it means to have high *expectations of ourselves.*"

A 28-year-old mother from Long Beach reported, "I can always tell the mood Benjamin is in by the way he *talks* when he is *playing.*"

It is my belief that to really understand and grasp the lasting effect of a phenomenon, you have to listen and digest the stories of those who are affected. I am confident that I have captured the essence of how people are impacted by having or not having an admired man in their life. I am equally honored and personally affected by having the privilege and opportunity to meet, for myself, some of the men that others have ordained to admire. Thompson and Thompson share profound wisdom in their statement, "To make a lasting impression, you need to share a personal story that makes an emotional connection with people—an authentic narrative that describes why you care and what you believe in an openhearted, down-to-earth way."[4] I believe that I have, in a genuinely caring way, managed to capture and share the stories that allow my readers to reflect upon their own meaningful and emotional connections with others, with the greatest of authenticity. I hope that this book inspires humanity in a manner that encourages men to be admired and to embody the skills I have shared as well as other skills—for the sake of humanity.

So, of course I have to add my contribution to this discussion. I have to name a man that I admire and explain why?

I admire my son, Chris L. Hickey, Jr. I admire my son because he is a hardworking, honest, role model, and loving father, who cares about his family.

Also, I would be remised if I didn't share that I also admire my daughter, Diana Sharice van Houwelingen. She is the most brilliant person I have ever met. And, she cares dearly about her Family. She makes her dad feel Special!!

Of course, I admire my son's loving wife and mother of his son, Lockell; as well as my daughter's very thoughtful, caring and attentive husband, Luke.

And, of course my wife, Sharron L. Hickey. I could not have chosen a better woman to berth my two wonderful children. I admire her dearly.

8

Review of Prior Research about Men

Admiration

IN GROUND-BREAKING RESEARCH, where functional magnetic resonance imaging (fMRI) was used to track the brain activities of subjects as they listened to different stories designed to evoke strong emotional reactions, including admiration of physical skills, affective neuroscientist and human development psychologist Mary Helen Immordino-Yang and Dr. Antonio Damasio suggested that feelings, such as admiration, are rooted deep within the brain, where basic traits like anger and fear reside. The research suggests that the region of the brain most affected by such emotional reactions, the posteromedial cortices (PMC), is also a major contributor to the maintenance of consciousness and the construction of self. In other words, the region of the brain that facilitates self-identity also regulates the emotional elements that accompany our admiration of others, which, again, clearly suggests a relationship between the admiration of others and self-identity and awareness:

> Social emotions such as admiration...play a critical role in interpersonal relationships and moral behavior...The experience of [this emotion] may also produce a sense of heightened

self-awareness that incites our own desire to be virtuous or skill-ful, or else gratitude for our own good circumstances.[1]

Moreover, "Admiration can be evoked by witnessing virtuous behavior aimed at reducing the suffering of others [known also as 'elevation'] or by displays of virtuosic skill."[2] The phenomenon of "self-awareness" is evident. Additionally, what this may suggest is that when an Admired Man is modeling admirable Quality/Behavior/Characteristics (QBC's), and being admired, they are also raising the level of "self-awareness" in the individuals who are admiring them. In a similar study conducted at Stanford University researchers expanded on the PMC/behavioral re-lationship by expounding not only on its influence on "self-awareness," to include how PMC engages in the mental construction of (internally directed) "autobiographic" mental representations (e.g., recall and/or imagination), as opposed to externally directed focus (e.g., arithmetic calculations).[3] Affectively, the PMC supports, "Social emotions—adapta-tions of emotional states to meet the needs of social situations...thought to be functions of the left hemisphere [of the brain]."[4]

As you have read, the expression of emotion in many of the stories shared is profound. It did not seem to matter whether the people I had the privilege of talking with face-to-face expressed a man they admired, or said they admired no man, the presence of emotion and self-reflec-tion was evident. I could not help but consider the aforementioned re-search by Brett L. Foster, Stanford University neuroscientist; Mohammad Dastjerdi of the Stanford University Cancer Institute; and, Josef Parvizi, associate professor of neurology at Stanford University, about the auto-biographic mental representations that are generated in the postero-medial cortices region of the brain as a result of one thinking about someone they admire.[5] I suggest that it is extremely likely that the mere asking of questions about admiration and one's father, for many of those I spoke with and who participated in the survey, may have stimulated the "autobiographic" mental representations in their consciousness. I could clearly see and feel the onset of emotion during my in-person interviews, in both the participants and myself. Additionally, Schaetti, Ramsey and Watanabe suggest a relationship between personal leadership (the bringing forth of "the highest levels of learning and creativity")[6] and self-reflection. They share, "Practicing Personal Leadership requires us to self-reflect with absolute honesty and integrity. We have to be willing to look at our motivations, our assumptions, our expectations."[7] Affectively, it is plausible that for some, the contemplation of what man a respondent admires may, in and of itself, stir the ingredients of leadership development along with self-reflection.

In research that takes a more focused perspective about the various roles that admired men tenure, (i.e., fathers, friends, mates, brothers, etc.), there exists an interminable library of journal articles and books that focus more specifically on how men in various roles affect others in their life; or in absentia.

Fathers

In this book the role of the father illuminates prominently, as you read. It is my hunch that "father" appears so adamantly in this study because of the very issues just discussed relevant to the affects of the stimulated PMC. It is highly plausible that the question "What man do you admire?" particularly followed by "Did you grow up with your father in your life?" may very well stimulate the "autobiographic" mental representations in one's posteromedial cortices (PMC) consciousness, which feasibly triggers emotions relevant to one's phenomenal childhood experience. While my focus is on the admiration of a man, and why, the results of my investigation reveal an overwhelming presence of both the physical and conceptual father in the consciousness of most people. Notwithstanding the focus of my examination, copious questions regarding the role and impact of the physical and/or conceptual father are luminous, reflected by the profoundly diverse research contributions over the past few decades.

The following represents only a minimal sample of the scholarly literature addressing the role of fathers in the life of their children, and how they affect the social, emotional, academic, and psychological development of their children.

Infancy: Assistant Professor of Psychology at the University of Wisconsin, Madison and member of the Society for Research in Child Development, Michael E. Lamb, suggests the father-son relationship is evident during the infancy stage of the child's development. While traditionally, particularly beginning in utero, it is the mother who has been dominantly recognized for her role in socializing the infant, primarily because of her biological affixation with the child and primary nurturing role, the social network of the child, including their relationship with the father, begins in the infancy stage of their life, and is profoundly influenced by the father's engagement and interaction with the infant. With respect to the child's role in social interaction and networking, Lamb argues that researchers are demonstrating that infants who at one time were assumed to be passive and receptive partners in social interaction are now viewed as playing a more active role. He nevertheless cautions us not to equate time spent with an infant with the quality of interaction; a point that applies to both parents. He thus concludes that "...empirical and theoretical considerations indicate that the amount of time spent together is a poor predictor of the quality of the infant's relationship with either mother or father...the extent of interaction is probably unrelated to its quality."[1]

The quality of the child's relationships is a dominant theme that permeates the literature addressing the father's role in the child's development.[2-14] For example, University of Massachusetts' Milton Kotelchuck asserts that developmental psychologists have virtually ignored the father's influence on the infant's early social development, instead studying fathers only in their absence.[15] Lamb elaborates on the need to not only examine the mother-child relationship, but also our need to appreciate the complexities of the father-child relationship.[16] Moreover, to better understand the socio-personality development of the infant's social world we must appreciate its complexity and multi-dimensionality.[17] Henry B. Biller, Department of Psychology, University of Rhode

Island, suggests a parallel alliance between the quality of the infant's relationship with parents (including the father), and that of future relationships.[18] For example, he argues, there is a direct correlation between infants who experience greater anxiety on separation from their mother, and infants who have little contact with their father. Furthermore, as fathering researchers Jacinta Bronte-Tinkew, Jennifer Carrano; and Lina Guzman conclude, the father's perception is another significant factor related to the father's role in his child's development.[19] In his exhausting examination of the *Phenomenology of Perception,* French phenomenological philosopher Merleau-Ponty articulates a relational connection between perceptions and body sensory,[20] therefore establishing again a relationship between perception, self-identity, self-reflection and the phenomenal characteristics of admiration. Others specifically identify: caregiving activities; paternal warmth; nurturing activities; physical care; and cognitively stimulating activities as the most significant domains of father involvement that are associated with the father's perception of what fathering constitutes.[21-22]

School-aged children: Charles Lewis, Lancaster University professor of psychology, discusses some of what I consider a profoundly comprehensive perspectives, in appreciation of the father's role in child development at this age, from a sociological standpoint. First, it is important to identify, distinguish, and clarify the differences between the psychological and the sociological approach to research on this topic. In doing so Lewis points out the two contradictory themes in fatherhood research of the 1970's, one from a psychological perspective, the other more sociological. He reminds us that while on the one hand psychological research suggests that men have a significant influence on their children's development, on the other hand there exists an alternative theme in the sociological literature that plays down the father's role in influencing their child's development. With respect to this dichotomy, it must be noted that Lewis' statements are intended to address the effect and influence of father involvement, not the accessibility, consistency, and frequency of father involvement.[1]

To add clarity to his point regarding the two perspectives, Lewis writes, "More often than not authors expressed two opinions simultaneously: that fathers provide an essential ingredient to the child's psychological development, but to understand fathers we need to grasp that other factors are involved."[2] And, it is the examination and analysis of these other sociological factors, both direct factors and indirect factors, that have helped advance the research addressing the father's role. This approach moves us away from the simple cause and effect relationship in the parent-child interaction.

Henry B. Biller and Jon Lopez Kimpton, from the University of Rhode Island, also recognize the social aspect of the child's cognitive development, noting that cognitive functioning cannot be isolated from other aspects of the child's development such as social and moral growth. With respect to the social aspects of cognitive development, and the father's influence on social and moral growth, the authors address what research reveals regarding father absence. For example, both for boys and girls, father absence (which they defined as two years of separation from father, though not necessarily consecutive) was related to relatively low ability in perceptual (motor and manipulative) spatial tasks. They also noted that the major disadvantage occurring with father absence for children is lessened paternal attention, including fewer opportunities to model mature decision making and problem solving, a profound affect on a boy's sex-role development, and, by extension, the development of implicit leadership skills. They argue that during the elementary school years, daughters are less influenced by father absence than are sons. Additionally, they point out a positive relationship between a son's occupational mobility during early adulthood and the father's support of physical-athletic development during childhood.[3] Although these studies undoubtedly illuminate the instrumental role played by the father it is important to note that they were conducted during an era prior to the 1990's when the hetero nuclear family norm was usually taken to be the norm, suggesting probable bias.[4]

More recently, a range of studies have examined the effects of a combination of father involvement and social environment on the development of school-aged children. An exploratory study of a sub-sample of 1,334 families with children between the ages of five and twelve was conducted by Brent A. McBride, Sarah J. Schoppe-Sullivan, and Moon-Ho Ho with the intent to examine the relationship between school, neighborhood, family-level resources, and children's academic achievement. More specifically, the goal of the study was to identify the role played by father involvement in mediating contextual influences on children's learning.[5] This brings into focus the topic related to the indirect influence the father has on his school-aged son's expanding social network.[6-11] Among the findings of this study, the research revealed "...a significant relationship between aspects of father involvement in their children's education and student achievement beyond that accounted for by mother involvement."[12]

In research conducted by Patterson, where assessments were conducted for possible differences between gay or lesbian parents, in contrast to heterosexual parents, it was concluded that there was no evidence, given comparable circumstances, of any significant compromise of the development of the children of the former parenting construct.[13] However, in another study, drawn from parent questionnaires, child interviews, and focus groups to investigate school incidents experienced by children of lesbian and gay parents, Vivien Ray and Robin Gregory found that students between the second and tenth grade expressed feelings of discrimination and frustration by their peers' lack of understanding about their families. Additionally, many of the students interviewed expressed feelings of being unsafe and a lack of confidence in their teacher's abilities to deal with homophobia. Clearly, more research is warranted on subjects related to this and other "non-traditional" family structures and environments.[14]

Adolescence: While a case can be made regarding the distinction between early school-age children and adolescents, for the teenager, being a more independently thinking and socialized offspring, research suggests that the effects of father involvement during infancy and the child's school-age development continues to predicate the adolescent child's social development. This is the case for both the father present and father absent adolescent. Additionally, adolescent boys are distinctly influenced by the relationship they have with their fathers, with the quality of the relationship having no less affect on the boy's development than during infancy and the school-age years.[1-8]

Diamond eloquently articulates the plight and complexities of the adolescent boy as follows: "Outrageous, conformist, turbulent, despairing, desperate, crazy, ecstatic—these words only begin to describe the breathtaking roller coaster of the emotionally intense, hormone-fueled teenage years."[9] Diamond goes on to assert a foundation from which the teenage boy starts to deal with his changing mind, body, and emotion. He continues:

> Boys are, moreover, faced with three essential tasks: to begin to formulate their own identities while incorporating all the changes they're undergoing; to separate from their families, particularly from their fathers; and to begin to come to terms with their feelings of loss.[10]

In support of Diamond's clinical as well as personal observations, recall Siegel's discussion on the changing adolescent brain:

> Brain changes during the early teen years set up four qualities of our minds during adolescence: novelty seeking, social engagement, increased emotional intensity, and creative exploration. There are changes in the fundamental circuits of the brain that make the adolescent period different from childhood. These changes affect how teens seek rewards in trying new things, connect with their peers in different ways, feel more intense emotions, and push back on the existing ways of doing things to create new ways of being in the world.[11]

Young adults: Further along on the path to adulthood, boys continue to experience changes in how they deal with family relationships, in particular with their fathers. Diamond proposes:

> ...young men need to begin to create an autonomous life where they can experience themselves as adult men able to function independently, apart from their families. This entails two tasks: finding their place in the world (which includes creating a career direction); and forming intimate, lasting love relationships. Neither is easy.[1]

And, both are affected by the young man's infant, school-age, and adolescent relationship with his father.[2-7]

Dennis Balcom eloquently points out a number of adverse effects due to "divorce, death, absences due to employment or military service, addictions, incarceration, and chronic physical or mental illness"[8] that father abandonment has on a son's own attempts at having intimate relationships with his own mate and children. In his discussion of the therapeutic strategies that may assist men in resolving issues of grief and shame, Balcom points out that the abandoned son's feelings are generally typified by emotional reactivity, characterized by the statement, "I'll never be like him!" Likewise, many abandoned sons simply disavow the importance of their fathers, which harkens back to our discussion about the phenomenology of perception and how it relates to self-identity, self-reflection and the phenomenal characteristics of admiration.[9] In either case, Balcom suggests that "Until the son acknowledges his unfulfilled needs and longing for his father, he can remain in turmoil about himself and his intimate relationships."[10]

The notorious Los Angeles area gang member (CRIPS), Monster Kody Scott[11] discussed his adolescent pain resulting from the treatment he received from his stepfather. While serving a six-year prison sentence at maximum security prisons, for armed robbery, assault, and illegal possession of a weapon, he shared that his mother disclosed to him that the man he grew up thinking was his father, Ernest Scott, was in fact not his "real" father. He was actually the son of the former football player for the Los Angeles Rams, Dick Bass, as a result of his mother's extramarital affair with the popular athlete. To this news, Monster began to recollect feeling mistreated by the man be believed was his father. He recounted his feelings about being left behind when Scott would take the other children on trips. After attempting to console his mother by repeating to her that her losing him to the streets was not her fault, upon her leaving for the day he contemplated to himself:

> As I lay on the slab I now said it over and over to myself, "It's not your fault." And I hated that muthafucka Scott and Dick Bass. What could Mom do? She could only be our father for so long. I do remember not being taken on any trips like the others and being treated differently by Scott. When the others were on trips, I would be alone and sad…Mom would pretend that the reason I couldn't go on the trips was that she wanted me with her because I was her favorite. She tried very hard to keep my spirits up, even when her's were down. Scott would take the others to Houston to visit his mother, their grandmother. But I was an illegitimate child and he was ashamed of me, hated me, Mom said. I never met my grandmother.[12]

Monster's recollection of his phenomenal pain and self-reflection is, of course, by no means unique to young men who have found themselves in his circumstance. Recall;

- 85% of all children who show behavior disorders come from fatherless homes – 20 times the average (Center for Disease Control)
- 70% of juveniles in state-operated institutions come from fatherless homes (Source: U.S. Dept. of Justice, Special Report, Sept 1988)

Cultural and socioeconomic factors: Considering that one of my goals of this book is to examine the human nature of feelings, it is important to acknowledge that the onset of many human feelings and particularly the articulation of human feelings are influenced and experienced within the context of cultural and socioeconomic factors. As men and boys develop within the environment of a particular family structure, their developing emotions and feelings are affected by the cultural context and relationships of the family. Given this reality, it is appropriate to acknowledge the possibility of differences, based on varying cultural and/or socioeconomic factors, in how men and boys may articulate feelings about what may seem on the surface to be very similar experiences.

In some of the earliest literature addressing the role of the father in child development there are a number of references with respect to the importance of taking into account cultural considerations and differences. Much of the focus is generally intended to either point out cultural social changes within mainstream Western society; that is, to contrast general differences with respect to family structure and practices, from the standards of Western Protestant norms; or, to use differences found among non-Western traditional practices as examples of "bad fathering."[1]

Professor of Child and Family Studies, Jaipaul L. Roopnarine, sets the stage for reexamining how we evaluate father involvement from a multicultural perspective in his examination of father involvement on the part of African American and African Caribbean fathers. Pointing out the doubtfulness of any singular characteristic being able to capture the ethos of both the African American and African Caribbean fathers' level of investment in the welfare of their families, Roopnarine suggests considerable variability in the family structure and context within which these men become fathers and develop a relationship with their children.[2]

In their discussion on generative fathering, William D. Allen and Michael E. Connor offer:

How African American men view their family experiences, *what* they are able or willing to do as family members, and even *when* they decide to do it are often directly affected by ethnicity.[3]

With respect to research methodology, Professor Alfredo M. Mirande points out two very distinctive conceptual errors to be avoided in deference to understanding the impact of ethnicity.[4] The errors they warn against are: (1) ignoring the potential effects of ethnicity—thereby assuming that all fathers are alike and, conversely, (2) assuming that ethnicity has the same effect on all members of a given ethnic group. Avoidance of such errors contributes to a higher level of research that is relevant and consistent with respect to representing the cross-section of family structures and functions in American culture. A number of other recent studies adhere to this approach to evaluating the father's role in the development of children in terms of accounting for cultural differences in their analysis of the father-son relationship.[5-9] With respect to this approach, Michael E. Connor of California State University, Long Beach, and Joseph White, of the University of California, Irvine discuss in denoting detail their perception that African American men are often shortchanged in most research on their involvement with their children. They write:

[A] more complete analysis of Black men will likely demonstrate that some of the men who were not involved with their children were not "deadbeat" per se, but were men bearing both psychological and physical scars—scars derived from daily interactions in an oppressive environment. The ugly remnants of these scars were passed on to their offsprings in terms of an emotional [and physical] distance between fathers and children.[10]

Nonetheless, in my opinion, the children of non-involved and/or absent fathers suffer in the meantime. Children do not understand the historical antecedents and influences of their father's condition. By the time the children are able to genuinely comprehend some of the historical and cultural factors that may contribute to the father's parental neglect, the damage is done, in spite of later attempts to educate or enlighten the child on the historical and cultural factors. Connor and White went on to suggest that the true love and caring involvement of black men in the lives of their children is actually ignored by those outside of the African American community, or unduly measured against traditional concepts of father involvement, rendering their involvement inadequate and often non-existent.[11] Esther Dermott adds, "In focusing on the different kinds of fathering involvement, it has been argued that a more expansive definition is required as restricting men's involvement with children to direct care is too narrow."[12] Brigham Young University professor Renata Forste and Jonathan Jarvis, of the University of Hawaii reveal that although research indicates that "black children are less likely to live with two biological parents than non-blacks"[13] their fathers are more likely to remain in contact with them as compared to white non-residential fathers.

Studies such as that of Forste and Jarvis bring to light the importance of not falling into the trap of overly focusing on the deadbeat dad.[14] It is my contention that the nurturing and involved fathers of most cultures and ethnicities must not be ignored or perceived as less important or worthy of discussion and attention. The father's effective influence is evident through their children, as suggested by the term "generative fathering."[15] Whereas, indeed there is a lot of attention focused on the deadbeat dad in the literature, these authors and others are generally suggesting that there is not enough written on the "good" black father. I would argue, however, that one can find traces of "the good black father" in the scholarly literature on good fathering in general, although such studies regrettably do not explore important cultural considerations specific to African American fathers. Unfortunately, among those studies that do address African American fathers in terms of their cultural distinctions, it is all too often the case that this is within the greater general literature as examples of the "bad" father. Such essentializing categorizations are of little use, and in fact can be said to be harmful. I contend rather that there is no "good" black fathering, or "good" white fathering. Likewise, there is no "bad" black fathering—just good fathering and the absence of good fathering, and the literature is pretty clear in identifying the Quality/Behavior/Characteristics (QBC) of good fathering. Whereas, certainly there are within this viewpoint of "good fathering and the absence of good fathering" cultural variations, it is important to avoid negative ethnic stereotypes typified by the language "bad fathering." Yet given the propensity to make cultural identifications along such categories as "good" and "bad" fathers, greater care should be taken to approach them equitably.

Similar to the Connor and White perspective, with respect to African American father involvement research,[16] Cabrera and Coll discuss this issue as it pertains to Latino father involvement. Referring to research conducted in the early 1990's, the authors point out that there has been a growing recognition of the inherent problem of judging the parent-child relationship of Latino families against the standards of Euro-American models of family structure and function.[17] Resulting from this growing awareness is a new view of Latino fathers and families. Replacing the extant perception of Latino fathers as machista-authoritarian, harsh, and overly disciplinarian, is recognition of Latino men being more flexible, adaptable, and caring. They also point out that one of the barriers that Latino men must overcome is the negative stereotypes that surround them, as a residual of earlier research distortions of their true involvement with their family and children. Bronte-Tinkew point out the problem of many immigrant fathers, experiencing a shift in family roles when arriving in this country, adding to other stressors such as: underemployment; unemployment; language barriers; shifts in identity roles; and barriers to services and information.[18]

Overall, it is my belief that too often research endeavors that seek to explain social/economic/cultural factors that affect father involvement direct attention away from what we know about the effects of a nurturant, caring, and actively involved father on the development of their children. If the focus were specifically on the development of the children, how would social/economic/cultural differences, with respect to father involvement, have any different affect on the social, psychological, and cognitive development of the children in American culture? Surely, the social/economic/cultural segmentations in American society have an affect on family time and financial resources. Families with more lucrative financial access are better able to take advantage of other contributing resources that affect their child's social, emotional, and cognitive development (for example, better schools and social settings). Conversely, families with less financial resources are correspondently at a disadvantage, with respect to their access to contributing resources. In a discussion regarding the homogeneous sample of 25 fathers in her study on "…how men conceptualized their role as 'worker' and 'father' and the extent to which reality matched the theory,"[19] Esther Dermott divulged, "The assumption here was not that creative parenting practices are limited to a particular family form but, because the push of economic necessity is often the reason that is given for adopting 'traditional' gendered forms of parenting, higher income levels might afford more possibilities."[20]

Moreover, in their study addressing the effects of a father's perception of his involvement, Bronte-Tinkew resolve that the perception of fathering is in fact affected by income, race/ethnicity, age, education level, and marital status.[21] Yet with respect to a father's quality involvement and the affect it has on a child's social, emotional, and cognitive development, research supports the fact that under any social/economic/cultural circumstance, children are positively influenced by fathers who are present, nurturant, supportive, engaged, and active with their children, particularly their sons.[22-27] Studies reveal that when fathers are not involved in a supportive and nurturing way in their children's lives, regardless of the social/economic/cultural differences found in American society, their children suffer.[28-33]

One need only to read the chilling manifesto, "My-Twisted-World" written by Elliot Rodgers, who engaged the 2014 Isla Vista killings. In this document Rodgers, the son of a wealthy father, shares a startling chronology of the deteriorating relationship with his father, and how it affected his feeling of self-respect and value. Speaking of his life at six-years-old, Rodgers reflected, "My father's new directing career was taking off quite well too, and he would go away a lot to direct commercials for prestigious companies, leaving my mother and the nanny to look after me. The only downside of this was my father's absence from my life. Despite this, I always looked up to him as a powerful and successful man." He later shared, "Very shortly after my seventh birthday, the news came. I believe it was my mother who told me that she and my father were getting a divorce; my mother, who only a few months before told me that such a thing will never happen. I was absolutely shocked, outraged, and above all, overwhelmed. This was a huge life-changing event…. My life would change forever after this. The family I grew up with has split in half, and from then on I would grow up in two different households. I remember crying. All the happy times I spent with my mother and father as a family were gone, only to remain in memory."

The expression of his feelings and emotions, associated with a feeling of loss and abandonment, are not in the least different from those shared by young boys and girls with considerably less affluence. He then shared his thoughts at the age of 17, after a number of tumultuous experiences with his two families; spending some time with his mother, and other time with his father and new wife, he resolved, "My misery became harder and harder to bear, and none of my parents understood my plight. My father thought that all was well with me. *How could he be so blind?…* He didn't care about how my life was turning out. I cursed him for it. My father never made any effort to prepare me for facing such a cruel world. He never taught me how to attract girls. He never warned me that if I didn't attract girls at an early age, my life would fall into a miserable pit of despair! Again…*How could he be so blind?* I asked myself constantly…I was very angry with father, but I hid my anger. I still needed him." Sadly, this story ends and begins with Elliot Rodgers going on a killing spree that resulted in the death of seven people, including himself. Chilling, to say the least. Particularly telling, with respect to Rodger's insidious "father-hunger," is his confession that it was his intent to also kill his father's wife, but that he decided not to go to their home, in fear of his father being there, and having to kill him as well. The idea of killing his father was beyond comprehension; outside of his demented state of mind. Moreover, as "crazy" as he was, father-hunger still prevailed. Clearly, there are other psychological factors involved here; my point is that the emotional trauma of parental abandonment, and associated feelings of despair, hopelessness, fear, and self-worthlessness, (among other disorders) are not shielded by affluence and social status. Tabloids are replete with other examples. In an almost undetectable way, Rodgers is alluding to (in his mind) leadership, or the lack thereof, on the part of his parents, particularly his father.

Even with the growing trend of leadership programs for college youth, there is research suggesting a significant link between the perceived circumstances at home and with parent(s), and the student's attitude and academic performance. For instance, Barling, Dupre, and Hepburn conducted a study of 134 college students and their parent(s) to evaluate the effect of parents' job insecurities on their children's attitudes and beliefs toward work. The authors cited other research that found that even at the young age of third and fourth grade, children are very observant of their parent's reactions and emotions relevant to work.[34] By this time in their lives, the children know where their parent(s) work, what they do, and perceive what their parent(s)' job satisfaction is.[35-37] Consistent with the findings of other research, Steele and Barling[38] found that, particularly when students identified more strongly with their fathers, there was profound evidence suggesting conditions that moderate the relationship between perceptions of parents' job security and the students' work beliefs and propensity for leadership. This may suggest that even in light of our institutional attempts to teach leadership, with all the scholarly references and material, the foundation for how young folk perceive occupational leadership is primarily formed at an early age, at home, modeled by their parents.

Alternative perspectives: Notwithstanding the overwhelming empirical research supporting the conclusions regarding the significant influence and role played by fathers on the psychological, sociological, cognitive, sex-role, and leadership development of their children, there are some who refute such notions on various levels. Psychology professor and author David C. Rowe emphatically asserts the position that after 100 years of behavioral genetic research, there is little factual support for the "common sense" proposition that child-rearing styles and family environment are formative of personality traits. He posits:

> Nonintellectual traits seem to be determined instead by genetic influences and by relatively specific environmental influences, most of which are not particularly tied to the family or parental treatment. Intellectual traits show modest family environmental influence, but that influence may diminish in importance after childhood.[1]

With similar tone, Herrnstein and Murray[2] and Pinker[3] question various issues related to the nature versus nurture influence on children, particularly with respect to intelligence and cognitive development, referring to genetic influences as being the primary determinate of personality and cognitive Quality/Behavior/Characteristics (QBC) in children. It is their position that parental involvement has minimal influence on personal and cognitive development. These positions run somewhat contrary to the prevailing literature tying parental influence of the father, as well as the mother, to the development of their children on a number of levels, including their personality and cognitive development. Surely, there are genetic influences involved; however, there is significant evidence supporting the influence of the child's social network, particularly the direct and indirect influence of the child's immediate family, having profound and lasting affect on the child's personal and cognitive development, at and over time.

It is important to note that several studies in the past 10 to 15 years have re-addressed the nature versus nurture debate. Recent studies have argued for the existence of a more integrative process in cognitive and emotional development. According to Elliot M. Tucker-Drob:

Recent research in behavioral genetics has found evidence for a Gene × Environment interaction on cognitive ability: Individual differences in cognitive ability among children raised in socio-economically advantaged homes are primarily due to genes, whereas environmental factors are more influential for children from disadvantaged homes.[4]

In another study, Tucker-Drob and K. Paige Harden share, "Parenting is traditionally conceptualized as an exogenous environment that affects child development. However, children can also influence the quality of parenting that they receive."[5] They add that:

Genetic and environmental factors differentially contributed to these effects. Parenting influenced subsequent cognitive devel-opment through a family-level environmental pathway, whereas children's cognitive ability influenced subsequent parenting through a genetic pathway. These results [of their research] suggest that genetic influences on cognitive development occur through a transactional process, in which genetic predisposi-tions lead children to evoke cognitively stimulating experiences from their environments.[6]

This line of research thus presents evidence for the need to consider new perspectives on the nature versus nature debate that depart from the traditional dichotomous understanding of human development.

Emotions/feelings: Balcom's descriptive applied research article on the absent father's effect on abandoned sons serves to illuminate and establish a grounded foundation from which to stage further discussion.

After a brief discussion of the social context of father abandonment, as mentioned above, Balcom highlights the adverse effects abandonment can have on the son's intimate relationships.[7] Krampe & Newton suggest the importance of the father's experience as a son; as such reflections and memories are invariably influential in their relationship with their spouse and children.[8] Balcom continues on to discuss therapeutic strategies that may assist men in resolving issues of grief and shame. My primary interests in this article, as it relates to feelings, center on issues of self-esteem, emotion, communication, perception, and self-consciousness. Furthermore, Balcom's acknowledgment of the role unacknowledged feelings can play in a son's emotional development is of significant relevance to the concept of feelings utilized in this book.[9]

In a very brief but succinctly relevant autobiographic case study on father-son mutual respect, Campbell discusses some of the dynamics of the relationship in the self-perceptual context of success. During a camping and hiking trip, "deep in the forests of the Pacific Northwest" under the tutelage of his 25-year-old son, Campbell found himself pondering on various notions of mutual respect between fathers and sons. He writes, "A son who in his own mind never matches his father's performance is vulnerable to a life that feels incomplete, unfulfilled, and unsatisfying, no matter how much he, the son, objectively accomplishes.[10] In this article the author brings to the conversation the element of value,[11-12] asserting that the perception of success in the son's mind is dependent upon his perception of what the father values. "If the father values only money, the son's only avenue to success is to make more of it than did the father."[13] Campbell adds that if this is not accomplished, the son "is doomed to a perpetual feeling of personal insufficiency."[14] While this is obviously a sweeping generalization, the implications, particularly in light of the study on abandoned sons, can be profound. Specifically, considering the notion that the abandoned son may likely become consumed in an insufficient and self-reflective distortion of what his father values and/or what constitutes success, within the self-perpetuating context of his germinating father-fantasies—á la Elliot Rodgers.

Floyd and Morman remind us that, "Far fewer studies have addressed men's affection with adolescent sons."[15] Wyatt adds to our understanding about the loss of a father in his autoethnographic case study chronicling his reflections on his relationship with his father both during his father's life and after his death. He began documenting his thoughts almost a year after his father's death. His opening words are:

> It is on days like today, in summer, that I remember him most: tanning himself in the harsh sun or swimming in the sea, so far out that I could glimpse him only between the waves; or as now, when the evening draws in, holding his whisky - half scotch, half water. The nectar of the gods, as he would say.[16]

Reflexivity, perception, memory, affection, and resolution are all embedded in the words of the author, as he opens the reflective door to his feelings, both past and present. In the final words of this writing the author shares, "My teenage son is in the room above me—I can hear his tapping at the computer keyboard and the beat of his music—and my twelve-year-old daughter sings as she skips up the stairs and slams her door."[17] With his initial words, the author invites the reader into the reflective visualization of a time filled with fondness and appreciation of his father's protective presence and shared humor. With his final words, the author "fast-forwards" the reader into the reality of his current protective post as a father who in turn reflects the present, bound in an inevitable surrender to the future. With these words the author closes the loop, acknowledging that the feelings associated with his relationship with his father not only affect the past and present, but the future as well. The next six pages of his story are more narrative memories accounting for the author's relationship with his father. Finally, the author again puts it all in perspective in terms of the lasting phenomenon of life; past, present, and future. He closes:

The story is finished, compressed into a few pages. I have worried over it, dreamed it, loved and hated it, and feel sad that it is done. The writing of it meant living it again. I imagine that there will come a time when I shall want to stop writing about my father, and I sense that I may be nearing that point, but for now, I am reluctant; because to stop narrating stories is to cease being alive and I don't want him, or me, to die yet.

In an hour or so the house will begin to awaken. The drone of a heavy metal soundtrack will filter through the ceiling; there will be footsteps on the stairs, followed by requests for money, friends, transport, or time. I cannot wait.[18]

This story also helps to illuminate the power of narrative, in addition to other data gathering techniques, in a comprehensive analysis of a phenomenon, particularly one that is both nebulous and material.

I have chosen to quote Wyatt's work so extensively in order to illustrate the goals I hope to achieve in this book with respect to unveiling the depth of feelings individuals express and/or exemplify about the man they admire, and why; both in the past, present and future.

Friends

Cohen extensively chronicles the plethora of literature that covers the portrayal of the experience of men friendship and intimacy. He explains that much of the literature on this topic portrays men as being inexpressive, rational, and competitive; lacking both "...an appreciation of and capability for intimacy." Influenced by a "...lifetime of male socialization." Cohen cites homophobic concerns that "...further trap men within narrow, somewhat superficial positions vis-à-vis other men." Although intimacy with women is far less restricted, it still "...falls short of women's abilities and expectation of emotional intimacy."[1]

Reid and Fine share very similar ideas about how men relate to one another, focusing on issues related to self-disclosure in men's relationship. Phenomena such as competition, vulnerability, homophobia, and marital status are expounded on in the context of explaining various perspectives on the matter. Specifically, on the topic related to how men share differently with men than women, the authors explain, "Concerns with disclosure reciprocity did not emerge in friendships with women to the same extent as in friendships with men, even though many men in our sample indicated there are few differences in what they talk about with their male and female friends."[2] Moreover, in order to maintain some sense of protection, "Some men admit to 'playing the listening role' and not sharing equivalent information that might make them appear 'weak' to their friends."[3]

Cohen's study explored alternative perspectives on why the expression of intimacy between men differed from women, and concluded that forces such as marriage, children and work may significantly account for a change in priorities for men; adversely affecting the time they have to bond with other men. He explains, "Without much time beyond the family and workplace to invest in new relationships, informants restricted much of their social and emotional life to their marriage."[4]

Mates

Clearly, from the literature on fathers, and how fathers impact the social/emotional development of boys as well as girls, it is understandable why a significant number of women survey respondents for this book would state that their father is the man they most admire. Not surprisingly, most of those who stated that their father was most admired also stated that they had their father in their life as a child. Following the father was friend, closely followed by husband. Along with those who said husband, an overwhelming majority stated that they did have a father in their lives, even if partially. What the literature suggests, as well as the account of the women I surveyed, is that women admire a man in their life, particularly those in which they have an intimate relationship, who most remind them of the Quality/Behavior/Characteristics (QBC) of a man who they admired as a child. This of course harkens on the neuroscience research that informs "admiration" as a social emotion, resides in the same area of the brain, the posteromedial cortices (PMC), which is also credited with regulating "self-awareness" and "autobiographic" mental representations. Therefore is seems more than reasonable that a man who most reminds a woman of favorable recollections of a past "Admirable" man in her life, particularly during childhood, will head the list of the present man she admires.

With respect to the role of the husband, John Gottman, a pre-eminent marriage researcher finds that two critical components for the success of a relationship are the presence of fondness and admiration, between the two partners, suggesting of course the presence of mutual admiration as having a positive influence on not only the bond of marriage, and/or other forms of affectionate relationships, but also on the individuals engaged in the relationship.[1]

In an on-line posting of letters from women to popular talk-radio host Dr. Laura Schlessinger, asking "what they admired most about their spouse," one responded shared:

> I thought this question was most appropriate. We just celebrated our anniversary. We have been married for forty-four years. One thing I admire about my husband is the way he has always been supportive of me. When I retired last year, he wasn't happy and didn't know if it was going to work, but he said I could do it and worked harder to make it possible. Marriage is a rocky road but we've worked it out. I never went home to mother and he never complained about me to his co-workers. He always compliments me even when I know I'm not in the best shape. We have seven children, three by c-section. I've had a full hysterectomy and two abdominal surgeries for colon cancer and he still tells me I'm hot and sexy (and I'm almost sixty-one). He always makes me feel loved and cared for. He's a hardworking man (not a male) and would do anything for me and our

family. These are just a few reasons why I Admire my husband so much.[2]

Other literature related to these roles of admired men as well as other roles were shared throughout the book, relevant to the chapter. Again, this is just a small sample of the wealth and variety of literature related to the study of men.

Leadership

Leadership development in youth: Burns remarked, "Leadership is one of the most observed and least understood phenomena on earth."[1] In his broad-range discussion on human development and leadership, Gardner outlined a meticulously articulated perspective regarding the process of leadership development. According to Gardner, leadership is a process that occurs within the minds of individuals who live in a culture. He points out the significance of the capacity to create, understand, and evaluate the stories that mediate the process of leadership development in the minds of individuals.[2] This point is a strong feature in the work of Shamir and Eilam,[3] who are emphatic in their argument that authentic leadership development is directly influenced by storytelling, for both the leaders and followers, on an aesthetic as well as practical level. They elaborate extensively on the research implications of storytelling and authentic leadership development, including the cross-cultural generalizability of this concept.[3]

Clearly, Komives, Lucas, and McMahon are correct in their assertion that, "There are widely divergent paradigms for what it means to be a good leader."[4] They add that some perspectives are centered beyond "good leaders" to consider "good leadership." In as much as leadership development in boys is directly influenced by what they experience, and the meaning made of the son-father relationship experience, a comprehensive overview of the leading theories and perspectives on various topics related to leadership styles and practices provides an excellent segue into a more focused attention and review of leadership literature specific to leadership development in youth. With respect to the phenomenal son-father relationship experience, it is actually the emotionally activated meaning of the father-self that accentuates authentic leadership development.[5] The students in a Steen, Kachorek, and Peterson[6] study are essentially divulging a collected set of implicit leadership theories, developed during the early stages of life and experience[7] related to one's meaning of self.

The father's role in leadership development: The work of Burns is the perfect place to start, particularly his discussion of the psychological matrix and the social sources of leadership. Burns points out that the father's role in developing self-esteem in his son, and the reciprocal interaction and effect of the son-father relationship experience, contributes ultimately to how self-esteem is reflected in the boy's leadership development.[1] Here, Burns strongly implies a process, beginning with the boy's sex-role development that has an effect on his self-esteem, which in turn functions as the basis of leadership development.

An exploratory study conducted by Bronfenbrenner[2] reported a significant relationship between parental and adolescent behavior, along sex roles, and the child's responsibility and leadership as rated by high school teachers. He also reported that leadership is more likely in families where fathers are more highly educated, and in which both parents are less rejecting, punitive, and less overprotective.[3] It is important to keep in mind, however, that because the Bronfenbrenner study dates back to the early 1960's; and given the many changes in gender roles since that era, including the (greater, but hardly widespread) acceptance of homosexuality, much of the thinking in this study could be considered as outdated.

Implications: Certainly, there are a number of implications deriving from this very brief summary of the literature regarding male development and the role played by fathers. I am immensely interested in one in particular, which pertains to looking at the subject from a different analytical lens. Of the literature I have reviewed, a significant number of the authors have suggested essential flaws in the research design and/or data gathering. Many speak of limited access to the father's account of the relationship with their children, resulting in research findings being primarily based on the account of the mother of the children and the children themselves. With respect to personality research conducted with an overemphasis on empirical methodologies, Shontz offered, "...personality research inherently requires solutions to methodological problems that are in some ways unique."[1] Furthermore, he adds "Theoretical problems are often ill-suited to empirical methods, and meaningful questions are often attached in scientifically meaningless ways."[2]

In my view, research that is able to access data from all parties would assist in the reliability and validity of research findings, including the depth and breadth of understanding derived. Additionally, I believe that many of the interpretations derived from these studies require reevaluation in the postmodern context. Thus, for example, Biller's[3] research findings regarding homosexuality as being primarily influenced by a negative father-son relationship is clearly outdated and thus requires revisions in line with more recent research findings.[4-6] Illustrating a more current perspective, Dermott asserts, "Increasing acknowledgement of gay fatherhood...is important because it not only presents an additional challenge to the actuality of having two biological parents as carers, but it does so publicly."[7] Similarly, "Critical and feminist theorists show that most leadership research, including studies of transformational leadership, continue to present prescriptions—heroic and post-heroic—as if they were gender neutral. The critics argue that, although there is a search for a different kind of leader—a 'post-heroic hero' who displays characteristics different from the traditional model—even this leader continues 'to enjoy the same godlike reverence for individualism associated with traditional models.'"[8]

Schaetti, Ramsey, and Watanabe shed light on a relationship between creative contemplation and personal leadership:

Mindfulness is about being aware, being "awake," and paying attention. Creativity is about bringing forth what's right for the

particular moment and cultivating our connection to our deepest source of joy and inspiration…the two principles are interde-
pendent and mutually connected. Each informs the other, each
sustains the other, each helps to call forth the other. Where the
two principles of Personal Leadership come together, we find
presence, the tangible experience of embodied aliveness.[9]

Sinclair concurs, "…a great deal of emphasis is placed on self-awareness
and acting from self-knowledge."[10] Additionally, she warns, "…leaders
need to step back and understand the wider processes by which certain
identities may be assumed for them. They may actively seek to repudiate
some identities or to cultivate unexpected ones—and this identity work
is likely to be more onerous for those unconsciously assumed to be in
predetermined identity positions—by ethnicity, gender, class or other
categorization."[11]

Revisiting gender considerations, Komives, Lucas, and McMahon
suggest that youth asked themselves, "How does my gender influence my
attitudes and behaviors? How does my experience as a man or woman
shape my worldview and how might it shape the worldview of others?"[12]
Clearly, these are considerably significant considerations in one's self
analysis and consideration of the man they admire. Additionally, these
questions offer considerable framing for self-reflection and construction of one's leadership development. The authors elaborate:

Historically, men's involvement in the development of children
has been limited because that role has been considered femi-
nine and nurturing…Likewise, those who hold conventional
leadership expectations…may be holding a traditional masculine paradigm that excludes many woman, as well as many men
who are very capable…. To understand how men and women
have come to be as they are, we can learn from children's development. The way we play in childhood establishes patterns of
how we work and communicate as adults.[13]

Moreover, the adult influence in the lives of children, (including the absence of an admirable man) plays a significant role in the way they develop and form relationships as adults. Sinclair shares a revealing account of how political leaders are influenced by family and parental structures:

> Research of leaders has found that a significant proportion of political leaders—men in particular—have had a period of childhood where the father has been absent.... As historical and psychoanalytic studies of leadership show, an absent father can influence the motivation for, and style of, leadership in several possible ways. One interpretation is that the child, without a strong paternal figure, fanaticizes about being the "big father" themselves...The mother may (perhaps unconsciously) convey an expectation that the child will be the father: "the man of the family." These conditions feed the child's emerging sense of themselves and what they need to do. In the narcissistic extreme, the adult quest for leadership is an endlessly repeated search for (the lost father's or mother's) admiration.[14]

My hope is that this book will serve to turn the tide on fatherlessness, and have men adopt an affirmative and conscious intentionality to acquiring and embracing the Quality/Behavior/Characteristics (QBC) of an admired man.

I am reminded of an awesome NBA Playoff performance by Los Angeles Clipper guard Austin Rivers, where he delighted the league with his profound performance against the Houston Rockets, in a pivotal home game. The overwhelming and obvious back story to Rivers' performance was the whole father-son relationship issue with his dad and Clipper head coach, "Doc" Rivers, who hired his son to be on the team, and represented the first father-son – head coach-player dyad in the history of the NBA. After the excitement of the game and Rivers' awesome 25-point on 10-for-13 shooting performance, it occurred to me that while the general public is pretty clear about the debilitating affects "fatherlessness" has on a child, we must not overlook the profound impact and affect a mindful, supporting and nurturing father can and does have on a child at and over time. Having such an experience as a child does much more than just balance out the negative affects of fatherlessness: It is not a zero-sum equation. Having such a relationship with a father does far more than just eliminate the disadvantage of not having a father in a child's life, and I believe that this point is well worth attention and focus. There are vast advantages for a child having a nurturing father in their life. In the course of our attention to pointing out the significance of fatherlessness, I think it is equally important that we illuminate and celebrate the vast advantages of a man being supportive and present in his children's lives. We should recognize and celebrate such experiences – and point it out when we see young fathers being fully present in their children's lives. Let them know of the long-range impact they are having – tell them that they are being, An Admired Man.

Be Admired!!!

NOTES

Preface

1. Aboim, S., (2010). *Plural Masculinities: The Remaking of the Self in Private Life.* Ashgate Publishing. (p. 5).

2. Patterson, C.J., (2004). Gay Fathers. In M.E. Lamb (Ed.), *The Role of the Father in Child Development* (pp. 397-416). Hoboken, New Jersey: John Wiley & Son.

3. Cabrera, N.J. and C.G. Coll. (2004). Latino Fathers: Uncharted Territory in Need of Much Exploration. In M.E. Lamb (Ed.), *The Role of the Father in Child Development* (pp. 98-120). Hoboken, New Jersey: John Wiley & Son.

4. Caldwell, L.D. and L. Reese, (2006). The Fatherless Father: On Becoming Dad. In M.E. Connor and J.L. White (Eds.), *Black Fathers: An Invisible Presence in America* (pp. 169-187). Mahwah, New Jersey: Lawrence Erlbaum Associates, Publishers.

5. Hickey, Chris L., (2013) "The Phenomenal Characteristics of the Son-Father Relationship Experience." *Dissertations & Theses.* Paper 22.

6. http://aura.antioch.edu/etds/22

7. Wengraf, T (2001). *Qualitative Research Interviewing.* Thousand Oaks, CA: Sage Publication.

8. Hickey, Chris L., (2013) "The Phenomenal Characteristics of the Son-Father Relationship Experience." *Dissertations & Theses.* Paper 22.

9. http://aura.antioch.edu/etds/22

10. Burns, J.M. (1978). *Leadership.* New York, NY: Perennial. (pp.74-75).

11. Work, J.W. (1996). Leading a Diverse Work Force. In F. Hesselbein, M. Goldsmith and R. Beckhard (Eds.), *The Leader of the Future*. New York, NY: Jossey-Bass, (p. 71 - 79).

12. ibid., (p. 73).

13. Beckhard, R. (1996). On Future Leaders. In F. Hesselbein, M. Goldsmith and R. Beckhard (Eds.), *The Leader of the Future*. New York, NY: Jossey-Bass, (p.125 – 129).

14. Schaetti, B.F., Ramsey, S.J., and Watanabe, G.C. (2008) *Personal Leadership*. Seattle, WA: FlyingKite Publication. (p. 4).

15. ibid., (p. 12).

16. Gottman, J. and J. DeClaire. (1997). *Raising an Emotionally Intelligent Child: The Heart of Parenting*. New York, NY: Simon & Schuster Paperbacks.(p. 20).

17. Jones, J. and W. D. Mosher (2013). Fathers' Involvement with their Children: United States, 2006-2010. *National Heath Statistics Reports*, no. 71. Hyattsville, MD: National Center for Health Statistics.

18. Patton, M.Q. (2002). *Qualitative Research & Evaluation Methods 3d Edition*. Thousand Oaks, CA: Sage Publications. (p. 482).

19. Benz, V. M., and Shapiro, J.J. (1998). *Mindful Inquiry in Social Research*. Thousand Oaks, CA: Sage Publications. (pp. 40-41).

20. Damasio, A. (1994). *Descartes' Error: Emotion, Reason, and the Human Brain*. New York, NY. Penguin Books. (p. 158).

21. Jawer, M.A., and M.S. Micozzi (2009). *The Spiritual Anatomy of Emotion: How Feelings Link the Brain, the Body, and the Sixth Sense.* Rochester, VT. Park Street Press. (p. 34).

22. Fox, M. (2008). *The Hidden Spirituality of Men: Ten Metaphors to Awaken the Sacred Masculine.* Novato, CA: New World Library. (pp. xi).

23. ibid, (p. 57).

Who Am I?

1. Hickey, Chris L., (2013) "The Phenomenal Characteristics of the Son-Father Relationship Experience." *Dissertations & Theses.* Paper 22.

2. http://aura.antioch.edu/etds/22

3. ibid.

4. ibid.

5. ibid.

6. ibid

Introduction

1. Hickey, Chris L., (2013) "The Phenomenal Characteristics of the Son-Father Relationship Experience." *Dissertations & Theses.* Paper 22.

2. http://aura.antioch.edu/etds/22

3. Osherson, S. (1986). *Finding our Fathers: The Unfinished Business of Manhood.* New York, NY: The Free Press. (p.60).

4. Cashman, K. (1998). Leadership from the Inside Out: Becoming a Leader for Life. Provo, UT: Executive Excellence Publishing. (p. 63).

5. Shamir, B., and Eilam, G. (2005). "What's your story? A life-stories approach to authentic leadership development, *The Leadership Quarterly*, 16(3), 395-417.

Chapter I: On Being Fatherly

1. Parke, R.D. (1981). *Fathers.* Cambridge, MA: Harvard University Press. (p. 11)

2. Hawkins, A.J., and Dollahite, D.D. (Eds.) (1997). *Generative Fathering: Beyond Deficit Perspective.* Thousand Oaks, CA: Sage Publication.

3. ibid.

Chapter II: Honesty Counts

1. Diamond, M. J. (2007). My Father Before Me: How Fathers and Sons Influence Each Other Throughout Their Lives. New York: W.W. Norton. (p. 159).

2. Ibid (p. 159).

3. Ibid (p. 159).

Chapter III: Loving Is So Admirable

1. Siegel, D.J. (2012). *The Developing Mind: How Relationships and the Brain Interact to Shape Who We are.* (Second Edition). New York, NY: The Guilford Press. (p. 175).

Chapter V: Nothing More Important than Family

1. Herzog, J.M. (2001). *Father Hunger: Explorations with Adults and Children.* Hillsdale, N.J.: The Analytic Press. (p. 51)

2. ibid, (p. 51).

3. ibid, (p. 81).

Chapter VI: L(ife)eadership Development Principles

1. Thompson, M.C., and B.S. Thompson (2012). *Admired: 21 Ways to Double Your Value.* Ashland, OH: Evolve Publishing, Inc. (p. 12).

2. Helgesen, S. (1996). *Leading from the Grass Roots.* In F. Hesselbein, M. Goldsmith and R. Beckhard (Eds.), *The Leader of the Future.* New York, NY: Jossey-Bass. (p. 39).

3. Komives, S.R., Lucas, N., and McMahon, T.R. (2007). *Exploring Leadership: For College Students Who Want to Make a Difference.* 2nd Ed. San Francisco, CA: John Wiley & Sons, Inc. (p. 3).

4. ibid, (pp.3-4).

5. Cashman, K. (1998). Leadership from the Inside Out: Becoming a Leader for Life. Provo, UT: Executive Excellence Publishing. (p. 15).

6. ibid, (p. 15).

7. Komives, S.R., Lucas, N., and McMahon, T.R. (2007). *Exploring Leadership: For College Students Who Want to Make a Difference.* 2ⁿᵈ Ed. San Francisco, CA: John Wiley & Sons, Inc. (p. 27).

8. Cashman, K. (1998). *Leadership from the Inside Out: Becoming a Leader for Life.* Provo, UT: Executive Excellence Publishing.

9. ibid, (p. 20).

10. ibid, (p. 18).

11. Thompson, M.C. and B.S. Thompson (2012). *Admired: 21 Ways to Double Your Value.* Ashland, OH: Evolve Publishing, Inc. (p. 60).

12. Benz, V. M., and Shapiro, J.J. (1998). *Mindful Inquiry in Social Research.* Thousand Oaks, CA.: Sage Publications. (pp. 40-41).

13. Merleau-Ponty, Maurice (2012). *Phenomenology of Perception.* New York, NY: Routledge. (p. 390).

14. Cashman, K. (1998). *Leadership from the Inside Out: Becoming a Leader for Life.* Provo, UT: Executive Excellence Publishing. (p. 76).

15. Herzog, J.M. (2001). *Father Hunger: Explorations with Adults and Children.* Hillsdale, N.J.: The Analytic Press. (p. 253).

16. Smith, G.J. (2005). *Life Lessons for Youth: Practical Stuff Every Young Person Needs to Know to Successfully Transition into Adulthood.* New York, NY: iUniverse, Inc. (p. 41).

17. ibid, (p. 41).

Chapter VII: Things that Matter

1. Thompson, M.C. and B.S. Thompson (2012). *Admired: 21 Ways to Double Your Value.* Ashland, OH: Evolve Publishing, Inc. (p. 9).

2. Work, J.W. (1996). *Leading a Diverse work force.* In F. Hesselbein, M. Goldsmith and R. Beckhard (Eds.), *The Leader of the Future.* New York, NY: Jossey-Bass. (pp.76).

3. Kouzes, J.M., and Posner, B.Z. (1996). Seven lessons for leading the voyage to the future. In F. Hesselbein, M. Goldsmith and R. Beckhard (Eds.), *The Leader of the Future.* New York, NY: Jossey-Bass. (pp. 101-108).

4. Thompson, M.C. and B.S. Thompson (2012). *Admired: 21 Ways to Double Your Value.* Ashland, OH: Evolve Publishing, Inc. (p. 191).

Chapter VIII: Review of prior research about men

General Admiration

1. Immordino-Yang, M.H., McColl, A., Damasio, H. and A. Damasio (2009). Neural correlates of Admiration and Compassion. http://www.pnas.org/content/106/19/8021. PNAS| May 12, 2009|vol. 106|no.19| (p.8021).

2. ibid, (p. 8021).

3. Foster, B.L., Dastjerdi, M., and J. Parvizi. (2012). Neural populations in human posteromedial cortex display opposing responses during memory and numerical processing. http://www.pnas.org/cgi/doi/10.1073/pnas.1206580109. PNSA| September 18, 2012 | vol.109 | no.109|15514-15519.

4. Siegel, D.J. (2012). *The Developing Mind: How Relationships and the Brain Interact to Shape Who We are.* (Second Edition). New York, NY: The Guilford Press. (p. 242).

5. Foster, B.L., Dastjerdi, M., and J. Parvizi. (2012). Neural populations in human posteromedial cortex display opposing responses during memory and numerical processing. http://www.pnas.org/cgi/doi/10.1073/pnas.1206580109. PNSA| September 18, 2012 | vol.109 | no.109|15514-15519.

6. Schaetti, B.F., Ramsey, S.J. and Watanabe, G.C. (2008) *Personal Leadership.* Seattle, WA: FlyingKite Publication. (p. 3).

7. ibid, (p. 7).

Fathers

Infancy

1. Lamb, M. (1976). *The Role of the Father in Child Development.* New York, NY: John Wiley & Sons. (p. 4).

2. Biller, H.B. (1976). The father and personality development: Paternal deprivation and sex-role development. In M. Lamb (Ed.), *The role of the father in child development.* New York: John Wiley & Sons.(pp. 89-156).

3. Biller, H.B.,. and Kimpton, J.L. (1997). The father and the school-aged child. In M. Lamb (Ed.), *The role of the father in child development.* (3rd ed.). New York: John Wiley & Sons. (pp. 143-161).

4. Diamond, M. J. (2007). *My Father Before Me: How Fathers and Sons Influence Each Other Throughout Their Lives.* New York: W.W. Norton.

5. Floyd, K. and Morman, M.T. (2003). Human affection exchange: II. Affectionate communication in father-son relationships. *Journal of Social Psychology,* 143(5), 599+

6. Lamb, M. (1976). *The Role of the Father in Child Development.* New York, NY: John Wiley & Sons.

7. Lamb, M. (1981). *The Role of the Father in Child Development.* 2nd edition. New York, NY: John Wiley & Sons.

8. Lamb, M. (1997). *The Role of the Father in Child Development..* 3rd edition. New York, NY: John Wiley & Sons.

9. Lamb, M. (2004). *The Role of the Father in Child Development.* 4th edition. New York: John Wiley & Sons.

10. Lewis, M., and Weinraub, M. (1976). The father's role in the child's social network. In M. Lamb (Ed.). *The Role of the Father in Child Development.* New York: John Wiley & Sons(pp. 157-184).

11. Morman, M.T. and Floyd, K. (2006). Good fathering: Father and son perceptions of what it means to be a good father. *Fathering,* 4(2), 113-136.

12. Newberger, E.H. (1999). *The Men They Will Become: The Nature and Nurture of Male Character.* Princeton: Princeton University Press.

13. Poulter, S.B. (2004). *Father You Son.* New York, NY: McGraw-Hill.

14. Roopnarine, J.L. (2004). African American and African Caribbean fathers; Level, quality, and meaning of involvement. In M. Lamb (Ed.), *The Role of the Father in Child Development.* (4th ed.). New York: John Wiley & Sons, pp. 32-57.

15. Kotelchuck, M. (1976). The infant's relationship to the father: Experimental evidence. In M. Lamb (Ed.). *The Role of the Father in Child Development.* New York: John Wiley & Sons, pp. 329-344.

16. Lamb, M. (1976). *The Role of the Father in Child Development.* New York, NY: John Wiley & Sons.

17. Parsons, T. (1964). *Social Structures and Personality.* London: The Free Press.

18. Biller, H.B. (1976). The father and personality development: Paternal deprivation and sex-role development. In M. Lamb (Ed.), *The Role of the Father in Child Development.* New York: John Wiley & Sons, pp. 89-156.

19. Bronte-Tinkew, J., Carrano, J., and Guzman, L. (2006). Resident fathers' perceptions of their roles and links to involvement with infants, *Fathering,* 4(3), 254-285.

20. Merleau-Ponty, Maurice (2012). *Phenomenology of Perception.* New York, NY: Routledge.

21. Dermott, E. (2008). *Intimate Fatherhood: A Sociological Analysis.* London: Routledge.

22. Morman, M.T. and Floyd, K. (2006). Good fathering: Father and son perceptions of what it means to be a good father. *Fathering,* 4(2), 113-136.

School-aged children

1. Lewis, C. (1997). Fathers and Preschoolers. In M. Lamb (Ed.) The role of the father in child development. (3rd ed.). New York: John Wiley & Sons, pp. 121-142

2. ibid, (p. 122).

3. Biller, H.B. and Kimpton, J.L. (1997). The father and the school-aged child. In M. Lamb (Ed.), The role of the father in child development. (3rd ed.). New York: John Wiley & Sons, pp. 143-161.

4. Lewis, M., and Weinraub, M. (1976). The father's role in the child's social network. In M. Lamb (Ed.). The role of the father in child development. New York: John Wiley & Sons, pp. 157-184.

5. McBride, B.A., Schoppe-Sullivan, S.J., and Ho, M. (2004). The mediating role of fathers' school involvement on student achievement, *Applied Developmental Psychology*, 26, 201-216.

6. Diamond, M. J. (2007). *My Father Before Me: How Fathers and Sons Influence Each Other Throughout Their Lives.* New York: W.W. Norton.

7. Keller, T. (1999). Images of the familiar: Individual differences and implicit leadership theories. *The Leadership Quarterly*, 10(4), 589-607.

8. Lamb, M. (2004). The role of the father in child development. (4th ed.). New York: John Wiley & Sons.

9. Lewis, C. (1997). Fathers and Preschoolers. In M. Lamb (Ed.), *The Role of the Father in Child Development.* 3rd edition. New York: John Wiley & Sons, pp. 121-142.

10. Lewis, M., and Weinraub, M. (1976). The father's role in the child's social network. In M. Lamb (Ed.), *The Role of the Father in Child Development.* New York: John Wiley & Sons, pp. 157-184.

11. Lewis, M., Feiring, C., & Weinraub, M. (1981). The father as a member of the child's social network. In M. Lamb (Ed.). *The Role of the*

Father in Child Development. 2nd edition. New York: John Wiley & Sons, pp. 259-294.

12. McBride, B.A., Schoppe-Sullivan, S.J., and Ho, M. (2004). The mediating role of fathers' school involvement on student achievement, *Applied Developmental Psychology*, 26, 201-216.

13. Patterson, C.J. (1992). Children of Lesbian and Gay Parents, *Child Development*, 63(5), 1025 - 1042.

14. Ray, V. and Gregory, R.(2001). School Experiences of the Children of Lesbian and Gay Parents, *Family Matters*, 59, 28 - 34.

Adolescence

1. Biller, H.B. (1976). The father and personality development: Paternal deprivation and sex-role development. In M. Lamb (Ed.), *The Role of the Father in Child Development..* New York: John Wiley & Sons, pp. 89-156.

2. Biller, H.B. and Kimpton, J.L. (1997). The father and the school-aged child. In M. Lamb (Ed.), *The Role of the Father in Child Development..* 3rd edition. New York: John Wiley & Sons, pp. 143-161.

3. Diamond, M. J. (2007). *My father before me: How fathers and sons influence each other throughout their lives.* New York: W.W. Norton.

4. Katz, E. (2002). At the still point of the turning world: a journey through the temporal dimensions of a father-son conflict. *Journal of Family Therapy*, 24, 369-384.

5. Osherson, S. (1995). *The Passions of Fatherhood.* New York: Fawcett Columbine.

6. Ogletree, M.D., Jones, R.M., and Coyl, D.D. (2002). Fathers and their adolescent sons: Pubertal development and paternal involvement, Journal of Adolescent Research, 17(4), 418-424.

7. Videon, T.M. (2005). Parent-child relations and children's psychological well-being: Do dads matter?, *Journal of Family Issues*, 26(1), 55-78.

8. Williams, C. (1991). *Forever a father, always a son: Discovering the difference a dad can make.* Wheaton, IL: Victor Books.

9. Diamond, M. J. (2007). *My father before me: How fathers and sons influence each other throughout their lives.* New York: W.W. Norton. (p. 110).

10. ibid, (p. 111).

11. Siegel, D.J. (2013). *Brainstorm: The Power and Purpose of the Teenage Brain.* New York, NY: Jeremy P. Tarcher/Penguin. (p. 7).

Young adults

1. Diamond, M. J. (2007). My father before me: How fathers and sons influence each other throughout their lives. New York: W.W. Norton. (p. 136).

2. Herzog, J.M. (2001). Father Hunger: Explorations with Adults and Children. Hillsdale, N.J.: The Analytic Press.

3. Ilardo, J. (1993). Father-Son healing: An Adult Son's Guide. Oakland, CA: New Hardinger.

4. Newberger, E.H. (1999). The Men They Will Become: The Nature and Nurture of Male Character. Princeton: Princeton University Press.

5. Osherson, S. (1986). Finding our Fathers: The Unfinished Business of Manhood. New York, NY: The Free Press.

6. Pollack, W. (1998). Real Boys: Rescuing Our Sons from the Myths of Boyhood. New York, NY: Random House.

7. Poulter, S.B. (2004). Father You Son. New York, NY: McGraw-Hill.

8. Balcom, D.D. (1998). Absent fathers: Effects on abandoned sons. Journal of Men's Studies, 6(3) (p. 285).

9. Merleau-Ponty, Maurice (2012). Phenomenology of Perception. New York, NY: Routledge.

10. Balcom, D.D. (1998). Absent fathers: Effects on abandoned sons. Journal of Men's Studies, 6(3) (p. 283).

11. Scott, K. (1993). *Monster: The Autobiography of an L.A. Gang Member.* New York, NY: Grove Press.

12. ibid, (p. 332).

Cultural and socioeconomic factors

1. Pleck, E. H. and Pleck, J. H. (1997). Fatherhood Ideas in the United States: Historical Dimensions. In M. Lamb (Ed.). *The Role of the Father in Child Development.* 3rd edition. New York: John Wiley & Sons, pp. 33-48.

2. Roopnarine, J.L. (2004). African American and African Caribbean fathers; Level, quality, and meaning of involvement. In M. Lamb

(Ed.), *The Role of the Father in Child Development.* 4th edition. New York: John Wiley & Sons, pp. 32-57.

3. Allen, W., and Connor, M. (1997). An African American perspective on generative fathering. In A.J. Hawkins and D.D. Dollahite, (Eds.), *Generative fathering: Beyond deficit perspective.* Thousand Oaks, CA: Sage Publication. (p. 53).

4. Mirande, A. (1991). Ethnicity and fatherhood. In F.W. Bozet & S.M.H. Hanson (Eds.), *Fatherhood and families in cultural context.* New York, NY: Springer, pp. 53-82.

5. Cabrera, N.J. and C.G. Coll. (2004). Latino Fathers: Uncharted Territory in Need of Much Exploration. In M.E. Lamb (Ed.), *The Role of the Father in Child Development* (pp. 98-120). Hoboken, New Jersey: John Wiley & Son.

6. Chow, H. (2007). Sense of belonging and life satisfaction among Hong Kong adolescent immigrants in Canada. *Journal of Ethnic and Migration Studies,* 33(3), 511-520.

7. Connor, M. and White, J. (Eds.), (2006). *Black fathers: An invisible presence in America.* Mahway, NJ: Lawrence Erlbaum Associates, Publishers.

8. Dumka, L. (2007). Interparental relations, Maternal employment, and fathering in Mexican American families. *Journal of Marriage and Family,* 69, 26-39.

9. Shwalb, D.W., Nakawaza, J., Yamamoto, T., and Hyun, J. (2004). Fathering in Japanese, Chinese, and Korean Cultures: A review of the research literature. In M. Lamb (Ed.).*The role of the father in child development. (4th ed.).* New York: John Wiley & Sons, pp. 146-181.

10. Connor, M. and White, J. (Eds.), (2006). *Black fathers: An invisible presence in America.* Mahway, NJ: Lawrence Erlbaum Associates, Publishers. (p.15).

11. ibid.

12. Dermott, E. (2008). *Intimate fatherhood: A sociological analysis.* London: Routledge. (p.23).

13. Forste, R. and Jarvis, J. (2007). "Just like his father": Family background and residency with children among young adult fathers. *Fathering,* 5(2). (p. 100).

14. ibid.

15. Connor, M. and White, J. (Eds.), (2006). *Black fathers: An invisible presence in America.* Mahway, NJ: Lawrence Erlbaum Associates, Publishers.

16. ibid.

17. Cabrera, N.J. and C.G. Coll. (2004). Latino Fathers: Uncharted Territory in Need of Much Exploration. In M.E. Lamb (Ed.), *The Role of the Father in Child Development* (pp. 98-120). Hoboken, New Jersey: John Wiley & Son.

18. Bronte-Tinkew, J., Carrano, J., and Guzman, L. (2006). Resident fathers' perceptions of their roles and links to involvement with infants, *Fathering,* 4(3), 254-285.

19. Dermott, E. (2008). *Intimate Fatherhood: A Sociological Analysis.* London: Routledge. (p. 3).

20. ibid, (p. 4).

21. Bronte-Tinkew, J., Carrano, J., and Guzman, L. (2006). Resident fathers' perceptions of their roles and links to involvement with infants, *Fathering*, 4(3), 254-285.

22. Cabrera, N.J. and C.G. Coll. (2004). Latino Fathers: Uncharted Territory in Need of Much Exploration. In M.E. Lamb (Ed.), *The Role of the Father in Child Development* (pp. 98-120). Hoboken, New Jersey: John Wiley & Son.

23. Chow, H. (2007). Sense of belonging and life satisfaction among Hong Kong adolescent immigrants in Canada. *Journal of Ethnic and Migration Studies*, 33(3), 511-520.

24. Connor, M. and White, J. (Eds.), (2006). *Black fathers: An invisible presence in America*. Mahway, NJ: Lawrence Erlbaum Associates, Publishers.

25. Forste, R. and Jarvis, J. (2007). "Just like his father": Family background and residency with children among young adult fathers. *Fathering*, 5(2), 97-110.

26. Pleck, J.H. and Masciadrelli, B.P. (2004). Paternal involvement by U.S. residential fathers: Levels, sources, and consequences. In M. Lamb (Ed.).*The role of the father in child development.* (4th ed.). New York: John Wiley & Sons, pp. 222-271.

27. Roopnarine, J.L. (2004). African American and African Caribbean fathers; Level, quality, and meaning of involvement. In M. Lamb (Ed.).*The role of the father in child development.* (4th ed.). New York: John Wiley & Sons, pp. 32-57.

28. Cabrera, N.J. and C.G. Coll. (2004). Latino Fathers: Uncharted Territory in Need of Much Exploration. In M.E. Lamb (Ed.), *The Role of the Father in Child Development* (pp. 98-120). Hoboken, New Jersey: John Wiley & Son.

29. Chow, H. (2007). Sense of belonging and life satisfaction among Hong Kong adolescent immigrants in Canada. *Journal of Ethnic and Migration Studies*, 33(3), 511-520.

30. Connor, M. and White, J. (Eds.), (2006). *Black fathers: An invisible presence in America.* Mahway, NJ: Lawrence Erlbaum Associates, Publishers.

31. Forste, R. and Jarvis, J. (2007). "Just like his father": Family background and residency with children among young adult fathers. *Fathering,* 5(2), 97-110.

32. Pleck, J.H. and Masciadrelli, B.P. (2004). Paternal involvement by U.S. residential fathers: Levels, sources, and consequences. In M. Lamb (Ed.).*The role of the father in child development.* (4th ed.). New York: John Wiley & Sons, pp. 222-271.

33. Roopnarine, J.L. (2004). African American and African Caribbean fathers; Level, quality, and meaning of involvement. In M. Lamb (Ed.).*The role of the father in child development.* (4th ed.). New York: John Wiley & Sons, pp. 32-57.

34. Barling J., Dupre, K.E., and Hepburn, C.G. (1998). Effects on Parents' job insecurity on children's work and attitudes *Journal of Applied Psychology,* 83, 112-118.

35. Abramovitch, R. and Johnson, L.C. (1992). Children's perception of parental work. *Canadian Journal of Behavioral Science,* 24, 319-332.

36. Kelloway, E.K., Barling, J., and Agar, S. (1996). Pre-employment predictors of union attitudes: The moderating role of parental identification, *Journal of Social Psychology*, 136, 413-415.

37. Piotrkowski, C.S. and Stark, E. (1987). Children and adolescents look at their parents' job. In J.H. Lewko (Ed.), *How Children and Adolescents View the World of Work*. San Francisco, CA: Jossey-Bass, 3-19.

38. Steele, J., and Barling, J. (1996). Influence of maternal gender-role beliefs and role satisfaction on daughters' vocational interests, *Sex Roles*, 34, 637-648.

Alternative Perspectives

1. Rowe, D.C. (1990). As the twig is bent? The myth of child-rearing influences on personality development. *Journal of Counseling and development*, 68(6). (p.606).

2. Herrnstein, R.J., and C. Murry (1994). *The Bell Curve: Intelligence and class structure in American Life*. New York, NY: Free Press.

3. Pinker, S. (2002). *The blank slate: The modern denial of human nature*. New York, NY: Penguin.

4. Tucker-Drob, E. (2011). Emergence of a Gene x Socioeconomic Status Interaction on Infant Mental Ability Between 10 months and 2 years. *Psychological Science*, 22(1). (p. 125).

5. Tucker-Drob, E. and Harden K. (2012). Early childhood cognitive development and parental cognitive stimulation: evidence for reciprocal gene-environmental transactions. *Developmental Science*, 15(2). (p. 252).

6. ibid, (p. 254).

7. Balcom, D.D. (1998). Absent fathers: Effects on abandoned sons. *Journal of Men's Studies*, 6(3), 283+.

8. Krampe, E.M., and Newton, R.R. (2006). The father presence questionnaire: A new measure of the subjective experience of being fathered, *Fathering*, 4(2), 159-190.

9. Balcom, D.D. (1998). Absent fathers: Effects on abandoned sons. *Journal of Men's Studies*, 6(3), 283+.

10. Campbell, D.P. (2005). Fathers, Sons, and Mutual Respect. *Leadership in Action*, 25(1). (p. 24).

11. Michie, S. and Gooty, J. (2005). Values, emotions, and authenticity: Will the real leader please stand up? *The Leadership Quarterly*, 16(3), 441-457.

12. Shamir, B. and Eilam, G. (2005). "What's your story? A life-stories approach to authentic leadership development, *The Leadership Quarterly*, 16(3), 395-417.

13. Campbell, D.P. (2005). Fathers, Sons, and Mutual Respect. *Leadership in Action*, 25(1). (p. 24).

14. ibid, (p. 24).

15. Floyd, K. and Morman, M.T. (2003). Human affection exchange: II. Affectionate communication in father-son relationships. *Journal of Social Psychology*, 143(5). (p. 600).

16. Wyatt, J. (2005). A gentle going? An autoethnographic short story. *Qualitative Inquiry*, 11(5). (p. 724).

17. ibid, (p. 725).

18. ibid, (p. 732).

Friends

1. Cohen, T.F. (1992). Men's Families, Men's Friends: A Structural Analysis of Constraints on Men's Social Ties. In P.M. Nardi (Ed.), *Men's Friendships: Research on Men and Masculinities* (pp. 115-131). Newbury Park: Sage Publication.

2. Reid, H.M. and G.A. Find (1992). Self-Disclosure in Men's Friendships: Variations Associated with Intimate Relationships. In P.M. Nardi (Ed.), *Men's Friendships: Research on Men and Masculinities* (p.146). Newbury Park: Sage Publication.

3. ibid, (p. 146).

4. Cohen, T.F. (1992). Men's Families, Men's Friends: A Structural Analysis of Constraints on Men's Social Ties. In P.M. Nardi (Ed.), *Men's Friendships: Research on Men and Masculinities* (p.129). Newbury Park: Sage Publication.

Mates

1. Schlessinger, L. (2012). For Listeners: What I Admire Most about my Spouse. http://www.drlaura.com/b/What-I-Admire-Most-About-My-Spouse.../726652544635687585.html

Leadership

Leadership development in youth

1. Burns, J.M. (1978). *Leadership.* New York, NY: Perennial. (p. 2).

2. Gardner, H. (1995). *Leading Minds: An Anatomy of Leadership.* New York, NY: Basic Books.

3. Shamir, B. and Eilam, G. (2005). "What's your story? A life-stories approach to authentic leadership development, *The Leadership Quarterly*, 16(3), 395-417.

4. Komives, S.R., Lucas, N. and McMahon, T.R. (2007). Exploring Leadership: For College Students Who Want to Make a Difference. 2nd Ed. San Francisco, CA: John Wiley & Sons, Inc.. (p.9).

5. Michie, S. and Gooty, J. (2005). Values, emotions, and authenticity: Will the real leader please stand up? *The Leadership Quarterly*, 16(3), 441-457.

6. Steen, T.A., Kachorek, L.V., and Peterson, C. (2002). Character strengths among youth. *Journal of Youth and Adolescence*, 32(1), 5-16.

7. Ayman-Nolly, S. and Ayman, R. (2005). Children's implicit theory of leadership. In B. Schyns and J.R. Meindl (Eds.), *Implicit Leadership Theories: Essays and Explorations*. Greenwich, CT: Information Age Publishing, pp. 227-274.

The father's role in leadership development

1. Burns, J.M. (1978). *Leadership*. New York, NY: Perennial. (p. 98).

2. Bronfenbrenner, U. (1961). Some familial antecedents of responsibility and leadership in adolescents. In L. Petrullo and B.M. Bass (Eds.), *Leadership and interpersonal behavior*. New York: Holt, Rinehart and Winston, Inc., pp. 239-271.

3. Zacharatos, A., Barling, J., and Kelloway, K.E. (2000). Development and effects of transformational leadership in adolescents, *The Leadership Quarterly*, 11(2), 211-226.

Implications

1. Shontz, F.C. (1965). *Research methods in personality.* New York: Appleton-Century-Crofts. (p. viii).

2. ibid, (p. 3).

3. Biller, H.B. (1976). The father and personality development: Paternal deprivation and sex-role development. In M. Lamb (Ed.), *The role of the father in child development.* New York: John Wiley & Sons, pp. 89-156.

4. Gottlieb, A.R. (2003). *Sons talk about their gay fathers: Life curves.* New York, NY: Harrington Park Press.

5. Patterson, C.J., (2004). Gay Fathers. In M.E. Lamb (Ed.), *The Role of the Father in Child Development* (pp. 397-416). Hoboken, New Jersey: John Wiley & Son.

6. Snow, J.E. (2004). *How It Feels to Have a Gay or Lesbian Parent: A Book by Kids for Kids of All Ages.* New York, NY: Harrington Park Press.

7. Dermott, E. (2008). *Intimate Batherhood: A Sociological analysis.* London: Routledge.

8. Sinclair, A. (2007). *Leadership for the Disillusioned: Moving beyond myths and heroes to Leading that Liberates.* Crows Nest NSW 2065 Australia: Allen & Unwin. (p. 32).

9. Schaetti, B.F., Ramsey, S.J. and Watanabe, G.C. (2008) *Personal Leadership.* Seattle, WA: FlyingKite Publication. (pp. 17-18).

10. Sinclair, A. (2007). *Leadership for the Disillusioned: Moving beyond myths and heroes to Leading that Liberates.* Crows Nest NSW 2065 Australia: Allen & Unwin. (p. 58).

11. ibid, (p. 140).

12. Komives, S.R., Lucas, N. and McMahon, T.R. (2007). Exploring Leadership: For College Students Who Want to Make a Difference. 2nd Ed. San Francisco, CA: John Wiley & Sons, Inc. (p. 153).

13. ibid, (pp. 154-155).

14. Sinclair, A. (2007). *Leadership for the Disillusioned: Moving beyond myths and heroes to Leading that Liberates.* Crows Nest NSW 2065 Australia: Allen & Unwin. (p. 60).

References

Aboim, S., (2010). *Plural Masculinities: The Remaking of the Self in Private Life*, p. 5, Ashgate Publishing.

Abramovitch, R. and Johnson, L.C. (1992). Children's perception of parental work. *Canadian Journal of Behavioral Science*, 24, 319-332.

Allen, W., and Connor, M. (1997). An African American perspective on generative fathering. In A.J. Hawkins and D.D. Dollahite, (Eds.), Generative fathering: Beyond deficit perspective. Thousand Oaks, CA: Sage Publication, pp. 52-70.

Ayman-Nolly, S. and Ayman, R. (2005). Children's implicit theory of leadership. In B. Schyns and J.R. Meindl (Eds.), Implicit Leadership Theories: Essays and Explorations. Greenwich, CT: Information Age Publishing, pp. 227-274.

Balcom, D.D. (1998). Absent fathers: Effects on abandoned sons. Journal of Men's Studies, 6(3), 283+.

Barling J., Dupre, K.E., and Hepburn, C.G. (1998). Effects on Parents' job insecurity on children's work and attitudes. Journal of Applied Psychology, 83, 112-118.

Barling J., and Mendelson, M.B. (1999). Parents' job insecurity affects children's grade performance through the indirect effects of beliefs in an unjust world and negative mood. Journal of Occupational Health Psychology, 4(4), 347-355.

Beckhard, R. (1996). On future leaders. In F. Hesselbein, M. Goldsmith and R. Beckhard (Eds.), The Leader of the Future. New York, NY: Jossey-Bass, pp. 125-129.

Benz, V. M. and Shapiro, J.J. (1998). Mindful Inquiry in Social Research. Thousand Oaks, CA.: Sage Publications.

Biller, H.B. (1976). The father and personality development: Paternal deprivation and sex-role development. In M. Lamb (Ed.), The role of the father in child development. New York: John Wiley & Sons, pp. 89-156.

Biller, H.B. and Kimpton, J.L. (1997). The father and the school-aged child. In M. Lamb (Ed.), The role of the father in child development. (3rd ed.). New York: John Wiley & Sons, pp. 143-161.

Bronfenbrenner, U. (1961). Some familial antecedents of responsibility and leadership in adolescents. In L. Petrullo and B.M. Bass (Eds.), Leadership and interpersonal behavior. New York: Holt, Rinehart and Winston, Inc., pp. 239-271.

Bronte-Tinkew, J., Carrano, J., and Guzman, L. (2006). Resident fathers' perceptions of their roles and links to involvement with infants, Fathering, 4(3), 254-285.

Burns, J.M. (1978). Leadership. New York, NY: Perennial.

Cabrera, N.J. and C.G. Coll. (2004). Latino Fathers: Uncharted Territory in Need of Much Exploration. In M.E. Lamb (Ed.), The Role of the Father in Child Development (pp. 98-120). Hoboken, New Jersey: John Wiley & Son.

REFERENCES

Caldwell, L.D. and L. Reese, (2006). The Fatherless Father: On Becoming Dad. In M.E. Connor and J.L. White (Eds.), *Black Fathers: An Invisible Presence in America* (pp. 169-187). Mahwah, New Jersey: Lawrence Erlbaum Associates, Publishers.

Campbell, D.P. (2005). Fathers, Sons, and Mutual Respect. Leadership in Action, 25(1), 24-25.

Cashman, K (1998). Leadership from the Inside Out: Becoming a Leader for Life. Provo, UT: Executive Excellence Publishing.

Chow, H. (2007). Sense of belonging and life satisfaction among Hong Kong adolescent immigrants in Canada. Journal of Ethnic and Migration Studies, 33(3), 511-520.

Cohen, T.F. (1992). Men's Families, Men's Friends: A Structural Analysis of Constraints on Men's Social Ties. In P.M. Nardi (Ed.), *Men's Friendships: Research on Men and Masculinities* (pp. 115-131). Newbury Park: Sage Publication.

Connor, M. and White, J. (Eds.), (2006). Black fathers: An invisible presence in America. Mahway, NJ: Lawrence Erlbaum Associates, Publishers.

Connell, R.W., (1995). *Masculinities*, University of California Press.

Damasio, A., (1994). *Descartes' Error: Emotion, Reason, and The Human Brain*. New York, NY. Penguin Books.

Dermott, E. (2008). Intimate fatherhood: A sociological analysis. London: Routledge.

Diamond, M. J. (2007). My father before me: How fathers and sons influence each other throughout their lives. New York: W.W. Norton.

Dumka, L. (2007). Interparental relations, Maternal employment, and fathering in Mexican American families. Journal of Marriage and Family, 69, 26-39.

Floyd, K. and Morman, M.T. (2003). Human affection exchange: II. Affectionate communication in father-son relationships. Journal of Social Psychology, 143(5), 599+

Forste, R. and Jarvis, J. (2007). "Just like his father": Family background and residency with children among young adult fathers. Fathering, 5(2), 97-110.

Foster, B.L., Dastjerdi, M., and J. Parvizi. (2012). Neural populations in human posteromedial cortex display opposing responses during memory and numerical processing. http://www.pnas.org/cgi/doi/10.1073/pnas.1206580109. PNSA| September 18, 2012 | vol.109 | no.109|15514-15519.

Fox, J. (2008). *Your child's Strengths: Discover Them, Develop Them, Use Them.* New York, NY: Viking.

Fox, M. (2008). *The Hidden Spirituality of Men: Ten Metaphors to Awaken the Sacred Masculine.* Novato, CA. New World Library.

Gardner, H. (1995). *Leading minds: An anatomy of leadership.* New York, NY: Basic Books.

Gottlieb, A.R. (2003). Sons talk about their gay fathers: Life curves. New York, NY: Harrington Park Press.

Gottman, J. and J. DeClaire. (1997). *Raising an Emotionally Intelligent Child: The Heart of Parenting.* New York, NY: Simon & Schuster Paperbacks.

Gottman, J.M. and N. Silver, (1999). *The Seven Principles for Making Marriage Work.* New York, NY: Three Rivers Press.

Greif, G.L. (2009). *Buddy System: Understanding Male Friendships.* Oxford, NY: Oxford University Press, Inc.

Hawkins, A.J. and Dollahite, D.D. (Eds.) (1997). *Generative fathering: Beyond deficit perspective.* Thousand Oaks, CA: Sage Publication.

Helgesen, S. (1996). *Leading from the grass roots.* In F. Hesselbein, M. Goldsmith and R. Beckhard (Eds.), The Leader of the Future. New York, NY: Jossey-Bass, pp. 19-24.

Herrenkohl, T. I., Sousa, C., Tajima, E. A., Herrenkohl, R. C., & Moylan, C. A. (2008). Intersection of child abuse and children's exposure to domestic violence. Trauma, Violence, & Abuse.

Herrnstein, R.J., and C. Murry (1994). *The Bell Curve: Intelligence and class structure in American Life.* New York, NY: Free Press.

Herzog, J.M. (2001). Father hunger: explorations with adults and children. Hillsdale, N.J.: The Analytic Press.

Hickey, Chris L., (2013) "The Phenomenal Characteristics of the Son-Father Relationship Experience." *Dissertations & Theses.* Paper 22.

http://aura.antioch.edu/etds/22

Ilardo, J. (1993). Father-son healing: An adult son's guide. Oakland, CA: New Hardinger.

Immordino-Yang, M.H., McColl, A., Damasio, H. and A. Damasio (2009). Neural correlates of Admiration and Compassion. http://

www.pnas.org/cgi/doi/10.1073/pnas.0810363106. PNAS| May 12, 2009|vol. 106|no.19|8021-8026.

Jawer, M.A. and M.S. Micozzi (2009). *The Spiritual Anatomy of Emotion: How Feelings Link the Brain, the Body, and the Sixth Sense.* Rochester, VT. Park Street Press.

Jones, J. and W. D. Mosher (2013). Fathers' Involvement with their Children: United States, 2006-2010. National Heath Statistics Reports, no71. Hyattsville, MD: National Center for Health Statistics. 2013.

Katz, E. (2002). At the still point of the turning world: a journey through the temporal dimensions of a father-son conflict. Journal of Family Therapy, 24, 369-384.

Keller, T. (1999). Images of the familiar: Individual differences and implicit leadership theories. The Leadership Quarterly, 10(4), 589-607.

Kelloway, E.K., Barling, J., and Agar, S. (1996). Pre-employment predictors of union attitudes: The moderating role of parental identification, Journal of Social Psychology, 136, 413-415.

Komives, S.R., Lucas, N. and McMahon, T.R. (2007). Exploring Leadership: For College Students Who Want to Make a Difference. 2nd Ed. San Francisco, CA: John Wiley & Sons, Inc.

Kotelchuck, M. (1976). The infant's relationship to the father: Experimental evidence. In M. Lamb (Ed.). The role of the father in child development. New York: John Wiley & Sons, pp. 329-344.

Kouzes, J.M. and Posner, B.Z. (1996). Seven lessons for leading the voyage to the future. In F. Hesselbein, M. Goldsmith and R. Beckhard

(Eds.), The Leader of the Future. New York, NY: Jossey-Bass, pp. 99-110.

Krampe, E.M., and Newton, R.R. (2006). The father presence questionnaire: A new measure of the subjective experience of being fathered, Fathering, 4(2), 159-190.

Lamb, M. (1976). The role of the father in child development. New York, NY: John Wiley & Sons.

Lamb, M. (1981). The role of the father in child development. (2nd ed.). New York, NY: John Wiley & Sons.

Lamb, M. (1997). The role of the father in child development. (3rd ed.). New York, NY: John Wiley & Sons.

Lamb, M. (2004). The role of the father in child development. (4th ed.). New York: John Wiley & Sons.

Lewis, C. (1997). Fathers and Preschoolers. In M. Lamb (Ed.). The role of the father in child development. (3rd ed.). New York: John Wiley & Sons, pp. 121-142

Lewis, M., Feiring, C., & Weinraub, M. (1981). The father as a member of the child's social network. In M. Lamb (Ed.). The role of the father in child development. (2nd ed.). New York: John Wiley & Sons, pp. 259-294.

Lewis, M., and Weinraub, M. (1976). The father's role in the child's social network. In M. Lamb (Ed.). The role of the father in child development. New York: John Wiley & Sons, pp. 157-184.

McBride, B.A., Schoppe-Sullivan, S.J., and Ho, M. (2004). The mediating role of fathers' school involvement on student achievement, Applied Developmental Psychology, 26, 201-216.

Merleau-Ponty, Maurice (2012). Phenomenology of Perception. New York, NY: Routledge.

Michie, S. and Gooty, J. (2005). Values, emotions, and authenticity: Will the real leader please stand up? The Leadership Quarterly, 16(3), 441-457.

Mirande, A. (1991). Ethnicity and fatherhood. In F.W. Bozet & S.M.H. Hanson (Eds.), Fatherhood and families in cultural context. New York, NY: Springer, pp. 53-82.

Morman, M.T. and Floyd, K. (2006). Good fathering: Father and son perceptions of what it means to be a good father. Fathering, 4(2), 113-136.

Newberger, E.H. (1999). The men they will become: The nature and nurture of male character. Princeton: Princeton University Press.

Ogletree, M.D., Jones, R.M., and Coyl, D.D. (2002). Fathers and their adolescent sons: Pubertal development and paternal involvement, Journal of Adolescent Research, 17(4), 418-424.

Osherson, S. (1986). Finding our fathers: The unfinished business of manhood. New York, NY: The Free Press.

Osherson, S. (1995). The passions of fatherhood. New York: Fawcett Columbine.

Parke, R.D. (1981). Fathers. Cambridge, MA: Harvard University Press.

REFERENCES

Parsons, T. (1964). Social structures and personality. London: The Free Press.

Patterson, C.J. (1992). Children of Lesbian and Gay Parents, Child Development, 63(5), 1025 - 1042.

Patterson, C.J., (2004). Gay Fathers. In M.E. Lamb (Ed.), *The Role of the Father in Child Development* (pp. 397-416). Hoboken, New Jersey: John Wiley & Son.

Patton, M.Q. (2002). *Qualitative Research & Evaluation Methods 3Edition.* Thousand Oaks, CA. Sage Publications.

Pinker, S. (2002). *The blank slate: The modern denial of human nature.* New York, NY: Penguin.

Piotrkowski, C.S. and Stark, E. (1987). Children and adolescents look at their parents' job. In J.H. Lewko (Ed.), How children and adolescents view the world of work. San Francisco, CA: Jossey-Bass, 3-19.

Pleck, E. H. and Pleck, J. H. (1997). Fatherhood Ideas in the United States: Historical Dimensions. In M. Lamb (Ed.). The role of the father in child development. (3rd ed.). New York: John Wiley & Sons, pp. 33-48.

Pleck, J.H. and Masciadrelli, B.P. (2004). Paternal involvement by U.S. residential fathers: Levels, sources, and consequences. In M. Lamb (Ed.).The role of the father in child development. (4th ed.). New York: John Wiley & Sons, pp. 222-271.

Pollack, W. (1998). Real boys: Rescuing our sons from the myths of boyhood. New York, NY: Random House.

Poulter, S.B. (2004). Father you son. New York, NY: McGraw-Hill.

Ray, V. and Gregory, R.(2001). School Experiences of the Children of Lesbian and Gay Parents, Family Matters, 59, 28 - 34.

Reid, H.M. and G.A. Find (1992). Self-Disclosure in Men's Friendships: Variations Associated with Intimate Relationships. In P.M. Nardi (Ed.), *Men's Friendships: Research on Men and Masculinities* (pp. 132-152). Newbury Park: Sage Publication.

Rogers, C.R. (1962). On Becoming a Person. Boston, MA: Houghton Mifflin Company.

Roopnarine, J.L. (2004). African American and African Caribbean fathers; Level, quality, and meaning of involvement. In M. Lamb (Ed.).The role of the father in child development. (4th ed.). New York: John Wiley & Sons, pp. 32-57.

Rowe, D.C. (1990). As the twig is bent? The myth of child-rearing influences on personality development. Journal of Counseling and development, 68(6), 606-611.

Schaetti, B.F., Ramsey, S.J. and Watanabe, G.C. (2008) *Personal Leadership*. Seattle, WA: FlyingKite Publication.

Schlessinger, L. (2012). For Listeners: What I Admire Most about my Spouse. http://www.drlaura.com/b/What-I-Admire-Most-About-My-Spouse.../726652544635687585.html

Scott, K. (1993). *Monster: The Autobiography of an L.A. Gang Member.* New York, NY: Grove Press.

Siegel, D.J. (2012). *The Developing Mind: How Relationships and the Brain Interact to Shape Who We are.* (Second Edition). New York, NY: The Guilford Press.

Siegel, D.J. (2013). Brainstorm: The power and purpose of the teenage brain. New York, NY: Jeremy P. Tarcher/Penguin.

Shamir, B. and Eilam, G. (2005). "What's your story? A life-stories approach to authentic leadership development, The Leadership Quarterly, 16(3), 395-417.

Shontz, F.C. (1965). Research methods in personality. New York: Appleton-Century-Crofts.

Shwalb, D.W., Nakawaza, J., Yamamoto, T., and Hyun, J. (2004). Fathering in Japanese, Chinese, and Korean Cultures: A review of the research literature. In M. Lamb (Ed.).The role of the father in child development. (4th ed.). New York: John Wiley & Sons, pp. 146-181.

Sinclair, A. (2007). *Leadership for the Disillusioned: Moving beyond myths and heroes to Leading that Liberates.* Crows Nest NSW 2065 Australia: Allen & Unwin.

Smith, G.J. (2005). *Life Lessons for Youth: Practical Stuff Every Young Person Needs to Know to Successfully Transition into Adulthood.* New York, NY: iUniverse, Inc.

Snow, J.E. (2004). How it feels to have a gay or lesbian parent: A book by kids for kids of all ages. New York, NY: Harrington Park Press.

Steele, J., and Barling, J. (1996). Influence of maternal gender-role beliefs and role satisfaction on daughters' vocational interests, Sex Roles, 34, 637-648.

Steen, T.A., Kachorek, L.V., and Peterson, C. (2002). Character strengths among youth. Journal of Youth and Adolescence, 32(1), 5-16.

The Fatherless Generation: http://thefatherlessgeneration.wordpress.com/statistics/

Thompson, M.C. and B.S. Thompson (2012). Admired: 21 Ways to Double Your Value. Ashland, OH: Evolve Publishing, Inc..

Tucker-Drob, E. (2011). Emergence of a Gene x Socioeconomic Status Interaction on Infant Mental Ability Between 10 months and 2 years. Psychological Science, 22(1), 125-133.

Tucker-Drob, E. and Harden K. (2012). Early childhood cognitive development and parental cognitive stimulation: evidence for reciprocal gene-environmental transactions. Developmental Science, 15(2), 250-259.

Videon, T.M. (2005). Parent-child relations and children's psychological well-being: Do dads matter?, Journal of Family Issues, 26(1), 55-78.

Wengraf, T (2001). *Qualitative Research Interviewing.* Thousand Oaks, CA: Sage Publication.

Williams, C. (1991). Forever a father, always a son: Discovering the difference a dad can make. Wheaton, IL: Victor Books.

Woititz, J. G. and Garner, A. (1990). Lifeskills for adult children: Deerfield Beach, FL: Health Communications, Inc..

Work, J.W. (1996). Leading a Diverse work force. In F. Hesselbein, M. Goldsmith and R. Beckhard (Eds.), The Leader of the Future. New York, NY: Jossey-Bass, pp. 71-79.

REFERENCES

Wyatt, J. (2005). A gentle going? An autoethnographic short story. Qualitative Inquiry, 11(5), 724-732.

Zacharatos, A., Barling, J., and Kelloway, K.E. (2000). Development and effects of transformational leadership in adolescents, The Leadership Quarterly, 11(2), 211-226.

Index

Made in the USA
San Bernardino, CA
14 July 2015